*Theology as Repetition*

# Theology as Repetition

JOHN MACQUARRIE IN CONVERSATION

Stephen Foster

☙PICKWICK *Publications* • Eugene, Oregon

THEOLOGY AS REPETITION
John Macquarrie in Conversation

Copyright © 2019 Stephen Foster. All rights reserved. Except for brief quotations in critical publications or reviews, no part of this book may be reproduced in any manner without prior written permission from the publisher. Write: Permissions, Wipf and Stock Publishers, 199 W. 8th Ave., Suite 3, Eugene, OR 97401.

Pickwick Publications
An Imprint of Wipf and Stock Publishers
199 W. 8th Ave., Suite 3
Eugene, OR 97401

www.wipfandstock.com

PAPERBACK ISBN: 978-1-5326-7693-2
HARDCOVER ISBN: 978-1-5326-7694-9
EBOOK ISBN: 978-1-5326-7695-6

*Cataloguing-in-Publication data:*

Names: Foster, Stephen, author.

Title: Theology as repetition : John Macquarrie in conversation / Stephen Foster.

Description: Eugene, OR: Pickwick Publication, 2019. | Includes bibliographical references.

Identifiers: ISBN: 978-1-5326-7693-2 (PAPERBACK). | ISBN: 978-1-5326-7694-9 (HARDCOVER). | ISBN: 978-1-5326-7695-6 (EBOOK).

Subjects: LCSH: Macquarrie, John. | Theology. | Theology—Process. | Existentialism.

Classification: BX4827 M25 F67 2019 (print). | BX4827 (epub).

Manufactured in the U.S.A.                                OCTOBER 30, 2019

Scripture quotations are taken from the Holy Bible, NEW INTERNATIONAL VERSION®, NIV® Copyright © 1973, 1978, 1984, 2011 by Biblica, Inc.® Used by permission. All rights reserved worldwide.

This book is dedicated to Marg Lodder who
has shown me the Grace of Being.

—Song of Songs 8:6

# In Appreciation and Memory of John Macquarrie

*On the one hand, we must firmly hold to the divine initiative in the work of man's salvation, and to the active operation of the Holy Spirit in this. Yet we have also to safeguard the freedom with which man makes the gift of salvation his own, or, to put it otherwise, makes a commitment of faith. The concept of "existence" together with the notion of Being at once transcendent of and immanent in all particular beings enables us to have some understanding of how man can live by a grace that he recognizes as coming from God, and yet in this experience can be most fully himself. It is the paradox of which St. Paul speaks when he bid us: "work out your own salvation with fear and trembling; for God is at work in you, both to will and to work for his good pleasure."*

—JOHN MACQUARRIE[1]

*Deus est unicuique intimus, sicut esse proprium rei est intimum ipsi rei.*

—THOMAS AQUINAS[2]

*The true deity is always ahead of us and we never catch him up with even our most ingenious and subtle arguments. Is this not part of God's love affair with his creatures, so to speak? He brushes past us, we glimpse him, we cannot doubt his reality. But we cannot grasp him or pin him down or turn him into another item in the catalogue of human knowledge.*

—JOHN MACQUARRIE[3]

---

1. Macquarrie, *Principles*, 336.

2. "Thomas says in one of his earliest works that God is innermost in each and everything, just as its own *esse* is innermost in the thing: *Deus est unicuique intimus, sicut esse proprium rei est intimum ipsi rei*" (Gilson, *Spirit of Thomism*, 69).

3. Macquarrie, *In Search of Deity*, 207.

# Contents

*Acknowledgments* | IX

*Preface* | XI

PART ONE: SITUATING MACQUARRIE'S THEOLOGY

Chapter 1: Pilgrimage in Theology | 3

Chapter 2: Establishing Dialectical Theism | 14

Chapter 3: Theology in a New Style | 41

Chapter 4: Dialectical Theism and Postmodernism | 59

PART TWO: ONTO-THEOLOGY: DIALECTICAL THEISM AND POSTMODERNISM

Chapter 5: The Problem with (the Violence of) Natural Theology (I) | 73

Chapter 6: The Problem with (the Violence of) Natural Theology (II) | 99

Chapter 7: Reason, Experience, and Revelation | 125

Chapter 8: Truth, Language, and Scripture | 153

*Bibliography* | 187

# Acknowledgments

WITHOUT THE CONTINUED SUPPORT of several people this volume would not have been written. Professor Macquarrie continued to be willing whether through visits at his home when I was in Oxford, or through correspondence when I was in Canada, to discuss many ideas that have found their way into this book. Many thanks to both Dr. Vincent Strudwick, and to Reverend Dr. Jane Shaw who in different ways helped organize the direction this project would follow. I am most grateful to Reverend Dr. Harriet Harris whose generous guidance, support, and constructive criticism have been invaluable.

Finally, this book would not have been possible without the love and encouragement of my wife Margaret. Marg has been a constant source of inspiration, help, and strength. Her love and her patience are unfailing! I dedicate this book to her. I love you very much!

# Preface

JOHN MACQUARRIE'S PHILOSOPHICAL THEOLOGY developed during a time of heightened secularism. He witnessed the reality that Christian theology was becoming less relevant to a scientific and technological age. Philosophically, Nietzsche's proclamation that "God is dead" was becoming more embedded in culture and theologically the legacy of Barth created a direction toward transcendence to the point of the absence of God; theologians argued for the "death of God," and "religionless Christianity," and a radical separation of philosophy and faith resolving to live by an extreme fideism. All of which allowed for theology to become absorbed in modern secularism as it compromised with the values of the age. Macquarrie developed his "dialectical theism" as a response to these trends. He argues for an existential-ontological relation between human existence and God, where God as (Holy) Being is disclosed through the phenomena of experience. In this sense, God is present and manifest in our experience, accessible through revelation and reason. He argues that the worldly context of secularism is best engaged through the incarnation and a sacramental view of the universe. Late in his life, Macquarrie explored these same themes in the context of postmodernism, finding that although offering some unique and creative observations, postmodernism is in many ways merely another form of modernism that is as challenged with the ongoing advent of secularism and atheism as the radical theology movement of the 1960s.

This book argues that Macquarrie's theology has much to say in relation to postmodern theology, and indeed shares many themes in common with postmodernism. His "dialectical theism" develops within the same historical and cultural context as postmodernism yet attempts a more constructive relationship with secular culture, taking seriously secularism and the need to found theology on concepts and language that acknowledge a shared context of experience between religious and non-religious views.

The book is divided into two parts. Part One situates the development of Macquarrie's theology from his beginnings up to postmodern times. Here I argue for the continuity and difference between Macquarrie's theism and other theological movements. In relation to postmodernism, I lay the foundation for a conversation between "dialectical theism" and postmodernism, focusing on general themes present in postmodernism that Macquarrie himself has identified in his book *Twentieth-Century Religious Thought*.

Part Two deals with Macquarrie's ontotheology, his grounding theology in phenomenological ontology. I cover the themes that are problematic in postmodern thinking as outlined at the end of Part One. These are, natural theology, reason and revelation, truth and language.

I use the heuristic of conversation to show how Macquarrie's theology is at once a presentation of the possibility of theology in a secular postmodern world and to show that it is through conversation, dialogue, and discourse that we work out our own salvation in communal existence. The heuristic of "repetition" operates to show that theology is always in progress; needing to retrieve the tradition and rethink it in new and relevant ways.

For better or worse, postmodernism is a movement that challenges the very foundations of our deepest convictions about truth and reality. This book extends Macquarrie's own investigation of postmodernism, carried out late in his own life, in a direction he himself did not pursue; namely how his "dialectical theism" as a method for doing theology is an antidote, on the one hand, for the skepticism (even nihilism) found in many postmodern thinkers and, on the other hand, the extreme fideism found in others.

Although radical and controversial in its own right, Macquarrie's philosophical theology offers a "third way," or a *via media*, between the polarities of skepticism and fideism found in postmodernism. I argue that the questioning of the foundations to truth and reality that is at the heart of much of postmodernism can benefit from Macquarrie's approach to theology. An important reason for this is that a "family resemblance" exists, so to speak, in the formative factors shaping postmodern thinking and Macquarrie's own "dialectical theism," especially the shared reliance on the phenomenological method. This makes Macquarrie a natural conversation partner with postmodern thinkers. As well, I (implicitly) make the (bold) claim that many of the innovative ideas found in postmodern thinkers have been anticipated in Macquarrie's "dialectical theism" in such a way as to allow for more constructive dialogue with (post)secular culture.

# PART ONE

*Situating Macquarrie's Theology*

*1*

# Pilgrimage in Theology

THINKING AND SPEAKING, ACCORDING to John Macquarrie, can only ever happen in a world of experience, they are worldly activities. So it seems appropriate to situate Macquarrie's thinking and speaking in a world of theology.[1] "Theology," of course, can be defined in many ways, but for Macquarrie it means generally a coherent thinking of the faith of the church. In this chapter we situate Macquarrie's theological thinking according to the influences that have given shape and form to his thought, that move him to think and to speak in response to what has been thought and spoken by others; for this is also what theology is, a conversation, a dialogue among those who share a common quest.

It is not insignificant that this worldly activity of theology was the original context for the Gospel; for certainly in the Christian faith, it is the incarnation[2] that is the "crux" of theology: God entering the world. In his *The Humility of God*,[3] Macquarrie offers the following observation:

---

1. "World" has a wide semantic range. Here I mean it in no specific existential (Heideggerian) sense or technical New Testament sense (from the Apostles Paul or John) as κτίσις or κόσμος. Rather, the sphere of theological thought in relation to Macquarrie's specific concerns is intended. These concerns will be unfolded through the pages of this thesis.

2. While accepting the word "incarnation" as part of the Christian tradition, it should be noted that Macquarrie has raised concerns over its limitation to represent the embodiment in Jesus Christ of the Second Person of the Trinity. He preferred the Greek word *enanthropoiesis* as capturing a more holistic union of God the Father and God the Son. Macquarrie, *Stubborn Questions of Theology*, 91.

3. Macquarrie, *Humility of God*, 22–24.

> This is why Christian theologians have never been willing to go along with rationalist and idealist philosophers who have sought to turn Christian teaching into a set of eternal truths. Theologians, have on the contrary, insisted on the particularity and concreteness of certain events, especially the event of Jesus Christ . . . One of the profoundest passages in all of literature is the prologue to St. John's gospel. It makes two great assertions. The first is a timeless or eternal truth: "In the beginning was the Word, and the Word was with God, and the Word was God" (John 1:1). The second is a particular historical truth: "And the Word became flesh and dwelt among us, full of grace and truth; we have beheld his glory, glory as the only Son from the Father" (John 1:14) . . . The meaning that is fundamental to the universe and is indeed identical with God has become flesh, and manifested its glory in a particular human person living in a particular locality at a particular period. This becoming flesh is what is meant by the term "incarnation."

However, different from the world in which the Word first becomes manifest and proclaimed, which was a world "full of gods," the context of Macquarrie's theology is a secular world, precisely a time that strives to live without gods or God. A time, according to some, where the word "God" has lost any and all meaning.[4] However, with the advent of a post-secular society, perhaps we have once again moved into a "world full of gods" and theology is called upon to again steer a course through a variety of possibilities. And one can suppose this is not dissimilar to the original context of the Gospel, where messiahs were announced everywhere. In the modern epoch, Nietzsche's announcement about the "death of God" began a movement that for some meant the impossibility of "God Talk" and for others unleashed a discourse where every kind of talk about God is possible. Yet, Nietzsche's madman is merely another messenger, since for Nietzsche Kant had killed God when he showed the arguments for the existence of God to be unsatisfactory. But Macquarrie does not see the announcing of the death of *this* God as the death of divinity. Instead, it allows the birth of a new way of thinking about God, one that escapes the grips of the old style natural theology called into question by Hume and Kant. Macquarrie's theology—as well as secular and post-secular theology in general—is to be read within the context of how to advance theological thought after Nietzsche's word, "God is dead."

---

4. This lost meaning of the word "God" is the subject of Macquarrie's lecture "How Theology Is Possible." This lecture will be discussed below.

Because theology is a worldly activity it is primarily about participation within a community that distinguishes itself from the secular "world" through its specific faith. So to speak, it is to be in the world but never merely of the world. Theology must also strive to be intelligible to a wider intellectual community that may not share the particular presuppositions of Christian faith. Theology, as an intellectual enterprise, shares with other disciplines the values of truth, consistency, and clarity of expression.[5] Theology must be able to "think" and "speak" meaningfully not only within its own community but to the secular community at large. This is the task of theology. Therefore theology is also a "step-back" from faith, subjecting faith to thought;[6] Macquarrie's philosophical theology is very much an attempt to indicate how this is possible.[7] It does not attempt to "prove" anything, but must point the way to a credible possibility. And, therefore, contrary to Heidegger who is his mentor in many ways, Macquarrie insists that theology "thinks." It is not merely a vocabulary for the subjectivity of faith. Neither is theology another "world-view," a concept that Macquarrie considers too rational and intellectual, or a philosophy in disguise that desires to abandon transcendence. Theology is itself an interpretation of reality through a hermeneutic of what and who that reality is. And, Macquarrie tells us, "Faith's name for reality is God."[8] *Theology* is a word about the Word, the *Logos*. Every *logos*, Macquarrie states—following Aristotle—"is at once *synthesis* and *diairesis*, putting together and taking apart."[9]

Macquarrie's theological development moves from a "narrow existentialism"[10] inspired by his early researches into Bultmann, to "existential-ontological" theism as an expression of his mature theology, as this is especially found in the second edition of his *Principles of*

---

5. Macquarrie, *Principles*, 1–3, 21–33.

6. Ibid., 1–4. The idea of a "step back" applies to the phenomenological reduction in Heidegger. Macquarrie follows Heidegger closely in this regard.

7. The idea of "indication" as a pointing toward something yet to be interpreted is very much in line with Heidegger's early idea of philosophy as "formal indication." In many ways, Macquarrie's philosophical theology—a descriptive approach—is a formal indication. However, as is often the case with Macquarrie, he ever moves beyond Heidegger in his method.

8. Macquarrie, *Paths in Spirituality*, 2nd ed., 30.

9. Macquarrie, *Thinking about God*, 75. We will see that in this sense of *Logos* we have the roots of deconstruction, which implies a construct that is pulled apart.

10. Macquarrie, "Pilgrimage in Theology," in *Theology, Church and Ministry*.

*Christian Theology*.[11] He developed the ideas expressed in *Principles* into later books, such as *In Search of Humanity*; *In Search of Deity*; and *Jesus Christ in Modern Thought*.[12] He would come to call his position in these later writings "dialectical theism," reflecting the central role of "dialectic" in his methodology as a way of ever engaging possible interpretations of reality. And yet, preserving "theism" as a reminder that we cannot fall prey to the pull of absolute immanence, the drive and desire is always toward the infinite future possibility of being.

Macquarrie's particular method of dialectic shares features of Socratic dialogue and the Hegelian resolution of opposites, without being comfortably resolved into any one of these different approaches. He often uses the strategy of opposition in reviewing ideas, and this too is with the intention of showing the need to find truth on both sides. So for example, when undertaking the existential analytic of the human being he uses polarities "within" the human subject as a heuristic device to show the dynamics of existence. But you see it in his review of philosophical and theological positions, for example, in his book *God and Secularity*, which sets these key words up as dialectical opposites, or in his review of postmodernism in *Twentieth-Century Religious Thought*, where a series of oppositions between modernism and postmodernism are analyzed in order to recognize the scope and limits of both. He is "Socratic" in that he is always entertaining the possibility to question received wisdom and dogmatic propositions. He is a pilgrim, a searcher, willing to dismantle—even deconstruct—certitudes that threaten to become idols of knowledge along his path. He is "Hegelian" in that his Socratic destruction is a step along the way toward unity of truth, of resolution of difference while celebrating diversity. He has a vision of the whole through the particular phenomena and his idealism is always checked by his existentialism.

Dialectical theism also preserves the word "theism," which had during this time fallen into disrepute because of its close associations with metaphysics[13] and its association with the radical transcendence

---

11. Macquarrie, *Principles*.

12. See Macquarrie's discussion on his desire to write a trilogy. "Life at Christ Church," in Morgan, *On Being a Theologian*, chapter 4.

13. The reason for this has to do with the association of "theism" with a speculative metaphysical theology. Macquarrie maintains metaphysics, but not in the speculative "rationalistic" sense of modernity. His metaphysics is grounded in phenomenological ontology and may be called "metaphysics of the other," in order to assure reference to the transcendent as opposed to the immanent.

and "otherness" of God. Theism was to be rejected in favor of a view of God more intimately connected with the world. But Macquarrie thinks theism can be descriptive of both the transcendence *and* immanence of God. "So, for me," he writes, "theism is not a bad word, and can be used both of Christianity and some non-Christian conceptions of God, both philosophical and religious. For instance, Hegel and Hartshorne are good examples of very different philosophers who claimed to be theists but whose conceptions of God were not of a supreme Ruler but much more closer to the Christian understanding."[14]

The radical criticism of theism shows a close association with ontotheology. This word—a major theme in Heidegger and postmodernism—has become a key word in the assault on "theism." This was not its original intention, however, and below we will consider Macquarrie's position in relation to its Heideggerian legacy. Yet we must say that although Macquarrie found no danger in using the word "theism" as descriptive of his own position, he would find no support in this from Heidegger. Yet, Heidegger does oppose the metaphysical reduction of God from transcendence to immanence and many attacks against theism undertaken in the name of ontotheology are in fact committing such a reduction. And in this opposition, Macquarrie is in line with Heidegger.

Macquarrie's theology must be situated in relation to the theological movements of the 1960s—specifically liberal theology, the radical theologies of "secular Christianity" and "death of God" theology, also referred to as "Christian Atheism." This situates his theology in relation to the past. But, Macquarrie's theology can be considered in relation to current trends in postmodern theology, which operate within the same tradition of post-Heideggerian phenomenological thought as does his own.[15] In doing so, we are not dealing with an artificial layering, or a leap of faith, when we bring modern trends like "death of God" theology into connection with postmodern theology. For, theologians who were schooled in the radical movement of "death of God" theology came to develop their thought in relation to various themes in postmodern theology.[16]

---

14. Macquarrie, *Twentieth-Century Religious Thought*, 400.

15. However, Macquarrie gives much more credence to the analytic tradition of philosophy compared to most postmodern thinkers.

16. Macquarrie points this out frequently in his writings. Also see Graham Ward, "Deconstructive Theology," in Vanhoozer, *The Cambridge Companion to Postmodern Theology*.

We find, for example, Hegel who was no stranger to the theme of the "death of God," still finding a voice in postmodern paradigms for theology as he did in the "death of God" theology in the 1960s. The same is true for Nietzsche, who has raised his philosophical head once again in the service of Christian theology through the work of Gianni Vattimo. And Heidegger seems always present in theology, either in a positive sense as we see in Rahner and Macquarrie or through his shadow as we see in many postmodern thinkers, for example, Levinas, Derrida, and Marion. The presence of the "Other" in Levinas is a return to the theme in Bonhoeffer's "religionless Christianity" and Christian Atheism. Derrida's view of "deconstruction," finds a place in the renewed movement of "death of God" theology and its call to the "end of theology," for example in the work of Carl Raschke.[17] For different reasons we can see a comparison with the thought of Marion, who revisits the idea of "death of God" through the teachings of Nietzsche and Heidegger. The "death of God" makes an appearance as well in the work of Mark C. Taylor's "a/theology,"[18] which is reminiscent of the original developments in "death of God" theology, but occurs within the context of deconstruction. Macquarrie often relates how the questions of theology are perennial questions, taking us over familiar ground from the tradition. We need to return to the tradition of philosophy and theology and seek insights that can be dialectically taken up, *repeated* in a manner similar to the way of Kierkegaard and Heidegger, so as to further our way in the pilgrimage of thought, correcting and promoting beneficial ways of thinking and speaking about God.

The presence of these various sources shows us the continuity of conversation in the theological tradition and its intersection with philosophy. But Macquarrie would see this as a necessary movement in the dialectic of thinking, which needs always to (re)turn to those who provoke and evoke thought. Returning to what has been thought and said in the past is not stale if one does so with the intention of taking up fresh insights in a new way. This intersection of the tradition and innovation of thought is at the heart of Macquarrie's philosophical theology.

Positioning Macquarrie in relation to the liberal and radical movements of the 1960s and the 1970s is to merely place him in the historical context when his theology developed. But there are traces of this tradition

---

17. Raschke, *The Alchemy of the Word*.
18. See, for example, Taylor, *Erring*.

reverberating in postmodern thought. Therefore to situate Macquarrie's theology in relation to postmodern theology is to set his position alongside later developments that share a commitment to some of the same historical and philosophical sources. Yet, these current trends share with secular theology and "death of God" theology a style and mood of thinking Macquarrie finds short-sighted.

Indeed, this is why dialectic is so important for Macquarrie since it allows thinking through alternative positions (oppositions) in order to further the development of theology. One needs to both be committed to the truth—and therefore take a position and defend it—and yet be open to the views offered by others and therefore open to reformation and correction. This is one way we recognize the plurality of expression, of *possibilities* of theology, while embracing the ideal of the unity of truth. And this places him clearly in the ranks of "modern theology." Macquarrie has always argued for unity as a goal of conversation and thinking in theology, this *in light of* the plurality of views.[19] He acknowledges the need for plurality, but he is not an advocate of plural*ism* in the sense of relinquishing the ideal of the unity of knowledge in favor of relativism. For Macquarrie, the pursuit of the ideal of unity is an axiological enterprise, one that is grounded ultimately in an ontological faith in the Beauty, Truth, and Goodness of creation.

Macquarrie is to be read in a scene of "theological crisis" (perhaps an overused phrase), to which he is at pains to respond. His is a correlational approach where "Athens and Jerusalem" *need* one another; where each tradition teaches the other its language and concepts.[20] With the advent and revelation of Christianity there can be no "Greek" thought separated from "Hebrew" thought.[21] Macquarrie does not merely follow trends; instead, he has always wanted to find ways for theology to respond relevantly to the cultural ethos. In some cases, this has caused him to follow a path contrary to what was in vogue. This can be witnessed by the fact that he was writing systematic theology when the idea of "system" in philosophy and theology was out of fashion. He continued to embrace and appropriate "Heidegger" even when Heidegger had

---

19. Macquarrie, *Theology, Church and Ministry,* 18. Also, Macquarrie, "Existentialism and Christian Thought," in Lefevere, *Philosophical Resources for Christian Thought,* 128.

20. Macquarrie, *Thinking about God.* Macquarrie, *An Existentialist Theology,* 3.

21. For different reasons, Macquarrie would embrace Levinas' idea that one needs to translate Hebrew (biblical) thought into Greek thought (philosophy).

become, and continues to be a scandal to philosophy. But even in this systematic appropriation of Heidegger, Macquarrie directs his concern toward a constructive approach which is not only a testimony of the Christian message but also an apologetic appeal to secular culture, which in many ways is a reading of Heidegger against Heidegger. For whereas Heidegger wanted theology to take seriously the separation of faith from philosophy, to reduce it to a positive science, Macquarrie recognizes that theology is cultural and therefore faith is only real faith in and through the culture one lives and moves within. It cannot be reduced to a method like a positive science but must be a path that leads one through actual phenomena to that which transcends, or saturates, phenomena. When Heidegger was waiting for and looking for "a god to save us," living in deferral, Macquarrie attempts to point a way to the God who is both present and manifest among us and also still on the way.[22]

It is important to note that Macquarrie does not adopt the phrase "post-secular" when describing our current "postmodern condition."[23] Neither does he use the phrase "post-Christian." For him theology must still move and respond to a "secular" culture: and Christianity is never something that we have passed through or overcome. Not unlike the recent movement of "Radical Orthodoxy," his response is itself historically and theologically situated in a return to premodern philosophy and theology and critical encounter with nineteenth-century theology, a return that was possible only after having passed through Barthian "neo-orthodoxy." Macquarrie, we have said, is not attempting to reinstate the liberal theology that fell out of favor after World War One, which came under the forceful attack of Barth, but to gather up the insights of such thinkers as Friedrich Schleiermacher and Rudolf Otto so theology is "embraced and given its character by the *saeculum*, or age."[24] Nevertheless, the perennial nature of theological questions and the inexhaustible riches of the gospel mean that the *saeculum* can never exhaust or absorb Christianity. Ironically, it is the secular that makes theology possible

---

22. Macquarrie would see as too one-sided the approaches of post-modern thinkers who exaggerate the idea that God *may be*, or, *is to come* but has not arrived and is not, perhaps cannot, be present. Richard Kearney and John Caputo are examples. This of course continues Heidegger's *waiting for (a) god*.

23. Commentators are careful to use the word "condition" as opposed to "situation" or "period," since the stress is on the effect of the times on our thinking and acting. Vanhoozer, ed., *The Cambridge Companion to Postmodern Theology*.

24. Macquarrie, *Heidegger and Christianity*, v.

even in a time of incredulity to transcendence. For with the "death of God," which comes as a consequence of the secular, comes the possibility to re-think the divine. So, in Macquarrie's dialectical theology we can never find a final disjunction between the "religious" and the "secular." As a theologian who embraces "secularity," he rejects (Christian) "secular theology" and (Christian) "death of God" theology as having a final, non-revocable word.

And in a way, Macquarrie can be counted among the *post*-modern theologians. For what is meant by the prefix "post-'? It is at once retrieval and moving-beyond previous positions, without being an outright rejection of them. So to be *post*-"secular," "modern," or "liberal" is not to have rejected outright the tenets of these movements, but to theologize in light of what has come to pass through this period of thought. It is about honoring tradition as well as "correcting" it, or "aligning" it with the questions of the day. Macquarrie sees continuity through difference between "modern" theology and "postmodern" theology, just as he sees continuity through difference between "liberal" theology and "radical" theology.[25] However, it is through this continuity with what is past that critical response to what has been said and thought is possible. Criticism is not mere rejection; it must offer something in its place. It is in the course of attempting to maintain continuity with what has been said before that one can have an ear for what is different. This makes dialogue possible. For outright rejection leaves no room for dialogue. In Macquarrie's estimation, one of the dangerous elements of the radical theology of the 1960s and (some) postmodern approaches to theology is the desire to reject tradition.[26] Dialogue requires one to define a position in relation to what is opposed. The opposition is key to the definition. The riches of theological positions and movements require one to engage critically alternate views, and this can only happen in light of theological tradition(s).

We have been speaking about theology in the singular, applying labels without definitions to distinguish movements of thought—"postmodern theology," "radical theology," "liberal theology"—it would be more accurate in a time that celebrates pluralism to speak of theolog*ies* (perhaps even a/theolog*ies*) since there is no one agreed upon *Theology* or negation of theology. Macquarrie himself acknowledged that we are

---

25. This is pursued below. However, I should indicate that the use of the singular "theology" is not to suggest that there is consensus in theology during these movements; one is probably better to speak in the plural and use the word "theologies."

26. Macquarrie, *Stubborn Questions*, 124.

ever confronted with a proliferation of theologies, and he seems to welcome such plurality for the basis of open conversation on the path to ecumenism.[27] In fact, as Macquarrie has pointed out in his *Principles*,[28] there is often more that unites theologians in their general concerns than separates them in their individual emphases within their method. We label theological positions too much, even too simply, using them perhaps to limit the value and relevance of a theological position, perhaps risking misleading ourselves and others into a dogmatic slumber that takes away our wits. We need to be sharp and see what is good and true in a theology and recognize what is dangerous and destructive to the richness and breadth of the Christian faith. He says, "The number of theological labels is very great, but they all tend to be somewhat vague and they overlap at various points... The wisest theologians avoid getting themselves labeled too precisely."[29] Macquarrie's pilgrimage as a theologian is a quest for what is "good and true and beautiful" without forgetting what is "dangerous and destructive" to the Christian faith. One can understand that his method of "dialectical theism" is meant to reflect his idea of always being a theological pilgrim, for it is a method that is designed to be both self-correcting and reforming and give impetus to an on-going quest without closure.

Indeed, because Macquarrie's method is *dialectical* it aspires to be neither *this* nor *that* without spiraling into relativism since it seeks always to balance both *this* and *that*: both immanence *and* transcendence; radicalism *and* conservatism; tradition *and* scripture; the individual *and* community; revelation *and* reason; *pistis* and *gnosis*; *poiesis* and *praxis*. Such polarities are limiting cases for his dialectical method. He avoids any dogmatic extremism in his theological method; choosing to not assume the only authentic choice is one side of the story only. It is necessary to move beyond any dogmatic fixed approach in order to get a handle on the type of theology one is dealing with.[30] This is necessary in order to assess the identity and differences of theological positions and to assess trajectories of thought and sympathetic leanings within the established theological tradition. This point will be further elaborated upon in the next chapter. For now, let it be said that there is in Macquarrie's

---

27. Macquarrie, *Thinking about God*, 71.
28. Macquarrie, *Principles*, 34.
29. Macquarrie, *Thinking about God*, 61.
30. Macquarrie, *Stubborn Questions*, 127.

philosophical theology a method that allows him a voice which fits neatly into the currents of contemporary theological debate. He is, let be said, an Anglican theologian whose method of "dialectical theism" opens a door for one to enter into conversation about the weighty matter of theology. He believes one can faithfully seek an understanding to the perennial question of what a proper balance would be between the doctrine of the "Total Otherness" of God and this same God's "Absolute Immanence." The crux of the matter for Macquarrie, we have said, is the Incarnation: which holds all things together. In placing his trust here as the symbol for what makes dialectical theology possible, he offers a theology that very much stands-out and announces itself as a witness for the relevance of the Christian faith for interpreting the meaning of our existence. In the next chapter we turn to the origins of Macquarrie's dialectical theism.

## 2

# Establishing Dialectical Theism

MACQUARRIE'S THEOLOGY, WE HAVE said, develops at a time of heightened secularity, in an environment that strives to live in the anonymity of God, or in the absence of God. With the advent of postmodernism, we are still passing through the secular in its various forms. Although postmodern theology invites the possibility of God, it lives in the space of the withdrawal of God, or in the deferred presence of God. The challenge for theologians, Macquarrie maintains, is to find a way to think and speak about God in a meaningful way and in a worldly context.[1] He recognizes that the polarity between "God" and "secularity" that is always in danger of pulling theology apart is ultimately a false dichotomy.[2] In its history, theology has often fallen victim to one side or the other of this polarity, or, in the context of deconstruction and postmodernism, one chooses to live with the ambiguity of undecidability where one can "rightly pass for an atheist," as Derrida and Caputo claim, while holding onto faith, *a* faith, in theism as a possibility, a *may be*. Although this perspective will not be totally alien to Macquarrie's theology, he will attempt to present a dialectic that is more affirmative of theism. More concretely, we cannot have a "world denying" theology that resides in some obscure transcendence, itself in danger of having no actual relevance to living and breathing beings. Neither can we have a "world affirming" theology that immerses us into an equally obscure immanence where we have perhaps only a trace or a glimpse of transcendence of that which is other than

1. Macquarrie, *God and Secularity*, 13.
2. Ibid., 14.

what is defined by the age. And so Macquarrie's theology stands between the "secular," which abandons God, and the post-secular, which claims to be open to any talk of God and gods and (I would add) attempts an antidote for those who are lost in deferral, waiting for a sign. His dialectical theology avoids these poles by offering a third way. It is a way of thinking that takes us to the intersection of theology and the secular, precisely in the world but not necessarily originating in a source that is of this world. Macquarrie theologizes in an age that believes while it doubts.

Secularity immerses us in the "everyday," the complacency of life. However, Macquarrie holds the view that now and again we are shocked-out of the malaise of the "everyday" into deeper concerns that provoke us to thought and questioning; questions which point to what underlies our everyday activity; questions about our own being, our actions, our values, our goals. And so, he cannot follow those theologians who want to abandon ontology to focus only on an ethical and social gospel, and we see Macquarrie follows a typical approach of existential theology in maintaining the role of "ontological shock"[3] as an occurrence that inevitably wakes us from our dogmatic slumbers and absorption into the banality of life.[4] Here we are confronted with that very Heideggerian theme of being shaken out of our inauthentic absorption in the "everyday" and moved toward thinking confronted with the authenticity of our transcendence. It is an old theme that some kind of shock is the beginning of thinking; we see it in diverse thinkers such as Plato and Levinas. However, Macquarrie speaks of a shock of the absence of something (i.e., God, or meaning) it is equally the shock of the presence of Nothing, or the shock of the presence of "Something" *rather than* Nothing. Indeed it can be experienced as an awareness of standing between Being and Nothing. Perhaps it is recognized as a lack of purpose or meaning, which moves us to probe the ontological questions; theologically it is sin, disorder in creation, defining lost-ness and alienation from oneself and others.[5] Becoming aware of our situation leads to *Angst*—anxiety about nothingness—"what is intended is awareness of the precariousness of existence which at any time may lapse into nothing or is already lapsing into nothing ... We become aware

---

3. Ibid., 15. This shock of "existence" or "non-existence" is fundamental. Macquarrie writes, "Tillich talked about the shock of non-being, the realization that one will cease to exist. I think myself that more primordial than the shock of non-being is the shock of being" (Macquarrie, *Two Worlds Are Ours*, 25).

4. Macquarrie, *Principles*, 86.

5. Ibid., 72.

of a nullity that enters into the very way we are constituted . . . The world too sinks to nothing, it gets stripped of the values and meanings that we normally assign to the things and events that belong within it, and it becomes indeterminate, characterized by the same kind of emptiness and nullity that we know in ourselves."[6] Although he does not use the expression, it is as if we are confronted with the always present possibility of the *tohu wa bohu* of existence.[7]

It is here, in the wider and deeper context of secularity that the question of God emerges as the innermost ontological concern and symbol of meaning. It is through the experience of the absence of God that we can begin to find a way to the presence of God; through our quest for meaning in existence, we begin to bridge the gap between Nothing (meaninglessness) and Being (meaning).

Macquarrie observes that it is during the rise of secularity that discussions about "God" reach the height of popularity, and books such as Bishop Robinson's *Honest to God* and Harvey Cox's *Secular Theology*, as well as Altizer and Hamilton's *Radical Theology and the Death of God* "are being eagerly read by surprisingly large numbers of people, many of them outside the Church."[8] So, ironically, in a time of heightened secularity the question of God becomes the "hot issue" in theology.[9] And here again, we see a connection to the present. For, the post-secular is supposed to be distinguished from the secular because of its renewed desire for God, a return to religion.[10] It is a time where the questioning of God[11] is again the topic of choice among many theologians and philosophers of religion. So, it seems that the desire for God and questions about God is relevant to culture regardless of whether we are in a secular (modern) or post-secular (postmodern) era. And for Macquarrie this means that there has never really been an absence of ontology; however, it may operate implicitly, tacitly, if not explicitly and thematically. Since they are

---

6. Ibid., 86.

7. The difference between Macquarrie and Levinas, who utilises the phrase *tohu wa bohu*, will be explored in later chapters of this book.

8. Macquarrie, *God and Secularity*, 18.

9. Ibid., 29.

10. Caputo, *On Religion*.

11. Caputo and Scanlon, *God, the Gift, and Postmodernism*; Caputo et al., *Questioning God*.

grounded in thought and decision, Macquarrie refers to these spectrums of alternatives as "hidden ontologies."[12]

During the theological debates of the 1960s, of which Macquarrie is a major voice, the themes of *secular* Christianity and even Christian *atheism* emerge where *secularism* and *atheism* point to the severing of transcendence and ontology from theology. Theological discussion was diverted away from God and "ontological matters"[13] (the being of God, the world, humanity) towards a focus on the "neighbor"[14] (other, ethics, community) and so *theoria* gave way to *praxis*. In current theological debate, this same concern is manifest in a "*post*-secular" environment. However, the concern for the "other," in a quasi-Barthian tone, has once again been extended to refer to God as the "Wholly Other" presence signified as a "trace" through the "neighbor," as one reads about this in Levinas and Derrida, for example. One can see here a revisiting of the "emptying" of God into the (human) world, as we witnessed in secularized Christianity. John Caputo, reflecting on the thought of Levinas, says: "The withdrawal of God from our view is always a matter of justice, of God deflecting our approach from God to the neighbor ... The *deflection* of God is the *translation* of God into deed ... it requires *doing* things, not philosophizing or theologizing them half to death."[15] Macquarrie prefers a dialectic between doing and thinking. He prefers a dialectic between the revelation that comes through the ethical challenge of the other *and* the ontological reflection on the Being of existence: the thinking about God *as* God.

Macquarrie's own theology develops between the poles of "revelation" and "reason," as this comes to us in the scene of the neo-orthodox/liberal theology divide. That is, he works out a theology that operates with the reality of the possibility of binaries, and yet he rejects a dualism, a division between, reason and revelation, as either/or. His approach is dialectical. It functions within the apparent antithesis of reason and revelation to show the mutual necessity of one for the other; this is the purpose of his dialectical theistic approach.

Macquarrie's first serious work in theology begins in the 1950s, when Barthian neo-orthodoxy was most influential. Because Macquarrie

---

12. Macquarrie, *God and Secularity*, 44.

13. Harvey Cox, *The Secular City*, cited in Macquarrie, *God and Secularity*, 16.

14. John A. T. Robinson, *The New Reformation*, cited in Macquarrie, *God and Secularity*, 17.

15. Caputo, *On Religion*, 137; italics in the original.

had found Barth's theology "insufferable,"[16] especially in relation to Barth's rejection of natural theology and *analogia entis*,[17] he moved in a different direction. He found himself drawn toward the existentialism of Bultmann, a theology that seemed more relevant to the individual in connection to the lived world. Bultmann was a fresh alternative to the Calvinism of Barth in Macquarrie's reckoning, and the philosophical grounding of Bultmann upon early Heidegger was a breath of fresh air. With the publication in 1955 of his book comparing Heidegger and Bultmann,[18] Macquarrie's theological development is evident. He seeks a philosophical language that gives us a strong existential and thorough ontological grounding. In this work, the similarities and differences between Heidegger and Bultmann are reconciled through the "Hegelianism" of F.H. Bradley, an early major philosophical influence on Macquarrie. Macquarrie touches on the relationship of Bradley's (mystical) ontology with Bultmann's existentialism;[19] and here we see Macquarrie developing a convergence of ideas that will be thematic for his future thinking. The central element of ontology (weak in Bultmann), and the concreteness of being-in-the-world (weak in Bradley) are gathered together through Heidegger. Heidegger becomes the very practical and theoretical key to the vision Macquarrie has for theology in a secular world. Heidegger's genius allowed for a phenomenological method of converse between ontology and existentialism. But Macquarrie wanted to ensure the integrity of his approach within the Christian tradition; in a sense, returning Heidegger to his sources.

Because of his weak handling for historicity and lack of concern for ontology, Macquarrie soon found Bultmann's "narrow existentialism" unsatisfactory. So, he was moved to undertake a study of the theological tradition, in order to fill-in this lack of historical insight he found in Bultmann's theology, especially as this related to the "historical Christ." Macquarrie wanted to grapple with the "frontiers of philosophy and theology."[20] Bultmann's theology was too modern renouncing as illegitimate the pre-modern resources of the Gospel, and too subjectivist, always in need of supplement from secular thought. This search culminated

16. Macquarrie, *Theology, Church and Ministry*, 2.
17. This will have our attention in chapter 5, below.
18. Macquarrie, *An Existentialist Theology*.
19. See especially the conclusion to Macquarrie, *An Existentialist Theology*, 241–43.
20. This was the subtitle of the book *Twentieth-Century Religious Thought*, which resulted from these researches.

in 1963 with the publication of his book *Twentieth-Century Religious Thought*,[21] which really lays bare the philosophical presupposition found in theological programs.

Macquarrie's concern to honor the theological tradition and yet to move the tradition into conversation with currents of the time will be a venture that continues in earnest from this point. But he is also aware that a "Christian-Socratic" approach is needed where it is appropriate to question the relevance of certain traditional ideas, to expose the philosophical foundation of theological thinking, leading one to seek fresh expression while remaining true to the original revelation of scripture and the tradition. The theme of the development of "existential-ontological" (or dialectical) theism is becoming established—where Macquarrie seeks a relevant vocabulary and concepts to "say again," *repeat*, in philosophical-theological terms, the Gospel. For, following Bultmann, Macquarrie believes that the mythical language of scripture no longer speaks to a secular world. However, unlike Bultmann, Macquarrie is not content to merely look for the existential significance of myth. There is indeed an existential message in scripture that still can speak meaningfully to us today, but also there are the ontological themes of scripture which need opening up. Mythological language was merely the pre-philosophical language attempting to express the dialectic of God and world. In a modern world, this language no longer fits our philosophical concepts. For instance, when we speak about the being of God, or the pre-existence and incarnation of Christ, or the being of human being, we need a language that allows a more coherent and relevant set of concepts that "repeats" the revelation of scripture. So Macquarrie stands in a hermeneutic tradition that asks not only "how do we read" scripture, but "how do we communicate" scripture? Theologians from the earliest traditions have been seeking this through the vocabulary of philosophy. Philosophical concepts and vocabulary have functioned apologetically to honor the doctrines of the Church. What is needed is a language—a contemporary situation of discourse—to bring this into expression and into our thinking.

1963, the same year that *Twentieth-Century Religious Thought* was published, saw the publication of one of the more controversial books of its time, Bishop Robinson's *Honest to God*, which brought the question of God, of how to think and speak about God, to the forefront of discussion. In Bishop Robinson's book, there is a depiction of God that Macquarrie

---

21. Macquarrie, *Theology, Church and Ministry*, 4.

considered close to his own, what may best be described as a panentheistic view; a view outlined in his inaugural lecture at Union Theological Seminary and would develop throughout his writing.[22] During a time when theology was considered by many to be impossible, in fact moving some radical Christian groups to deny the existence of God,[23] the question of the possibility of theology was ever present in Macquarrie's thinking. This question of the impossibility or possibility of theology was grounded in the central theological concept of God, as God had come to be conceived through the influence of modern philosophy, which was very critical of revelation and was grounding itself in reason. This was the legacy of the Enlightenment, especially of Kant.[24]

Macquarrie says the question of God "was in my mind during most of my years at Union, especially after the theological world was thrown into confusion by the appearance in 1963 of John Robinson's famous paperback, *Honest to God*."[25] Macquarrie's thinking was converging with some of the radical trends that were shaking the foundations of Christian theology at the time. Other trends he felt were dangerous, and yet, as we will see, he acknowledges that he shares some of the concerns expressed within them.

Macquarrie speaks of a narrow form of radical theology,[26] and this is where he would place the "death of God" theologians in vogue during the 1960s and still influential today. Narrow because it has a particular focus and ideology at its center. A broader form of radical theology is identified by Macquarrie; a movement that is much older, exemplified in the Reformation but dating back to the eschatological expectation spoken of in the scriptures.[27] He says that both narrower and broader radical theologies are attempts "to accomplish what Nietzsche called a 'transvaluation of all values,'" though they may understand this differently. He says: "All the essential categories of radical theology—the new, the future, the transvaluation of values, the rejection of the existing order (including "religion," in so far as this has become a part of that order),

---

22. Macquarrie tells us he sent a copy of his lecture to Robinson. Macquarrie, *Theology, Church and Ministry*, 6.

23. For example, Altizer and others in the "death of God" movement.

24. A discussion of the relevance of Kant will be part of a later discussion, when we deal with Macquarrie's view of "religion."

25. Macquarrie, *On Being a Theologian*, 34.

26. Macquarrie, *Thinking about God*, 62.

27. Ibid.

the new society of the kingdom of God—all these are grounded in the eschatological expectation."[28] Certainly, Macquarrie's comments hold up today, with postmodern theology (and philosophy) that functions very much within the category of eschatology and apocalyptic thought. Postmodernism, in Macquarrie's assessment, would be another radical approach to theology in a narrow way, a topic to which we will return.

It has already been stated that Macquarrie's theology has important points of contact with radical theology and liberal theology. "Radical theology is a theology of revolution . . ."[29] Macquarrie says, and this is also the context for the publication of Macquarrie's *Principles,* which he describes as revolutionary.[30] Indeed, he believes the application of Heidegger's thought to theology allows for radical developments. In *Principles* he says, "a truly radical theology lives in the tension of faith and doubt,"[31] that is, between faith and trust in the unity and wholeness of truth and the Socratic destruction of certainties.[32] And this is appropriate to Macquarrie's theology. "Death of God" theology is not radical in this sense since it resolves the tension by abolishing God; which holds in question whether it can be called "theology" at all. However, many of the categories that Macquarrie uses to characterize radical theology also apply to his own philosophical theology, which is offered as a new style that is focused on "future possibility," through the "values" of openness and commitment and mediation.

However revolutionary or radical Macquarrie's theology is intended to be, he also speaks of it as continuous with the theological tradition, with the "content of revelation . . . that has been held in the community of faith."[33] Macquarrie's approach respects scripture and the theological tradition as formative factors, and therefore as presuppositions to any theology. In many ways, this separates Macquarrie from postmodern approaches that, like "secular theology," are very critical of tradition. Not unlike the Reformers, Macquarrie reacts to the tradition with the idea

28. Ibid., 65.
29. Ibid., 63–65.
30. Macquarrie, *Principles,* 117.
31. Ibid., 158.
32. Macquarrie's approach reminds of the biblical mandate to be compassionate and patient with doubts (Jude 22), "I do believe; help me overcome my unbelief" (Mark 9:24).
33. Macquarrie, *Principles,* 34.

of correcting it,³⁴ but does not reject it outright. Macquarrie's theology is held in tension through what we might call a "radical conservatism." Such tension, however, is not to be considered a form of dogmatism, it is dynamic; it is dialectical. For it is precisely "tension," as *via media* between extreme positions, between "faith and doubt," which is central to Macquarrie's method; this can be illustrated through his proposed approach in his *Principles*. "So we must steer a middle way between an extreme Augustinianism (or Calvinism) and Pelagianism, though without necessarily embracing any of the historical forms of so-called "semi-Pelagianism," or "synergism."³⁵

However, many of the categories he applies to radical theology, we have said, apply to him. But his primary concern for his theology is similar to traditional approaches, providing "a bridge between everyday thinking and experience and the matters about which a theologian talks: it will relate religious discourse to all other areas of discourse."³⁶ It is precisely in a culture that expresses the absence of God that our quest for God can begin. Macquarrie's revolution in theology is a radical re-thinking of the tradition that attempts to end a certain way of thinking about God and preserve the theological tradition while making it relevant to secular society. In this way, Macquarrie sees his theology as a new beginning and a new way of thinking.

In 1961, when Macquarrie was first commissioned to write his *Principles of Christian Theology*,³⁷ he still considered himself a "liberal theologian"; by the time *Principles* is completed he has strong doubts about liberal theology. This could clearly be seen in 1967, a year after the publication of *Principles* when Macquarrie produced another book he considered a turning point in his theological development.³⁸ This book is called *God and Secularity* and is an apologetic against liberal theology,

---

34. There is a connotation with the word "correction" that suggests arrogance. It is suggestive of Heidegger, who speaks of philosophy as a "corrective" to theology. However, we need to keep in mind that what is meant by such a correction is a way of reform, a way of re-thinking central ideas to suit the temper of the times and to realign with the tradition itself. In Macquarrie's method there is the hope of coherence, intelligibility, and relevance. His *Principles* was commissioned to be a systematic theology in contemporary mode.

35. Macquarrie, *Principles*, 336.

36. Ibid., 57.

37. Macquarrie, *On Being a Theologian*, 22.

38. Macquarrie, *Theology, Church and Ministry*, 6.

which by this time he considered empty of any real substance, and is an attempt to continue his defense of "traditional Christianity."

Liberal theology was much in vogue during this time, with its repetition of nineteenth-century themes and renewed interest in the writing of Schleiermacher and also Harnack, whom Macquarrie identifies as the culminating figure of liberal theology in the nineteenth century.[39] Macquarrie characterizes liberal theology broadly as "openness to secular culture," being "especially open to the insights of the natural sciences, and likewise of psychology and sociology." And, "It has welcomed and responded to exchanges with philosophy. It has welcomed and responded to the historical criticism of the Bible and the sources of Christian faith."[40]

Macquarrie also states that liberal theology is easily reconcilable with evolution and progress, downplays sin and is very optimistic in its outlook.[41] He states that the question asked by liberal theology is: "How can I both be a Christian believer and a child of the modern world of the intellect, receiving its well-established findings and remaining open to its constantly new discoveries?"[42] Macquarrie does not think it wise for theology to accommodate itself to current trends only for the sake of being current. However, it must respond to the cultural situation, and liberal theology attempts this, and in his way, Macquarrie joins their company. The focus must be on the substance of the Gospel being expressed in terms relevant to the times, not on making the Gospel fashionable. The difference still requires the seeking of meaning and truth to prepare for conversion (*metanoia*): and this same seeking for meaning and truth leads one always to the path of conversation.

The broad outlines of liberal theology are also present in Macquarrie's thought. For example, Macquarrie has been influenced by scriptural criticism, especially through demythologization, and his whole method is structured around openness to the secular. However, he has always attempted to take sin more seriously than what we find in liberal theology,[43] or in some postmodern thinkers like Levinas.[44] Some have criticized

39. Macquarrie, *Thinking about God*, 61.
40. Ibid., 62.
41. Ibid.
42. Macquarrie, *Thinking About God*, 68.
43. Although in his summary of the five doctrines that theology cannot afford to do without, he does not mention sin directly: Creation, incarnation, sacrament, ecclesiology, and eschatology.
44. Macquarrie, *Twentieth-Century Religious Thought*, 465. Though in Levinas we

Macquarrie for having too negative a view about the state of the human race,[45] which is central in Macquarrie's thought for the quest for God (although, as mentioned, Macquarrie does distance himself from the Calvinist/Barthian view which he finds too destructive a view of humanity and of the Christian faith). There is a degree of rationalism in Liberal theology that Macquarrie believes extends too far.

We are children of the Enlightenment, Macquarrie says, but he does not believe the Enlightenment establishes absolute standards for thought.[46] And, as a good disciple of Heidegger, the influence of modern philosophy is also seen through Romanticism, in the role of the "imagination." For Macquarrie imagination allows for the active role of the intellect in a creative way, recognizing the creative tendencies of thought and language to contend with reality and rational thought. Imagination, therefore, is essential to constructive theology allowing for the possibility of "theory," as a "seeing" and a "vision" of the whole. But it is here, in the use of imagination so closely connected to reason, where concerns over conceptual idolatry and the question of the ability to have a clear description of phenomena independent from interpretation arises. Macquarrie neglects to discuss this in any detail. However, we will return to these questions in our review of his discussion of postmodernism, and his concern over the subjective and projective tendencies of thought found in modern and postmodern philosophy and theology.

Macquarrie reads Liberal theology as a compromise with modern philosophy, and modern culture generally, letting categories of modern thought set the agenda for theology. Macquarrie does not seek such a compromise, but he engages secular culture to show that the imminent and present concerns of any culture are the perennial concerns in theology. Macquarrie believes that theology requires philosophical grounding,[47] philosophy opens possibilities of expression for theology, and indeed he does not consider the concerns of philosophy and theology to have been opposed from the outset. We see the tension in Macquarrie where, on the one hand, he wants to liberate theology from Enlightenment rationalism; while on the other hand, he restricts theological claims which conflict with the authority of scientific reason. But he restricts scientific reason

---

must not mistake this for reducing the impact of evil, morally and metaphysically.

45. Kee, *The Way of Transcendence*, 50–51.
46. Macquarrie, *On Being a Theologian*, 17.
47. Macquarrie, *Twentieth-Century Religious Thought*, 476.

too and maintains there is in human experience more than scientific empiricism;[48] he maintains that imagination allows for constructive ontological insights that Rationalism or Empiricism does not allow. This is the value of philosophy, to expose presuppositions so to transcend their limits while living among and through the language and concepts that allow us to converse with others. He shares the *questions* of liberal theology but not the *method*.

The influence of (modernism and) the Enlightenment on Macquarrie's thought is evident, but his desire to move beyond the limits of Enlightenment thinking is equally apparent. His view on "miracles," for example, can serve as a case study where he appears to offer a typical liberal interpretation (following Bultmann) but where his dialectical theism moves him in a different direction. Bultmann's demythologizing acknowledges that the way of viewing the miraculous as portrayed in the language of scripture conflicts with modern science and therefore appears to suggest that miracles are a violation of what we call "laws of nature." Therefore, in this reading miracles are theologically possible, but they are scientifically impossible. That is to say, miracles are mythological, requiring existential interpretation, by definition outside possible study through methods of science. Macquarrie broke away from Bultmann's existential view, claiming it is too narrow in its approach. As well, he insists that miracles are not the intervention of God into nature.[49] In Macquarrie's dialectical theism God is both immanent and transcendent. It makes no sense to speak of miracles as a violation of the laws of nature, since this would be God working against himself, and therefore contradictory. Such a way of describing miracles as a violation of natural laws is a sign of the dualism of modernism invading Christian theology. Miracles are a revelatory event; they are rare phenomenal occurrences that happen when God is revealed in a particular and surprising way through various beings in the world. We see the world more deeply through the miraculous and this appears to conflict with the expectation of a universal and general behavior of phenomena described through "laws of nature." Miracles are ontological events requiring existential interpretation, they are not repeatable regulative phenomenological events described through science. In this way, Macquarrie wants to save the appearance of miracles without compromising the language of scripture and that of empirical science.

48. Macquarrie, *Theology, Church and Ministry*, 20–27.
49. Macquarrie, *Principles*, 247–53.

In fact, he will contrast the "essential" thinking of theology with that of the "calculative" thinking of the empirical sciences. His is an attempt at a renewed discourse, where the transcendent and the immanent can meet without the exclusion of culturally conditioned worldviews.

This is Macquarrie's "methodological hammer" an appropriation of Nietzsche's hammer ("for once to pose questions here with a *hammer* and perhaps to receive for answer that famous hollow sound which speaks of inflated bowels . . . which are here touched with the hammer as with a tuning fork . . ."[50]), and the hammer of Jeremiah ("Is not my word like fire . . . and like a hammer that breaks a rock in pieces?"[51]), smashing the narrow categories which set the limits of both liberal theology and Enlightenment philosophy: diminishing the tendency toward idolatry. This world is all too ambiguous, too mysterious to fit into any set of definite categories; the Gospel is too rich in its truth to be reduced to one expression of dogma. By designating his approach as "*philosophical* theology," Macquarrie is purposely stepping into the ring of controversy.[52] It is a perennial question, "what has Athens to do with Jerusalem?" As we have said, he is critical of those who call for the independence of theology from philosophy. Heidegger and Barth are typical. Barth extends the call from the arena of theology, and Heidegger from the standpoint of retrieving an authentic philosophy.[53] And yet, it is very difficult to understand how Barth's *Church Dogmatics* could be constructed without the tools of philosophical reasoning,[54] and Heidegger's philosophy is very much grounded in Christian theology.[55] Our postmodern situation is still within the orbit of Barth and Heidegger in its call for a separation of the philosophical *logos* from theology.[56] Macquarrie would be in league with Levinas who wanted to teach philosophy to speak Hebrew, to translate Greek into Hebrew in order to escape the overarching rationalism of the Western philosophical tradition.

50. Nietzsche, *Twilight of the Idols*, 31–32.

51. Jeremiah 23:29, NIV translation.

52. Macquarrie, *Principles*, 21–25.

53. Yet, Heidegger is also challenging theology to heed Paul's call to avoid the folly of worldly wisdom.

54. See Macquarrie's comments on Barth. Macquarrie, *Principles*, 16–18.

55. This particular theme will be taken up below.

56. I am thinking of those philosophers and theologians Macquarrie addresses in his recent paper on postmodernism. See his Macquarrie, *Twentieth-Century Religious Thought*, 447–76.

Liberal theology represents this view also present in Heidegger, Barth, and in postmodern theology generally. Barth's concern for the separation between philosophy and theology has to do with a view of revelation that grounds theology in knowledge not accessible to reason, and hence for him, there can be no natural theology. But Macquarrie's phenomenological approach does not set-up revelation and reason in opposition, as either/or. Many postmodern theologians who develop their ideas within a phenomenological method revert to the warfare of "Athens and Jerusalem" and have not progressed beyond Enlightenment categories of the separation between revelation and reason. Macquarrie follows a long tradition that believes the authority of the Gospel is not compromised through philosophy (culture) as a medium of discourse. Macquarrie uses Heidegger (against Heidegger) to bring philosophy into the service of theology.

There is in Heidegger's philosophical approach a view of thinking and knowledge that in many ways mirrors "revelation."[57] Heidegger develops a form of "essential" thinking that is receptive to truth (*alétheia*), a way of thinking he considers more original and primary than the thinking that has dominated Western metaphysics, which Heidegger says has been dominated by a form of thinking he refers to as "calculative" or "representational" thinking. This kind of thinking constitutes what Heidegger calls the onto-theological character of philosophy and has brought to us the reduction of truth to scientific reasoning. But this thinking has become an idol, trying to convince us that only its view is the right and true picture of reality. Yet, this reductionist type of thinking is a stubborn part of our Western philosophical and scientific heritage. This has been made clearly evident with the emergence of the so-called "New Atheism." Macquarrie considers reductionism of this sort a dimming down of reality. Macquarrie will insist that theology needs to be receptive to another more essential way of thinking, a way of thinking we will elaborate on in due course.

Considering Macquarrie's affinity to Heidegger and his pointed criticism of Barth, it is worth pointing out the irony that there is a structural

---

57. Macquarrie, *God Talk*, 166–67. Macquarrie quotes Laszlo Versenyi "The quasi-biblical tone of Heidegger's pronouncement is quite appropriate to what he is trying to say. For in his conception of thought-as thought by Being, for Being and of Being-the importance of the thinker as a self-certain subject is as much reduced as it is in the biblical conception of revelation—of God, by God and for the greater glory of God. At the same time, in and through biblical revelation, man obtains a new dignity as the preserver of the truth of Being, called by Being into the preservation of its truth."

similarity[58] between Barth's view of "revelation" and Heidegger's thinking of truth as *alétheia*, a thinking that is supposed to hearken back to the pre-Socratics but does so through a theological lens. Of course, Barth's hermeneutic of revelation positions him to argue for the wholly otherness of theology from philosophy, and Heidegger uses his analysis of "essential" thinking as a way of distinguishing the priority of philosophy from theology. We find a reading of this in Macquarrie,[59] which allows him to navigate through the "infinite qualitative difference" of Barth and Heidegger and their insistence on the separation between "Athens and Jerusalem."[60]

In *Principles*, Macquarrie comments, "the present mood between theologians and philosophers tends to be one of suspicion and standoffishness, as each remembers the injuries which his discipline has received or is supposed to have received at the hands of the other. Both theology and philosophy are determined to maintain their autonomy."[61] The situation has not changed much, Levinas' hope to translate Hebrew into Greek notwithstanding. Ironically, in postmodern theology the call for the autonomy of theology from philosophy is situated philosophically, stemming from the tradition of "father Heidegger."[62] Perhaps equally as ironic is Macquarrie's call for a positive relationship between theology and philosophy that is to be situated in the tradition of Heideggerian existential ontology.

Macquarrie says:[63]

> So I am claiming that a positive relationship between theology and philosophy is certainly good for theology, and probably good for philosophy as well. This relationship may well differ from what it customarily was in the past, and we must think of it as much in terms of a healthy tension as in terms of an alliance. But I do not believe that any theology can stand without philosophically defensible foundations, and so, no worthwhile theology can be delivered from the duty of conversing with philosophy.

58. See Zuidema, "The Idea of Revelation," 71–84.

59. Macquarrie, *Principles* and Macquarrie, *Thinking about God*.

60. We will see this in his use of *analogia entis* in opposition to Heidegger and Barth. See chapter 5.

61. Macquarrie, *Principles*, 22–23.

62. See the paper by Hankey, "Theoria versus Poesis," 387–415.

63. Macquarrie, *Principles*, 24–25.

Conversing, or conversation we said above, opens one up to possibilities of meaning and truth held in tension between dialectic of theology and philosophy.[64] A few comments are in order here.

Customarily, reason and faith have been held in opposition, or, when philosophy has been taken seriously by theology, it was often as a "handmaiden." Macquarrie breaks away from this traditional opposition. Heidegger also rejected the traditional opposition between faith and reason, however he opposed faith and philosophy as two different "sciences."[65] Macquarrie is suspicious of pursuing and categorizing theology and faith as "sciences."[66] Nevertheless, his breaking away from the view that faith and reason are opposed ways to knowledge or independent sources of knowledge, is radical along Heideggerian lines in its attempt to overcome the difference. In doing so he is also implicitly returning Heidegger to the premodern tradition of Christianity. Overcoming Modernity (metaphysics and theology), and overcoming Heidegger's version of ontotheology.[67] He is offering a new beginning, a new style natural theology. This new beginning is possible only because of phenomenology and mirrors the work of Heidegger's overcoming of the forgetfulness of Being. When Macquarrie speaks of a "healthy tension" in the above passage, he is alluding to the role of dialectic that is prevalent throughout his approach. The need for theology to be built upon philosophy allows for its apologetic success.[68] Although Macquarrie is not claiming that revelation is to be grounded in reason, he gives reason a corrective role in relation to revelation.[69] Indeed, an outcome of Macquarrie's view of reason and

---

64. More on this in chapter 7.

65. See his essay "Phenomenology and Theology," in McNeill, *Pathmarks*, 40ff.

66. Macquarrie, *Principles*, 3–4.

67. Heidegger's view is not completely outside the traditional Thomistic understanding of faith and reason, where he sees philosophy operating separately from faith. Macquarrie's view of reason and revelation needing one another is in a way more radical in this sense.

68. The use of the word apologetic needs to be handled carefully in Macquarrie. He is against apologetics as a form of superior argument, defeating other worldviews (see Macquarrie, *Theology, Church and Ministry*, 14). However, philosophical theology has as its goal the outlining the conditions for interpreting existence. For Macquarrie, theology can offer an interpretation of the situation of human existence which answers the concerns of those on a quest for meaning. In this sense, theology is apologetic by offering a way of interpreting existence that is both consistent with experience and meaningful for our lives.

69. Macquarrie says, against (early) Barth, that revelation must be vindicated by reason. Interestingly, he argues that revelation is ultimately vindicated by the faithful

revelation will be their cooperation since reason can and must be influenced by revelation. But always for Macquarrie theology is "reasonable" and not a form of fideism. Finally, Macquarrie speaks of the need for a conversation between theology and philosophy. However, in this passage, the assumption is that conversing means cooperation. It seems quite possible—indeed the present mood suggests it—that conversation between theology and philosophy can take place where no goal of cooperation is intended and acknowledgement of difference is the goal. Such a pursuit of autonomy in Macquarrie's assessment is a foil for any progress in theology and philosophy. However, in both of these disciplines, God as a horizon of (im)possibility must be a continuing conversation.

God, who is the subject of conversations among theologians, is the on-going enterprise that justifies *theology*, what Macquarrie calls "God-talk," an Anglo-Saxon interpretation of the Greek roots of this word.[70] And this conversation has always occurred in light of the impossibility of "God-talk." "God-talk" attempts to address the "possibility of the impossible"—where the limits once imposed on theology are being "overcome" in postmodern and post-secular thinking. This is why we write "(im)possibility," where the pre-fix is bracketed and renewed attention is given to openness to the possibility of discussing what might be considered out of the question. The brackets suggest that the logic of rational scientific discourse is not being abandoned, merely limited so other possible logics of discourse (such as "faith') can be pursued: the logic of an essential thinking beyond the strictures of the calculative thinking mentioned above. Here we see the shadow of Kant. A neo-Kantianism runs through the tradition that informs Macquarrie's view. Already in 1963, when the debate about the impossibility of "God Talk" and the very meaning of the word "God" was raging through academia, Macquarrie was talking about the "possibility" of theology, and overcoming the limits that it imposed upon itself. He titles his inaugural lecture at Union Theological Seminary: "How is Theology Possible?" This required him to search for a method,

---

community (Church), when we get to the discussion of reason below it will become evident that Macquarrie is very much a proponent of a species of "rational theology," what he refers to as the ideal of a "reasonable religion," where reason plays the role of a "corrective." In the use of the language of "correcting," and "corrective," we see the influence of Heidegger who makes a similar claim in "Phenomenology and Theology." Macquarrie, *Principles*, 17–18.

70. Macquarrie, *God and Secularity*, 13; and Macquarrie, *Thinking about God*, 7.

finding in phenomenology the benefits that are still being tapped today in postmodern theology.

So in his reaction to liberal theology, Macquarrie does not consider returning to a naïve "pre-modern" mythology denying the contribution of modern philosophy and science. Nor does he embrace "neo-orthodoxy," following in the line of many Barthians who became disillusioned with liberal theology.[71] Although he considered Barth's theology interesting spiritual reading,[72] we have noted he also considered his theology too negative in relation to its view on culture and humanity. Barth's theology does not speak to the needs of those Christians in a secular world and the consequences of his theology, Macquarrie suspects, informs too much of what is lacking in postmodern approaches. There is a certain "world denying" aspect to it that he is uncomfortable with.

What of Macquarrie's response to "death of God" theology? Here again, we find some similarities between the concerns of Macquarrie and those of the "death of God" theologians. For example, a certain theological deconstruction must be carried out. Concepts of God must be destroyed—God as problem solver, absolute power, necessary being, as Monarch. This is Macquarrie's shared heritage of Socratic-Heideggerian destruction, carried forward in Derridean deconstruction. Also, the experience of God today is of God as hidden, absent, and silent, and amounts perhaps more to a lack of experience of God, or a deferred experience of God, or a displaced experience of God, or merely to a theology of "perhaps," as this is articulated by John Caputo through his reading of Derrida. Situated in this "perhaps" God does not "exist," strictly speaking Macquarrie would agree, God is not to be found through any ontological investigation. The idea of God's existence is more akin to a haunting, God is better understood through a "hauntology," in Derrida's phrase, a haunting of what may-be, or may-come, but is unforeseeable; if found, God is found through a promise, a future fulfillment of a past event. But there is no metaphysics of pure presence, no God "here and now," so to speak. And again, all of this will have our attention in chapter 8, for now it is enough to say that this way of thinking and speaking about God is found in secular and post-secular thinking, where Macquarrie observes there is equally a strong desire for the presence of divinity while experiencing

---

71. Barth had influenced theologians who carried some of his views to extremes, as we see in the "death of God" theology, "theology of hope," and even today in postmodern theology.

72. Macquarrie, *On Being a Theologian*, 105.

a lack of the divine in experience as expressed through traditional ideas and language: what Macquarrie refers to as "God-Talk." Macquarrie accepts that we live through recurrent deaths of inadequate images of God. Again, that the conceptual idols we make must always die so that the true object of thought and action might emerge, come to life, is a shared theme with "death of God" theologians. Finally, both share awareness that our language about God is always inadequate and imperfect.

In 1966, when the first edition of Macquarrie's *Principles of Christian Theology* was published,[73] *Time* magazine carried a cover asking the question for everyone to ponder: "Is God Dead?"[74] The question, of course, relates to the radical theological movement, which took as its point of departure the philosophical idea of the "death of God." This movement was grounded, as we have mentioned, in some of the ideas of Hegel, Nietzsche, and Heidegger. Macquarrie distinguishes two general understandings of "death of God" theology: one that is connected with Hegel, and his "speculative Good Friday" and the other with Nietzschean nihilism.[75] In the former, Hegelian sense, we have a thinking that celebrates the "eternal self-giving of the Absolute Spirit as it goes into the realm of the finite." This is a philosophical and affirmative view, building upon a Lutheran hymn, which "in a bold exercise of the *communicatio idiomatum* wrote of the death of Jesus that "God is dead."[76] This is the more original idea of the death of God, not Nietzschean or nineteenth-century atheism. These later ideas were popularized by William Hamilton and Thomas Altizer, who took initiative from Nietzsche while remaining indebted to Hegelian immanentism and dialectic. So, in "death of God" theology there is a "Hegelian-Nietzschean" convergence of ideas.

The theological background to such radical movements as "death of God" theology and to Macquarrie's own thought is the same: both working within and shaking off the shackles of such theologians as

---

73. Second edition, 1977. No further revisions are made after this.

74. April 8, 1966.

75. Nihilism is a rich concept and has a wide range of meanings. Its application is not necessarily narrowed to a sense of meaninglessness of existence. It can refer to the renunciation of the worldly, in favour of affirmation of the spiritual, or it can refer to the repudiation of a theistic view of God, a God far-off and totally transcendent, unconnected to the process of history. Such a theistic view conceptualises God after the manner of metaphysics, so the "death of God" can refer to the death of metaphysics and what Heidegger referred to as "ontotheology."

76. Macquarrie, *Twentieth-Century Religious Thought*, 399.

Barth, Bonhoeffer, Bultmann, and Tillich,[77] yet both constructing a "new theology,"[78] perhaps by pushing them farther and demanding more from their thought than the original authors were willing to entertain. William Hamilton, borrowing the words of Langdon Gilkey to summarize his own theological heritage, states:[79]

> From Barth this movement has accepted the radical separation of the divine and the secular, of God and ordinary experience, and so of theological language and philosophy; and it approves his further separation of Christianity and religion, and the consequent centering of all theological and religious concerns solely on Jesus Christ. From Tillich it has accepted the campaign against theism, and against personalist and mythological language about God. From Bultmann categories in theology, which polemic needed only to be enlarged to include biblical-kerygmatic as well as objective-interventionist theological language about God to become very radical indeed. It also agrees with Bultmann that objective ontological and dogmatic language about God is impossible, with the consequence that theological language is reduced to language about the figure of Jesus Christ and about man's self-understanding.

In this connection, we are reminded about the radical theology of the 1960s where the general belief is that the apocalyptic elements of Christianity have been undermined through compromises with philosophy. We see the desire to break away from metaphysics in favor of ethics and social-political concerns. Radical theology is guilty of "carrying accommodation to the cultural mood to the furthest lengths."[80] According to radical theology, philosophy seeks universal rules, utilitarian responses

---

77. Certainly these do not exhaust the influences on Macquarrie's theology, but these theologians are the "giants" of Protestant thought who influence the next generation and in many ways cast their shadow upon theology for the next two decades. As Macquarrie notes, the trouble for theology is that it is often busy with responding to the theology of the previous generation (Macquarrie, *God and Secularity*, 18).

78. The word "new" suggests a modern approach to theology, but see Macquarrie's comments on radical theology in Macquarrie, *Thinking about God*.

79. Hamilton, "The Death of God Theologies Today."

80. Macquarrie, *Thinking about God*, 70. In Macquarrie, *Principles*, Macquarrie questions whether "death of God" theology can be considered radical theology at all since it cuts itself off from theology (*God*-talk) by denying the possibility of talking or thinking about God. Not only is it questionable whether it is *radical* theology, but whether it is *theology* at all.

to general possibilities. Apocalyptic requires decision, an either/or approach to the here and now.

However, Macquarrie strongly opposed the "death of God" movement as too much of a worldly surrender to secularization, leading to the destruction of the Christian faith. Theology must participate in culture with the notion of transforming it always as a goal. His is an eschatological view of theological participation in secular culture not a surrendering to its values. He says about this movement "their teaching so exalted the "horizontal" in Christianity that the "vertical" was put very much in second place.[81] This concern to properly balance the immanent and the transcendent is always central to Macquarrie's theology and is a predominant theme in his *Principles*, which was published in light of this controversy.

As always, Macquarrie's guide is Heidegger. Heidegger interpreted Nietzsche's word "god is dead" to mean much more than the advent of atheism. For both Heidegger and Macquarrie the "death of God" refers to the end of the Platonic order of universal essences and truth, indeed, any rationally conceived absolutes whatsoever. For Heidegger, and many who follow him, the "death of God" has philosophical consequences beyond the theological. It is a word that ushered in a new order of thinking and an end to Enlightenment metaphysics. In this way, Macquarrie follows Heidegger. However, Heidegger's thinking leads him to announce an end to philosophical theology, whereas Macquarrie follows a different path; for Macquarrie this is the new beginning of theology. Heidegger takes opportunity with the "end of metaphysics" to separate "Being" from "God." Macquarrie finds in this "end" a beginning where "Being" can be properly reunited with God. Yet it must be noted that the "God" Heidegger rejects is also the "God" Macquarrie rejects.[82] This "God" of the metaphysicians, the Wholly Transcendent Monarchical god, *is* dead. But Macquarrie refuses to remain silent about God and Heidegger refuses to speak about God in any direct sense, resulting in all his speech about the "divine" being lost in ambiguity.[83]

---

81. Macquarrie, *On Being a Theologian*, 38.

82. *Causa sui* the ground of being in philosophy—Macquarrie extends this to theology as a rejection of a Monarchical God who is absolute transcendence and the god of immanence kenotically absorbed into the world. For Macquarrie the death of these gods is liberating for theology.

83. Macquarrie, *In Search of Deity*, 153–67 and Macquarrie, *Heidegger and Christianity*.

Within this form of radical theology, there is a call to an end to theism and to metaphysical speculation. Therefore, it is a form of atheism articulated as the death of the transcendent God, and a call to a gospel of Christian atheism, since it is only through eliminating theism that humanity is free to discover its own transcendence. Altizer: "It is God himself who is the transcendent enemy of the fullness and passion of man's life in the world, and only through God's death can humanity be liberated from that oppression which is the real ruler of history."[84] Macquarrie would reject this (Monarchical) God too. But he sees referring to this as "atheism" in any absolute sense as an unnecessary surrender of theology to a philosophical concept of God at the hands of secular culture. Atheism, Macquarrie insists, "must always be understood in relation to what it denies."[85] Christian atheism denies too much, according to Macquarrie.

The view that the transcendence of God blocks the way to human transcendence seems to be a common theme in this form of radical theology, as it is in postmodernism when Derrida speaks of his philosophy blocking the way to all theology.[86] In both cases we see the danger of the reduction of the transcendent to the immanent, to the ego: the *difference of the Other* to the *identity of the Same*. Macquarrie would agree that an overemphasis on the transcendence of God is dangerous, as can be witnessed in his suspicion about Barth. However, he avoids any attempt to reduce God to immanence as a corrective to this view, and neither is he willing to champion atheism as a means of liberating human beings from an ill-conceived subservience.[87] Therefore the path Macquarrie will take is that it is only in holding a view of God as both transcendent and immanent that any proper view of human transcendence is possible: what is required is a *dialectical* Theism. Although Macquarrie holds to the ideal of the unity of truth and Being, his metaphysics is not a metaphysics of "identity," as we see in the tradition of rationalism, neither can we say it is better characterized as a metaphysics of the "other."

---

84. The quotation is from Altizer's *Gospel of Christian Atheism* and is quoted in Macquarrie's *Twentieth-Century Religious Thought*, 433. Macquarrie refers to the "death of God" theology in a variety of writings. For example, Macquarrie, *God and Secularity*; Macquarrie, *Thinking about God*; and Macquarrie, *Twentieth-Century Religious Thought*.

85. Macquarrie, *Principles*, 117.

86. Macquarrie, *Twentieth-Century Religious Thought*, 449.

87. Ibid., 433.

Instead, his is a theology of difference that anticipates unity because unity can only ever be experienced and expressed through difference. It is a metaphysics that is always on the way to transcendence and never a closed totality. In this way, it seeks the other (neighbor) of radical theology and postmodernism while not losing the goal of the unity of thought which must be metaphysical (ontological).[88]

The reduction of transcendence to immanence is a theme central to "death of God" theology found in Altizer and others. But the "death of God" theologians avoid an opportunity since this reduction carries within it the way to a dialectical theology. Macquarrie comments:[89]

> There are two ways, perhaps not compatible, in which Altizer visualizes the death of God as actually happening. One is the incarnation of Jesus Christ. God gives up his transcendent being to enter the realm of the finite. This is *kenosis*, self-emptying. The other way of speaking is less mythological, more metaphysical, following the teaching of Hegel. God or Absolute Spirit pours himself out into the realm of the finite. Put another way, there is a movement of the sacred into the profane, which is at the same time an impregnation of the profane by the sacred. This dialectic is called by Altizer the *coincidentia oppositorum,* a phrase derived from the fifteenth-century mystic, Nicholas of Cusa. It is hard to see how this complex patchwork of ideas could have the contemporary relevance that Altizer and his supporters claimed for it.

*Kenosis* in this model assumes an exhaustion of transcendent divine nature. In some writers, like Jean-Luc Marion, we read of a saturation of phenomena by the divine: phenomena that cannot hold or exhaust transcendence.[90] There is self-giving in this model, but no renunciation of transcendence as in Altizer's view. Marion's view will have our attention later, but it suggests always a remainder of transcendence. Macquarrie will argue something similar, that is, immanence is always the way of transcendence, never the absorption or replacement of it. But against

---

88. That Macquarrie will see metaphysics and ontology together divides him from postmodernism generally, especially Levinas and Derrida.

89. Macquarrie, *Twentieth-Century Religious Thought*, 434. It must be mentioned that the two ways Macquarrie mentions, the incarnation and Hegel's dialectic are themselves certainly at work in Macquarrie's triune structure of Being. This will be outlined in chapter 5 when we deal with the issue of Natural Theology.

90. Macquarrie will identify this (along with Dubose) as God's *outrance,* or "excess" (Macquarrie, *Stubborn Questions*, 117).

Marion he will argue that this is precisely a God *with* Being, or God *as* (Holy) Being. For "holy"[91] points to the difference, the remainder, beyond that in which it participates.

To anticipate what will become more thematic in chapter 6, a few statements about the role of the "holy" in relation to "difference and unity," and "immanence and transcendence" should be flagged. In *Two Words Are Ours*, Macquarrie observes that the "holy" acts as a unifying phenomenon.[92] He says, "The mystery of holy being draws us to itself and into itself."[93] This because of the deep affinity between unity and difference (Infinite and finite). Although the word "God" is the primary reality for Christianity, Macquarrie will say that this particular word has its true significance in that it indicates that God is *"holy* Being," to call "God" *Being*, as Macquarrie explicitly does, is to recognize the "holy or sacred reality at the heart of all being that is essential to religion and makes the significant difference between religion and a true atheism."[94] Being and the "holy" are connected for Macquarrie, as they are for Heidegger. Although, as we have stated previously, Macquarrie takes advantage of the hermeneutic ambiguity of Heidegger's ontological language, (re)turning it to the service of Christian theology, he is in agreement with Heidegger's words: "Only from the truth of Being can the essence of the holy be thought. Only from the essence of the holy is the essence of divinity to be thought. Only in light of the essence of divinity can it be thought or said what the word "God" is to signify."[95]

Returning to Altizer, the similarity that is drawn here between the incarnation of Jesus into the flesh, and of Hegel's Absolute Spirit participating in the finite process of history is one of the ways we see a confusion of biblical categories with philosophical models. The two are homogenized through the theme of the reduction of transcendence to immanence, of the Other to the Same. To Barth this is the danger of mixing philosophy and theology, the only result will be obfuscation. And in Macquarrie's assessment, Altizer attempts to usher in the death of

---

91. The role of "the holy" will be further elaborated upon in due course. It will be an important factor in how Macquarrie is aligned (for example with Levinas) and yet stands apart from postmodern thinkers who identify as "atheist" or offer a version of "theism." This will be dealt with in chapters 5 and 6 below.

92. Macquarrie, *Two Worlds Are Ours*, 240.

93. Ibid., 243.

94. Macquarrie, *Heidegger and Christianity*, 100.

95. Ibid., 61.

theology. Macquarrie's dialectical theism will attempt to use dialectic as an antidote to such extremism.

Certainly, Hegel's view, adapted by Altizer, is dialectical, but the movement is to an exhaustion of transcendence. The *coincidentia oppositorum* ends with the dissolution of opposites in a fullness of Identity: this is its goal, a Totality, a Totality rejected by both postmodern thinkers and Macquarrie. It is possible, of course, to view the dialectical movement as a continuous inexhaustible infinite movement. Perhaps along the lines of Process Theology, and Macquarrie's view of the coincidence of opposites bears a resemblance to the dynamic process found in this view, however he wants to retain an idea of transcendence through immanence that he feels is lost in Process thought. There is no exhaustion of transcendence, neither is there a complete saturation through immanence. Dialectical theism recognizes the coincidence of opposites in (our knowledge of) God. And in (Holy) Being, which needs particular beings to manifest.

More needs to be said. For now, it is good that we merely point this out as a central issue, and to say, that what Macquarrie shares with the biblical writers is an awareness of God's constant presence with creation—from the beginning. It is a presence that must be dialectical in its movement, where creation and providence cannot be separated.[96] The incarnation of Jesus is a special case of this, which Altizer confuses with an inauguration of God's absorption into the world bringing an end to transcendence. Whereas for Macquarrie it is the beginning of the possibility of theology, it is the possibility of a new expression of love and knowledge. But the incarnation does not usher in a renewed experience of clear and distinct ideas. It requires a faithful dialectical thinking.

In Macquarrie, this is especially connected to the main theme of paradox. "In a coincidence of opposites, which we might also call a "paradox," we find ourselves situated between two truths which appear incompatible, yet each of which appears to have a powerful claim. We cannot simply dismiss the one and retain the other, yet we may not be clear about how they can be reconciled."[97] Macquarrie is willing to venture a dialectic tension to maintain difference and not simply a Hegelian resolution of difference to unity. Macquarrie's criticism of Altizer is similar to his concern with postmodernism. About Altizer, he comments that it is doubtful that the complex medley of ideas he uses has the contemporary relevance

---

96. Macquarrie, *Principles*, 211ff, 239ff.
97. Macquarrie, *Christology Revisited*, 13–14.

he assumes. Radical theology was worked out in a philosophical reaction to system, to coherent totalities. Something similar also distances Macquarrie from postmodernism, which sides too much with fragmentation. As we mentioned earlier, Macquarrie's concern for system in *Principles* is one of the ways his approach is set apart from the radical theology of his day and this difference can be extended to the work of "deconstruction" in theology today. Nevertheless, Macquarrie would be in agreement with Altizer, and postmodernism in its various expressions, that any systematic totality, grounded in a rationalist system, as a speculative metaphysics, is to be rejected as a foundation for theology as too much of a flattening out and spatialization of the divine. But, is this the only method of Totalization? Is there another way to indicate something universal? We have seen that in Macquarrie's view of the role of the "holy," the answer is "yes!" This is Macquarrie's project in his new style philosophical theology.

It may be true of Altizer that his ideas have not been worked out in the coherent and intelligible way Macquarrie thinks is essential for a systematic theology, nevertheless, the *crisis* in theology which motivates "death of God" theology is also that which motivates Macquarrie's new beginning in theology. In commenting on these trends, Macquarrie quotes Schubert Ogden as saying: "However absurd talking about God might be, it could never be so obviously absurd as talking of the Christian faith without God."[98] How to talk and think about God is the question that is at the heart of Macquarrie's work. Even with these differences, it is true that Macquarrie and "death of God" theology agree that classical theism is the "central problem for theology in our time,"[99] and Macquarrie will attempt to reconstruct theology in a new style as a corrective to the old style of traditional theism. However, Macquarrie would disagree with Ogden when he says, "If theology is possible today only on secularistic terms, the more candid way to say this is to admit that theology is not possible at all."[100] It is Macquarrie's conviction that the possibility of theology requires grounding theology in secular language and philosophy; otherwise, the relevance of theology is to be held in question. This is not to say that he is an advocate of secular Christianity, here he agrees with Ogden that this is a bankrupt approach. No, secular thought and

---

98. Macquarrie, *Twentieth-Century Religious Thought*, 436.
99. Ibid.
100. Ibid.

language need to open the way to theology proper, and here a bridge is built between current trends and biblical faith.

"Not the death of God," Macquarrie says, "but the end of a certain way of thinking about God."[101] This crisis has to do with the loss of relevance of the Gospel in a secular world. Macquarrie's response to this crisis is to work to reinstate an ontological foundation, to boost the stress on the ethical life that had come to dominate "secular" theology. This ontological foundation has as part of its apologetic function a refusal to allow secularism to set the limits to experience (existential phenomenology) and reality (ontology). Macquarrie's ontology will not revert to the old style dualism of the *super*-natural over the natural. He is moving toward a "sacramental naturalism": a re-enchantment of nature, where the "holy" is an experiential response to our being-in-the-world.[102] His task is to hold existentialism and ontology in dialectical unity.

---

101. Ibid.

102. It will be seen, however, that this experience is itself ambiguous.

3

# Theology in a New Style

HAVING DISCUSSED THE TRAJECTORY of Macquarrie's theology, we can now examine the formative factors for his "new beginning" in philosophical theology, his new style natural theology. By speaking of a new style Macquarrie is concerned with method, with laying the philosophical presuppositions required for the possibility of theology. Our discussion in this chapter will signal ideas and themes elaborated on in Part Two.

Macquarrie discusses six formative factors for theology,[1] "experience," "revelation," "scripture," "tradition," "culture," and "reason." These factors are heuristic principles that also display the tension that theology must maintain as explication of faith in the world. That is, theology is busy with how to witness and make relevant the *kerygma* to the contemporary situation. The task of theology, as an intellectual enterprise, is to consider carefully methods of thinking and speaking that best express its content. Therefore, thinking, language, and theology go together, but in theology, which is a word of the Word, language plays a vital role.[2] The content of our speaking and thinking in theology refers to God, who cannot be conceptualized, who escapes all our categories of thinking, and who, as the Infinite, transcends our finitude. Because of this, theology is held in question.

To hold theology in question is not merely a matter of identifying its subject matter, as may be illustrated by the common appearance of

---

1. Macquarrie, *Principles*, 4–18.
2. Macquarrie's philosophy of language will be a main focus in chapter 8.

prolegomena under the heading "What is Theology?"[3] For as we have seen in a previous chapter, theology appears impossible, for how does one think and speak about what cannot be grasped? However, Macquarrie is not deceived by such appearances. His constructive and positive approach also takes very seriously the reality of paradox and ambiguity, yet he is not willing to settle for a theology of the "impossible."[4] He is not advocating a faith in spite of reason, a leap of faith against all appearances. He wants to show the possibility of theology through a re-evaluation of our thinking and speaking about God. In some ways, this will mean a returning to traditional ideas, such as *analogia entis*,[5] performing a repetition to bring new insights to a received but controversial idea. And, it will include reconsidering "reason" and "revelation" in a dialectic unity,[6] a return to a pre-modern alliance of reason and revelation or a rejoinder to a postmodern approach. Macquarrie wants to take this apparent impossibility of theology as a speaking and thinking of God and show not only its possibility but also its reality. The appropriate method will, Macquarrie insists, allow us "to see the possibility of theology as a meaningful and important area of discourse." But he does not want to be accused of "showing that theology is a possible study of the possible," rather he wants to show "that theology is possible as a study of the most concrete reality."[7] In following this approach, he wants to avoid getting lost in abstractions; therefore Macquarrie is not limiting the area of study of theology, but expanding our awareness of the mystery and awesome nature of our *experience* of reality. His hope is to step beyond the limits of a secularized view of nature and humanity, and into a "sacramental universe."[8] He wants to show that the phenomena of experience are saturated with the Presence of Being. And although he will not say this is a "pure" presence, he refuses to allow the calculative thinking of scientific

---

3. We will have occasion to discuss further the meaning of the word "theology" below, when we discuss Macquarrie's view of theology. It is interesting to note that the development of prolegomena accompanies the acceptance of the "pagan" word "theology." From its outset theology has been held in question. "What is its subject matter?" "How is theology possible?" "How is talk of God possible?"

4. In this context the "impossible" is a form of radical fideism.

5. We return to this in chapter 5.

6. We return to this in chapter 7.

7 Macquarrie, *Studies in Christian Existentialism*, 10, 12.

8. Macquarrie *A Guide to the Sacraments*, chapter 1.

empirical-rationalism to limit the arena of thinking and speaking or to allow a mystical-fideism to hinder the way to clarity.

Macquarrie's discussion of the factors that give form to theology begins with *experience* and ends with *reason*. These factors are not to be confused with the traditional polarities of empiricism and rationalism: they have a wider reference. However, it will be central to Macquarrie's epistemology to overcome the extremes of traditional empiricism and speculative reason. The theological method[9] he chooses to accomplish this is a variety of phenomenology combined with a "constructive use of reason," which is also "corrective," and is "dialectical in character."[10] Phenomenology is a method of description, and Macquarrie follows it as departure from the traditional use of demonstration and proof in natural theology, which laid too much emphasis on speculative reason and abstraction.[11] Phenomenology as a philosophical method is a *way* of thinking. It attends to the "things themselves," and in this way, it has characteristics that are—so to speak—"docile and receptive," allowing phenomena to be revealed. However, phenomenology requires an active bracketing of presuppositions and attitudes that can prejudice our understanding of the matter we are thinking about and observing and therefore is also rigorous, "strict and disciplined."[12] Macquarrie is clear in his view that there is no knowledge without presuppositions, no theology without assumptions,[13] however, he is convinced that compared to both empiricism and rationalism phenomenology allows things to show themselves, while attempting to avoid doing violence to them by shaping them too much in our own image.[14] Phenomenology allows this, Macquarrie adds, "as far as is possible," that is to say, within the limits of the ambiguity of experience and the constructive use of reason. In this way he follows Husserl who developed phenomenology for the purpose of correcting

---

9 Macquarrie, *Principles*, 33–39.

10. Ibid., 16, 33, 38. Macquarrie is always careful to distinguish descriptive (i.e., philosophical, phenomenological) theology from interpretive (i.e., symbolic). Dialectic is associated with interpretation, more than description, and Macquarrie's use of the term reason bridges the distinction between descriptive and interpretive theology. The roles Macquarrie gives to the function of reason will be discussed below.

11. Macquarrie, *Principles*, 15–16.

12. Macquarrie, *Heidegger and Christianity*, 77.

13. Macquarrie, *Principles*, 43.

14. This is a central theme of chapters 5 and 6.

the errors of positivism and rationalism, which attempts to clean up any ambiguity, creating abstractions out of concrete experience.

However, there is always ambiguity in the application of any method, allowing for diverse possibilities. Although softened by the time the second edition of his *Principles* appears,[15] Macquarrie's reliance on existentialism is still present. Existentialism, he tells us elsewhere,[16] "is a style that may lead those who adapt it to very different convictions about the world and man's life in it." Perhaps this is true of any style of philosophizing. Macquarrie's insistence that the world, God, and humanity are "ambiguous" seems to make it inevitable that there will be various convictions. In relation to human existence, Macquarrie writes that, in our "modern times we seem to be far as ever from an agreed understanding of what man is or who we are, and the great conflicting ideologies of our time reflect different understandings of what constitutes a genuinely human existence—the understandings that we find in humanism or Christianity or Marxism or Buddhism or in plain unsophisticated and unthinking hedonism."[17]

God's actions are also ambiguous; this is true whether he is acting through miracle, providence, or revelation.[18] In relation to the "world," the situation is similar. "In the long run, the picture must be acknowledged to be ambiguous, in the sense that no finally conclusive proof in support of his conviction can be offered by the theist, or for that matter, by the atheist who has been calling attention to other elements in the picture."[19] Macquarrie admits that in his new style natural theology his phenomenological method, relying on description, may point in directions not desired for a Christian theology. It may, for example, point toward a Sartrean view of Being as Nothingness:[20]

> In face of these conflicting views, we can only try to follow the phenomenological method, that is to say, to put aside as far as we can presuppositions and interpretations, so that we are confronted with the phenomena of human existence as they show themselves; and when we have tried to expose ourselves

---

15. Macquarrie, *Theology, Church and Ministry*, chapter 1. See also, Morley, *John Macquarrie's Natural Theology*, chapter 4.
16. Macquarrie, *Existentialism*, 2
17. Macquarrie, *Principles*, 59.
18. Ibid., 250, 273.
19. Ibid., 55.
20. We will return to this in chapter 6.

honestly to the phenomena, and to describe them as they give themselves, being especially careful not to omit what we may not want to see, then we can turn to the problem of interpretation.[21]

Let us outline what advantages Macquarrie sees in the phenomenological method. When Macquarrie uses the word "phenomena" he seems to use it to mean any experience of any kind whatsoever. However, human beings are experienced differently from other beings-in-the-world. "Men, cats, trees, rocks all *are*; they have being, we come across them in the world. But as far as we know, only man is open to his being, in the sense that he not only is, but is aware *that* he is, and aware too, in some degree, of *what* he is."[22] As human beings we both are interpreted and interpret, we have our existence disclosed to us and we disclose our existence to others.

Macquarrie's theological method is given in three movements: "phenomenology," "interpretation," and "application."[23] Orthodoxy and orthopraxy is possible only when the three harmonize together in an intelligible and coherent way; which is the goal of Macquarrie's new style natural theology. In this way, Macquarrie would offer *a* view that is consistent with experience and is internally coherent in its argument and assumptions. But it is never raised to the level of exclusivity.

Macquarrie tells us phenomenology is description, but it is not interpretation. Therefore, following Husserl, he insists one needs to be rigorous in the sense that we are to bracket our natural inclination to interpret, to assign value and meaning. We are to remove "concealments," "distortions," "and whatever else might prevent us from seeing the phenomenon as it actually gives itself.[24] Macquarrie claims that there are three main advantages to this approach. "The first advantage," he tells us, "is that it begins at the right place, with the phenomena themselves."[25] To be conscious of phenomena, Macquarrie insists, is to be related to phenomena in a world, it is not an inner representation of the phenomena in an objectifying sense. However, even here ambiguity creeps in for we are still dealing with the appearance of phenomena to our consciousness.

21. Macquarrie, *Principles*, 60.

22. Ibid., 60.

23. This threefold methodology is the rationale for the division of the work in three parts: Philosophical theology (phenomenological); Symbolic Theology (Interpretation), and Applied Theology (Application).

24. Macquarrie, *Principles*, 35.

25. Ibid., 35.

Can we have a "pure" apprehension of the phenomena, form without subjective content? Macquarrie struggles with this, on the one hand, he wants a description of the phenomena without the screen of subjectivity, "the object itself," and for that to be possible our consciousness must be emptied of any preconceived notions. Phenomenology is a non-objectifying science. In his discussion of this, Macquarrie is at pains to say we are to eliminate our presuppositions "as far as possible." "No thinking can be without presuppositions, or entirely uninfluenced by previous thinking." Macquarrie goes on to tell us that interpretation is a necessary part of Christian theology, however, in order to truly think along with the tradition we need to begin with our own convictions, "we should not allow presuppositions or ideas taken over from the history of philosophy or theology to dominate our minds to such an extent that we never really face the phenomena but remain content with some ready-made interpretation."[26] Therefore, "we can decide about this only if, so far as possible, we let ourselves be confronted by the phenomena. So we look at the phenomena as they show themselves, trying as far as possible to see and describe them as they are, without distorting prejudices."[27]

What is left unsaid is how we rid ourselves of the formative factors of our thinking—tradition and culture—both of which are encompassing and defining influences. So here we are called to bracket the unbracketable. Macquarrie is in a position not dissimilar to Husserl. One major criticism that Heidegger launched against his former teacher was precisely that we cannot bracket these influences on our thinking. Heidegger's phenomenology was developed along hermeneutic lines to embrace the unavoidable presence of tradition and culture, and Macquarrie is often walking a fine line between these two giants of phenomenology.

Yet, we understand what Macquarrie is after. He is willing to acknowledge ambiguity in our awareness of God, man, and world, but he is attempting to find a way out of the conflicting views of these phenomena that especially avoids the old style epistemology of subject-object reduction—"the world as picture" as Heidegger called it. He offers interpretation as a separate movement in his methodology because he wants to make it clear that we need to personally work through experience as "purely" as is possible. We must, through the disclosure of the "things themselves," come to our own understanding of the phenomena. It is

26. Ibid.
27. Ibid.

evident from his own statements, that Macquarrie sows the seed of doubt about whether this is possible: description *without* interpretation is not possible, however desired it may be. In this regard he is not really dissimilar to Derrida who was critical of any "pure phenomenal presence." We are always already in a world of temporality and interpretation. There can be no "pure presence," we are confronted always with a trace of phenomena passing us by already temporal and becoming.

Macquarrie offers a second advantage, which is not unconnected to the first. However, our criticism may suggest that the second advantage of phenomenology is equally problematic. Phenomenology is conducive to clarity. Description conducted as outlined above will allow a clearer view of what man, sin, God, revelation, history, etc. point to.[28] Here, we get the further contact of phenomenology as a formal indication. That is to say, we are still endeavoring to withhold our presuppositions and prejudices, but are merely indicating, pointing to, phenomena that show themselves as "sin," "God," "revelation," "history," etc. Clarity, in this context, would suggest that our interpretive structures cloud the phenomena. Description allows us "to see what these words mean, or how they refer, or in what context of experience they have their home, so to speak."[29] Macquarrie is speaking metaphorically, of course, when he speaks of *seeing* "history," "sin," and "revelation." But the mere fact that what is in question is whether these phenomena are realities indicates that not everyone who looks is going to *see* phenomena as "sinful" and "fallen," or recognize an event as revelation. Always, judgment is involved. Later we will deal with Macquarrie's comments about the struggle for clarity in language and the lack of clarity in the works of many postmodern writers. However, what distances Macquarrie from postmodernism is that he suggests that interpretation and description can be separate cognitive functions. And although there is difficulty in this, our language should—within limits—be capable of expressing clearly the phenomena as it appears.

So here again when one describes phenomena with theologically laden terms, we are moving within a trajectory of always already in a tradition and are also interpreting phenomena accordingly. Macquarrie is not in favor of deductive approaches to theology. He wants description to take the place, not of logic, of *logos*—ordered thinking that both constructs and deconstructs—but of logical *proof*, of thoroughgoing

28. Ibid.
29. Ibid.

rationalism and deductive thinking. Especially Kant's discussion of the inconclusiveness of the arguments for the existence of God has impressed Macquarrie. Yet, Macquarrie spans the modern Kantian antinomy and the postmodern *aporia* systemic to philosophical theology, through his dialectic of the *coincidentia oppositorum* which is foundational to his new style philosophical theology.

Kant, as well, made it clear that our view of the world is equally ambiguous, possible of widely differing interpretations. Kant's influence in demonstrating the shortcomings of logical argument in these matters have had enormous impact on theology, and Macquarrie sees in dialectical theism a method to gain back a way to discuss these issues with intellectual integrity. The "ground" phenomenology moves along, Macquarrie claims, is dialectically "more secure."[30] That is, it is not an objective reality but a mediated experience, a differentiated historical-temporal manifestation of phenomena. Yet, this security is part of the ambiguity of the structure of being that is revealed through temporality, or, in a postmodern mood through the trace and interpretation of situation. Yet, it is more secure because it does not require the abstraction of logical argumentation for its legitimacy. Instead one merely has to look and see the phenomena as presented. But there is danger lurking here, and Macquarrie repeats his previous caution. "No doubt description too is fallible, and as we have already seen, it can be distorted by uncritically accepted presuppositions. But phenomenological description (the expression is almost pleonastic) at least aims at a degree of care and precision which would seem to lay a firm foundation for any study."[31]

Has Macquarrie really offered us a more reliable method? He has said we should avoid distorting our description of phenomena with presuppositions, but we have no way of guaranteeing this, we can only attempt "as much as possible." But, what *is* possible here? If we go back to the factors that Macquarrie says are formative for theology, and therefore formative for *theological thinking*, will we find that the possibility for theology overcomes the ambiguity of experience, or has he already entered into a postmodern hermeneutic of "nothing outside the text'?

Phenomenology puts all of us on "common" ground by merely indicating the phenomenon. One is pointing and saying "there" and "here" are places that we need to concentrate for contextualizing ourselves, the

30. Ibid., 37.
31. Ibid., 36.

meaning of existence. Each person can look and ask what can "this" mean, what can "that" mean, what are the possibilities for the phenomena? But, always there is ambiguity with possibility. Phenomenology is supposed to allow for clarity *in light* of ambiguity. In fact, we might say, that in "showing" the phenomena, we are lighting-up ambiguity—the plurality and manifold possibilities of meaning in phenomena itself. Macquarrie's view suggests that when we venture an authentic openness to meaning in our experience, openness to revelation and therefore to truth (*alétheia*), we are confronted not with fixity, but a fluidity of possibility. Through human being, meaning enters into the world, but it does so partially, in bits and pieces requiring all the formative factors of theology to patch it together.

Our experience is formed through a variety of ways, as Macquarrie's discussion of the formative factors suggests. Through *revelation*, I am faced with that which is other than myself. Through *scripture*, I participate in the original record of revelation and share in the "memory" of a community. Through the *tradition* of the Church, I learn the meaning of revelation and the possible interpretations and applications of scripture. Through *culture*, all these factors come up against other possibilities of meaning, through which I am shaped and called to participate publically in the renewal and re-creation of culture. Through all of these in various ways, there is formation of how meaning can be disclosed. Because it can be disclosed only through the world, it needs these cultural, traditional, historical forms to do so. How then can description not be shaped and formed by interpretive structures?

All the formative factors are dynamic, there is no *arché* experience since we are always already within them, thrown into the world, as Heidegger likes to remind us. They inescapably structure our view of the world. An authentic description and interpretation of phenomena will bring us into confrontation with the radical contingency of existence; there is no *ahistorical* or *atemporal* necessary phenomena. For Macquarrie, this means not a new piece of knowledge added to what we already hold true, but it is a "seeing deeper," beyond the appearances a realization of the finitude of existence: it signals transcendence, pointing beyond what appears. This seeing deeper is a conversion type of experience. It requires us to convert our old way of seeing to something new because although always embedded in our world we can see "below," "beyond," or "behind" what it is that we have previously experienced, as this is also an inherent reality of human transcendence.

This contingency is not merely epistemic. For Macquarrie cognition carries with it affective states. Like Schleiermacher, Macquarrie does not detach "feeling" from "thinking" as a cognitive activity. As mentioned in a previous chapter, through our awareness of radical contingency we experience *Angst*; which is a heuristic principal in Macquarrie. We become aware of the possibility of nothingness, shocking us to move forward on a quest. Macquarrie's view of faith does not allow us to merely add God into our view of the world as an additional piece of a puzzle, even if it becomes the dominant heuristic piece, replacing Nothingness with Being. Faith is a way of existence. It requires a renewed epistemological orientation. It allows us to see differently and otherwise, we are not privy to new information, to secrets, but to depth of awareness and atonement. Seeing in-depth will expose the foundations upon which my view of the world is grounded. Such an experience can begin, as Macquarrie tells us, because of *Angst*, Kierkegaardian-Heideggerian Dread. But, it needs also a Kierkegaardian-Heideggerian "Repetition," an idea Macquarrie appropriates as "existential thinking."[32] Seeing in-depth requires a reformation of my view, a conversion, sustained through a repetition.

Such experience is dizzying, Macquarrie acknowledges, and carries with it ambiguity and therefore the possibility that phenomena may lead *not* to an experience of grace, but to an experience of Nothing. Leaning on the words of Kierkegaard to illustrate this state of affairs Macquarrie offers: "One may liken dread to dizziness. He whose eye chances to look down into the yawning abyss becomes dizzy . . . Thus dread is the dizziness of freedom, which occurs when freedom gazes down into its own possibility."[33] Yet, ambiguity is evident only through the interpretation of what is indicated, what is described. Once we have named it "Grace" or "Nothing" it has been interpreted and given meaning. Through our freedom to name our experience we take responsibility for any valuation attached to these experiences.

Macquarrie's philosophical theology requires one to have a predisposition toward Being as graceful, of the possibility of seeing the trace of God in the individual beings. Macquarrie says this possibility is *apriori*, we have built in us a quest for wholeness, not nihilation and oblivion. Such a quest would privilege a view of Being and not Nothing, of grace and not dread. Macquarrie says that eventually everyone will have an

---

32. This will be discussed in more detail below.
33. Macquarrie, *Existentialism*, 66.

experience of dread, a dark night of the soul; it is, in this way, inevitable: inevitable, but not invincible.

This means that for people who do not have an experience of grace, (Sartre for example) the universe remains unintelligible for only through the grace of Being does the universe have intelligibility, where the ambiguity gets resolved through faith into meaning. In *Principles* Macquarrie offers the following:[34]

> To adapt the words of St. Augustine, human existence makes sense if being grants what it commands, that is to say, if there are resources beyond our human resources to help us fulfill the claims that our very existence lays upon us . . . It has already been said however that human existence considered in isolation does not make sense and that the most acute atheistic philosophers are consciously philosophers of despair . . . Even the philosopher who preaches despair does not usually shoot himself but finds some limited areas of "engagement," as he may call it . . . The man of faith, for his part, is not to be thought of as complacently anchored by his faith, for any faith worthy of the name will be subject to testing, and will not be a permanent possession but an attitude that has to be continually renewed . . . Neither the man of faith nor the man of unfaith (if we may use the expression) has certitude . . . But while we cannot know with certitude the answers to the enigma of human existence, we cannot help coming to some decision about how we are going to understand ourselves, for the very fact that we have to exist, to adopt policies of action, to pursue goals, and to choose standards of value means that implicitly we have already chosen to understand ourselves in one way or another.

Macquarrie's method shows that by pointing to the phenomena we are confronted with ambiguity, the phenomena in itself are undecidable—we need to wrestle the truth out through interpretation—this implies violence.[35] This violence is not a "wrenching or distorting,"[36] but a stretching of language, a "driving of words and constructions beyond their everyday usages so they become creative and illuminating . . . thereby achieving that kind of unconcealment which is the coming to be of truth (*alétheia*)."[37] Violence, therefore, involves going beyond the

34. Macquarrie, *Principles*, 80, 81.
35. Macquarrie, *God Talk*, 147ff. Macquarrie, *Heidegger and Christianity*, 99.
36. Macquarrie, *God Talk*, 160.
37. Ibid.

familiar and routine opening new levels of meaning. Macquarrie emphasizes the ambiguity of phenomena and the fact that language always has a meaning *more than* we are capable of expressing, "human language labors altogether under great poverty of speech" causing us "to turn to that stretching of language . . ."[38] in order to express transcendence.

This moves us to wonder about the danger of subjectivism, which is what the phenomenological method was to guard against. In any interpretation we must have a pre-understanding, a frame of reference, "we do not come with a mind that is a *tabula rasa*. We come to any text or any phenomenon with some idea of what it is about and where it belongs in a 'world.'"[39] There is circularity, to which we add something new, a new understanding that widens and deepens our initial beginning point. It is circular, from the known to the unknown and back to the known,[40] but it is not because of this "subjective." Instead, it is a reciprocal relationship between phenomena and experience. This points to not only the circular nature of interpretation but to its repetitive character where one takes up something new and experiences it in relation to what has been known and recognizes possibilities that are original: this is the dialectical character of hermeneutics.

Phenomenology first "lets us see," and only after does it apply interpretation. This, of course, is the ideal, and as mentioned Macquarrie realizes that presuppositions and prejudice are stubborn characteristics of our thinking and experience.[41] However, the stress is "as far as possible" to allow us to see the phenomena, and this is meant to move theology out of the realm of the "possibility of the possible" (a shadow of idealism) and into theology as the "possible study of the most concrete reality." Therefore, pure speculation is to be avoided. Speculative reason becomes abstraction, theory detached from the lived situation. *Theoria*, which too often takes the form of conceptual violence applied to the phenomena, is very much tied to the metaphysical tradition Macquarrie wants to move beyond. Yet, he is also not interested in privileging *poiesis*[42] in opposition

---

38. Macquarrie, *Principles*, 193.

39. Macquarrie, *God Talk*, 149.

40. Macquarrie, *Principles*, 36ff.

41. This is evidenced by the central role of tradition and culture as formative factors of theology as inescapable presence in any knowing.

42. In relation to theology the distinction between *theoria* and *poesis* is grounded in the perennial question of the relationship between philosophy and theology (faith). Post-Heideggerians adopting Heidegger's onto-theological criticism of philosophy and

to *theoria* as Heidegger did later in his life, and many postmodern Christians are doing in his wake. Said differently, he has no desire to privilege *passion* over *intellect*. Macquarrie thinks such trends are a result of the abandonment of the philosophical *logos* in theological thought.[43] He is not interested in abandoning theoretical thought, however, it needs to be located within *praxis*: there can be no abstract theory replacing a living theology.

The later Heidegger turned to poetry to express thinking. Poetry for Heidegger became the "particular form of language which in a signal way lights up Being."[44] Heidegger's turn to *poiesis* is a response to the forgetfulness of Being, and many postmodern theologians confine themselves to this way of thinking, working within the space provided by Heidegger. Macquarrie, however much he relies on Heidegger, does not limit himself in this way. John Milbank has written a defense of this move toward *poiesis*. He says, "poiesis may be the key to . . . a postmodern theology. Poiesis . . . is an integral aspect of Christian practice and redemption. Its work is the ceaseless re-narrating and "explaining" of human history under the sign of the cross."[45]

Although Macquarrie would agree that *theoria* needs to be located in practice (he is always a liturgical thinker), theology as a "step back" is nevertheless capable of some distance and objectivity, whereas *poiesis* does not allow for theoretical distance.[46] The method of phenomenology, Macquarrie insists, requires this distance. But, it also allows for a systematic approach to theology. In many ways, Macquarrie's view of theology

theology, want to separate philosophy from theology. Macquarrie is critical of this, and stands out from the present generation of theologians working in Heidegger's shadow. Although Macquarrie joins postmodern theologians in opposing an Enlightenment form of reason that attempts to give a totalizing picture of everything, he is not opposed to theory at all costs. As we shall see, the role he gives to imagination and constructive reason will move him in the general direction of building systems of thought.

43. However, one thing we need to consider is whether Macquarrie's constructive reason is not merely a species of this tradition where *theoria* dominates, where Idea dominates over Word.

44 Macquarrie, *Heidegger and Christianity*, 89.

45. Quoted in Hankey, see above page 28, note 62.

46. In Macquarrie, *Theology, Church and Ministry*, Macquarrie criticizes "the notion of a detached or value-free study of religion and theology," he claims "that some minimal sympathy must be present" (13). Theology as a "second order language" cannot be detached, however it does have a "distance" from faith (12). This is Macquarrie's view of theology "stepping back," as it were, looking at faith with distance but not detachment.

is similar to Milbank's "re-narrating and explaining of human history under the cross." However, the fact that postmodern theology does not permit the "step-back" and instead connects phenomenology with faith, means theology and faith cannot be distinguished in a coherent way and the re-narrating and historical look become too interweaved with subjectivism as opposed to a primal revelation and living tradition.

These are subtle differences, but they are significant in our situating Macquarrie in the space between modernism and postmodernism. In his phenomenological method, Macquarrie says he follows the initiative of Husserl, who could be considered to be the "father" of phenomenology and perhaps there is a connection between Husserl's view of phenomenology as a communal activity and Macquarrie's emphasis on community as the authority for theology. The fact that Husserl believed his method was a breakthrough allowing for the "realization of the *idea* that governed philosophy from its inception"[47] is not far from Macquarrie's own view that his new style natural theology would overcome the forgetfulness of God.[48] However, it is more accurate to say that he is following the early Heidegger. The distinction is important because Heidegger's move away from Husserl was considered by him to be a "new beginning" in phenomenology, and it begins precisely where Husserl was not initially interested in going. It is the *epochē* that is the point of departure of Heidegger's "new beginning." As Merleau-Ponty has commented, "the whole of *Sein und Zeit* springs from an indication given by Husserl and amounts to no more than an explicit account of the "naturlicher Weltbegriff" or the "Lebenswelt" which Husserl, towards the end of his life, identified as the central theme of phenomenology."[49]

But, we need to dig deeper. Heidegger's "new beginning" in phenomenology has been shown to rely quite heavily on Christian sources; not only the New Testament, but the writings of many diverse thinkers in the Christian tradition such as Augustine, Aquinas, Luther, Pascal, Kierkegaard, and others.[50] His method of textual exegesis is said to have been inspired by Karl Barth.[51] In his early work, Heidegger was referred to by Husserl as a Christian theologian and Heidegger always acknowledged

47 Smith, *Husserl and the Cartesian Meditations*, 2.

48. Macquarrie, *Principles*, 116.

49. Merleau-Ponty, *Phenomenology of Perception*, vii–viii.

50. Van Buren, *The Young Heidegger*; Kisiel, *The Genesis of Heidegger's* Being and Time; Caputo, *Demythologizing Heidegger*.

51 Steiner, *Martin Heidegger*, 73.

this as his beginning.[52] Without this Christian theological beginning, he claims, his philosophy in *Being and Time* would never have come about. Other connections can be made to Heidegger's involvement with Christian sources in his later philosophy and we will have reason to mention these in relation to Macquarrie's views on language and thinking.

The significance of these comments in the context of Macquarrie's phenomenological method is that it has been claimed that the reason theologians find such an affinity with Heidegger's philosophy is that they are, as it were, "looking in the mirror."[53] Macquarrie himself makes a reference to the biblical beginnings of Heidegger's existentialism.[54] Macquarrie's own attempt at a "new beginning" in theology, mirrors Heidegger's "new beginning in philosophy" in many ways. But there are differences. Macquarrie appropriates Heidegger with the purpose that theology has to be intelligible to other ways of thinking. This is to say, the apologetic value of theology is that it can speak to other intellectual disciplines, contributing and sharing in a goal of the unity of knowledge.[55] For Heidegger, none of these disciplines can be said to "think" at all. Macquarrie sees theology not only as rigorous thinking but in sharing in the goal of the unity of knowledge. This goal, however unrealizable or deferred, should always direct our thinking and its expression in language. In this, he expects more from his method than Heidegger was concerned with. It is interesting to note that Macquarrie, who is attempting a re-expression of the Christian faith in a way more relevant to both Christian and secular thinkers is involved in a demythologizing of Heidegger,[56] making more

52. Heidegger, *On the Way to Language*.

53. Derrida, *The Gift of Death*, 23. Also see Caputo, *Demythologizing Heidegger*, 173.

54 Macquarrie, *An Existentialist Theology*, 240.

55. Macquarrie, *Principles*, 21.

56. I borrow the phrase from John Caputo, whose work *Demythologizing Heidegger*, has as part of its purpose exposing the debt Heidegger owes to Christian theology. There is irony in the title, of course. Bultmann, who borrowed much from Heidegger developed the method of "demythologizing" the New Testament in order to make it more relevant to a modern time. Macquarrie, although critical of Bultmann in many ways, works within the tradition of demythologizing of the Gospel, and is closer to modernity than to postmodernity. Yet, in building his theology on the foundations of both early and later Heidegger, he is at once indicating the affinity between the Gospel and Heideggerian thought. In this way he interprets Heidegger in light of fundamental biblical themes, which are, after all, the root of much of Heidegger's thinking. His implicit acknowledgement of this affinity between Heidegger and Christianity shows Macquarrie's relevance to postmodern theologies that attempt a demythologizing of

explicit the formative Christian content that lies implicit in Heidegger's thought.

Macquarrie does not enter the postmodern debate regarding the deconstruction of Heidegger, laying bare Heidegger's unpaid debt to his sources. He thinks of Heidegger as offering a reconstruction, retrieval, of the description of authentic (Christian) existence. He does this in spite of Heidegger's protests about connecting philosophy with faith. But neither Macquarrie nor those involved in the deconstruction of Heidegger's thinking accept Heidegger's protests.[57] Macquarrie mentions the affinity between Heidegger and Christianity with little commentary, instead reading him as one who "secularized" Christian views of humanity and the world, and therefore, a source useful for a new approach to theology. He does not enter the debate of the deconstruction of Heidegger because Heidegger's approach suits his own program of a needed secular vocabulary, operating as "neutral ground" to build an intelligible apologetic theology for our age. However, we need to notice that Macquarrie's *secular* vocabulary borrowed from Heidegger's *secularization* of Christianity is handled in a manner that in many ways clears up the distortions caused by Heidegger's philosophy of Being, which in its final form became more concerned with a paganism that is hostile to the Gospel.[58]

All this is mentioned not to minimize Macquarrie's originality, but to point out that the concepts and vocabulary he develops in his philosophical theology, which are obscure and difficult, have their origin in a thinking that has its *arché* in Christian sources, but it *telos* in another direction. Macquarrie is attempting to show a way where this end point can remain in and make an apologetic contribution to the Christian tradition while appealing to a secular culture. He is pursuing a *rapprochement* between theology and philosophy. So, whereas Heidegger secularizes Christian concepts only to leave behind Christian thinking, Macquarrie begins with Heidegger's secularization only to end with a "new beginning" for Christian thinking, which may not be so new, but perhaps a repetition, a reappropriation, a recovery, or a retrieval of a way of thinking that is already implied in the Gospel. Therefore, Macquarrie's

Heidegger.

57. Macquarrie is quite critical of Heidegger's onto-theological stance, separating biblical faith from philosophy. He mentions that Heidegger's view does indeed offer a closer connection between faith and philosophy than Heidegger recognises or admits to. See Macquarrie, *Heidegger and Christianity*, especially chapters 4 and 7.

58. Macquarrie, *Heidegger and Christianity*, chapter 7.

use of Heidegger's "new phenomenology" as a way of thinking, which attempts to think as much as possible without presuppositions, may be laden with the most significant of values if indeed it is a way of thinking that is structured through an original Christian view of time, history, death, fallenness, conscience, logos, and transcendence, all of which are central concepts to Heidegger.[59] For that reason, Macquarrie's intention of establishing a non-religious secular grounding for theology is suspect. This is all the more puzzling since he both explicitly and implicitly acknowledges the Christian foundations of Heidegger's "atheistic" analytic and yet is determined to consider his phenomenological description as neutral. Indeed, with his protests about the limits of *poiesis* as an approach to theology, Macquarrie will follow a not dissimilar approach with his reliance on Schleiermacher to navigate through the difficult connection between "faith" and "reason," the affective status of a philosophical *logos* for theology.

Macquarrie's use of phenomenology is meant to allow him a new approach (style) to doing theology, laying the philosophical foundations for explicating the Christian faith. I have argued that Macquarrie finds in Heidegger a method and vocabulary for doing theology in a secular world, and that this is primarily because Heidegger's major concepts are a secularization of New Testament themes. Macquarrie's philosophical theology is, in many ways, a creative reinterpretation of Heidegger's philosophy involving a returning of Heidegger's concepts to their original source. And so we find philosophy grounding theology. This is not merely methodological. For the key word for Macquarrie's philosophical position is Being: Being attends all thinking and ontology is pre-theological. Therefore the possibility for any theology is dependent upon ontology: and for Macquarrie, a *true* ontology is possible only after the Gospel.[60] This *is* ontotheology, and although our discussion of this will be deferred until later chapters when we elucidate Macquarrie's philosophical theology proper, we must now acknowledge in the context of *situating* Macquarrie's theology that this reliance upon ontology places him at odds with the trends of postmodernism, which generally speaking find any ontotheology to be the destruction of both philosophy and theology:

---

59. See "Existentialism and the Christian Vocabulary," in Macquarrie, *Studies in Christian Existentialism*, 127–36.

60. In this way, his dialectical approach centering on the incarnation has something similar to Hegel.

and, as we have said, have them thinking within Heidegger's shadow. To the question of postmodernism, we now turn.

4

# Dialectical Theism and Postmodernism

IN MACQUARRIE'S ANALYSIS OF postmodern philosophy and theology, he engages a diverse group of thinkers,[1] who have contrary views from one another. So it is interesting to note just what these thinkers share in the common spirit of postmodernism. Of course, Macquarrie lays out themes present in postmodernism generally; which we will come back to below,[2] but can we say something definitive about a common consensus which motivates these thinkers as a group? If we can identify such consensus, an origin (*arché*) of thought, then to hold true to what has been stated above Macquarrie will share this formative factor with postmodernism. Again, this is not to ignore difference in favor of identifying these various thinkers, but only to show that the ambiguity Macquarrie sees functioning in the world of discourse about religion and philosophy functions here as well. Typical of Macquarrie's approach in his own comments about postmodernism, we will be painting with broad strokes aiming to avoid empty characterizations. But the intention is a comparison of themes, so we can ask whether the difference between Macquarrie's theological project and postmodernism is one of degree or one of kind?

---

1. For example, Levinas, Lyotard, and Derrida as representative philosophers interested in religious and theological themes. He engages the theologians Taylor, Ward, and Marion, who are interested in philosophical themes.

2. Perhaps we can generalize and say Macquarrie sees modernism as too much of a compromise with secular rational metaphysics and he sees postmodernism (as a reaction to modernism) emphasizing too much the individualism of modernity with its skepticism about things epistemological and ontological.

Post-Enlightenment, Postmodern thinking with its Post-secular stance rises up against the Enlightenment "prejudice against prejudice," as Hans-Georg Gadamer called it, still within "modernity as a thriving project."[3] We are presently thinking against the backdrop, or better, within the context of secular modernity. It is not insignificant that in one of his last books, Macquarrie had identified the prejudice of Enlightenment methods of knowledge (with its prejudice in favor of the methods of natural science, and its illusion of neutrality) as the most "stubborn question" facing theology.[4] He says, for example, "people in our own time are deeply influenced in their thinking by the Enlightenment, though we have denied that it is not impossible to break free of it in some cases. I think we are now at a sufficient distance from the Enlightenment to be able to think critically about it. Is this not shown by the rise in recent years of "postmodernism," no doubt itself open to damaging criticisms but not without some justification when contrasted with "modernism"? It would be a betrayal of whatever was of value in the Enlightenment if we were to accept slavishly and uncritically everything it has bequeathed to us."[5] Macquarrie does not speak of the post-secular,[6] only of the changing face of the "largely secularized world,"[7] which itself calls us to be "enlightened by the Enlightenment"[8] a calling that can have us question the prejudices underlying the Enlightenment itself.

Each of the thinkers Macquarrie engages is operating in a time characterized by the bankruptcy of secular thought, especially defined as a way of thinking dominated by a view of autonomous, universal, neutral

3. Smith, *Introducing Radical Orthodoxy*, 32.

4. Macquarrie, *Stubborn Questions*, xi.

5. Ibid., 157.

6. Macquarrie's discussion of the secular is similar to Charles Taylor's in *A Secular Age*. Taylor distinguishes three ways of construing the secular. The first, is what was found in medieval culture where the secular was merely "the age" in which we live, and the idea of God was never really in question. A second idea of the secular can be found in modernity and the Enlightenment, where there is the view of a neutral reason, of objectivity separate from subjectivity, where public is secular and is divided from private belief. This secularity is thought to be a/religious. A third sense can be found in postmodernity, in the public square of pluralism and the global village religious belief is merely one option among others, where what is contested is the plausibility or the credulity of any and all beliefs. Macquarrie does not create a taxonomy of the secular in Taylor's sense, but much of his discussion of the secular oscillates between the second and third senses of the secular Taylor identifies.

7. Macquarrie, *Stubborn Questions*, ix.

8. Ibid., 157.

reason common to all people (believer or non-believer) and this is a rationality that is assumed to be separated from *faith*. It is the question of the relationship between reason and faith. And this is precisely the context of Macquarrie's philosophical theological project. Macquarrie is no more interested in maintaining an old style method of philosophical theology where reason functions as a neutral autonomous agent and faith is taken to be the belief in the supernatural, allowing us to go where reason cannot. All thinking, postmodernists and Macquarrie agree, is "faith-filled." All theology is reasonable, but such reason is a reception, it receives what it is given: it receives the *light* of reason. Reason is perfected through faith: in a post-secular, postmodern, post-Enlightenment world, faith is the *arché* and *telos* of reason.

When Macquarrie reviews the relationship between modernism and postmodernism he does so through a series of contrasts of binary pairs. This is typical of Macquarrie's method of dialectical thinking, but instructive too since it requires us to define both modernism and postmodernism in relation to the other. If we must think as post*moderns*, we must do so still as children of the Enlightenment.

Macquarrie begins his discussion of postmodernism by observing that although it is a difficult term to define, postmodernism "has something to do with the creation of a *fin-de-siècle* mentality in which there is a rejection of the past and an intense expectation of the new."[9] The advent of postmodernism has been brought on, Macquarrie suggests, by modernity itself. "Perhaps the end of the twentieth century with its ambiguous record of progress and retrogression"[10] has created the opening for what we now call the post*modern*. So, postmodernism "is not necessarily 'anti-modern'" and in fact can be considered to be "continuing an age-old quest."[11] Therefore, Macquarrie states "in the history of these subjects there is never a complete discontinuity or an absolutely new beginning . . . we shall also find that there have been foreshadowings in the twentieth century and even earlier ideas that are resurfacing among the postmodernists."[12] His statement is reminiscent of the words of Ecclesiastes: "Is there anything of which one can say, 'Look! This is something new'? It was here already, long ago; it was here before our

---

9. Macquarrie, *Twentieth-Century Religious Thought*, 447.
10. Macquarrie, "Postmodernism in Philosophy of Religion and Theology," 9.
11. Macquarrie, *Twentieth-Century Religious Thought*, 476.
12. Ibid., 448.

time."[13] However, he finds a prevailing spirit—one that has a sense of the apocalyptic (an intense expectation of the new)—and in their revisiting of age old questions a view that is "anarchic or verging on nihilism."[14] Macquarrie's description of postmodernism as an attempted rejection of the past finds support in Hugh Silverman's comment that to "name itself *post*-anything . . . announces the previous time is at an end, that a new time is on the rise, and that it is self-consciously *avant garde*";[15] and Macquarrie points out the very word "postmodern" is polemical since "you automatically put all your contemporaries out of date."[16]

Is there a tension, we might ask, in the understanding of postmodernism, both to acknowledge its heritage grounded in the past but to do so through a radial rethinking, perhaps even rejection, of the past? Macquarrie thinks so. To the point, perhaps, that the past has become unrecognizable through new forms of thought and language. Such a view has moved Macquarrie to say that in some cases the writing of postmodernists are so convoluted and disconnected to what is familiar that what they have to say "would be dismissed as gobbledegook."[17]

We find at least one opposition to Macquarrie's view that postmoderns do not acknowledge their past, we discover with this thinker that the intention to break from the past is not absolute; that in fact there is an awareness and endorsement of the roots and source of postmodern thought. We find this in Derrida. Derrida, speaking about such a source and origin (can one say foundation?) for his thought, writes emphatically: "Yes, there is much of the ancients in what I have said. Everything perhaps."[18] Macquarrie, we have seen, wants to rethink the tradition, to "pay it forward"; he wants to have the ancient knowledge reverberate in the present. Certainly, this is what Derrida is suggesting—as any good "follower" of Heidegger would do. The goal of Macquarrie's new style and "repetitive" thinking fits with this. "Tradition, as everyone knows, can become dead and mechanical, so that growth and healthy development are inhibited . . . The function of tradition that has been stressed here is interpretation, and interpretation needs to be done over and over

---

13. Ecclesiastes 1:9–10 (NIV).
14. Macquarrie, *Twentieth-Century Religious Thought*, 476.
15. Silverman, *Derrida and Deconstruction*, 154.
16. Macquarrie, *Twentieth-Century Religious Thought*, 447.
17. Ibid., 459.
18. Silverman, *Derrida and Deconstruction*, 1.

again."[19] Perhaps he fails to give credit to postmoderns who believe they are on a similar path philosophically. Macquarrie points out the influence of pre-modern thinkers (Plato, Eckhart, Aquinas) and modern thinkers (Descartes, Hegel, Marx, Nietzsche, Wittgenstein, Heidegger) on postmodernism, and Derrida is in agreement that these thinkers are "influences which have inspired their thinking."[20] And so there is a shared awareness that dialectical theism and postmodernism are continuing on a previously shared path.

Macquarrie's dialectical position falls between the most general of oppositions of "modernism" and "postmodernism." Of course, he struggles with the difference, and as is typical with his own style avoids definition and offers a description of the difference between these two "movements." We will return to this below. However, we need to state that what he would reject with the label postmodern, is perhaps its tendency to rebel too much against coherent thought, tradition and (Derrida's comments notwithstanding) the sources of its own thinking. Macquarrie sees postmodernism as a special case of modernism, and I would liken his position on the matter to be in agreement with a (postmodern) thinker who writes: "I am interested not in the abolition of modernity but in the continuation of modernity *by another means*, and that is how I interpret what nowadays is called postmodernity."[21]

It may be that Macquarrie's dialectical theism, indeed his new style philosophical theology is not to be identified as postmodern; but it certainly is modernism *by another means*. However, we cannot be too hasty in distancing Macquarrie from postmodernism. We have at least one writer who identifies Macquarrie with this movement. "The conceiving of the divine in a postmodern phase of language may be advanced by the work of John Macquarrie, whose theology is based on antifoundationalist philosophical thought. Macquarrie is not interested in giving philosophical and theological support to the idea of classical theism."[22] So be it. This is the range of Dialectical Theism. It can acknowledge its debt to "moderns" like Bradley, Heidegger, and Bultmann but be open to and inspired by "postmoderns" like Nietzsche, Kierkegaard, Levinas, and Derrida. We could add that central to a thinker like Lyotard's

---

19. Macquarrie, *Principles*, 13.
20. Macquarrie, *Twentieth-Century Religious Thought*, 472.
21. Caputo, *Philosophy and Theology*, 37.
22. McKnight, *Postmodern Use of the Bible*, 203–4.

presentation of postmodernism (as incredulity toward the metanarrative of modernism) is a view of language adapted from Wittgenstein and his theory of Language Games. The very theory Macquarrie[23] uses to advocate the legitimacy of the "logic" of theology, the possibility of theology in a world of secular discourse. And, we could say that Macquarrie accepts the criticism of ontotheology Heidegger and postmodernism advance while refusing to allow Heidegger and postmoderns like Marion to define ontotheology in such a negative way that it becomes a block to his own dialectical theology. And more, we could include that Macquarrie's view of the existential threat of nothingness has ontological reverberations in Levinas' view of the threat and horror of the *il y a* and Derrida's *khora* dangling us between existence and non-existence, being and nothing.

Now, we have already mentioned that although Macquarrie's own philosophical approach is a new style, therefore having this similarity with postmodernism's "new beginning," Macquarrie considers his own method to be more inclusive of the historical tradition of philosophical theology than he sees in postmodern thinking generally. Whereas Macquarrie presents postmodernism as attempting a rejection of the insights of the past to follow other possibilities, Macquarrie's repetition requires looking for renewed insights and possibilities from within the tradition.[24] This renewal could be seen as radical from the standpoint of the old style philosophical theology, but the intention of both Dialectical Theism and postmodernism is a rethinking of modernity *by another means*. Macquarrie declares that for postmodernism whatever is "modern" is dated, obsolete; therefore as we have said he distinguishes postmodernism beginnings as polemical. Macquarrie has the reputation of not being a polemicist,[25] always entering into dialogue with others openly and without belligerence. We must observe, however, that one could describe Macquarrie's dialectical theology as polemical along the Heideggerian lines of renewal; and this makes the difference between his new style philosophical theology and the *avant garde* approach he describes as *post*modern one of degree and not one of kind.

Consider that in his new style natural theology, Macquarrie breaks with the old style tradition of philosophical theology when he follows Schleiermacher in replacing the proofs of God's existence with an analysis

---

23 Macquarrie, *Principles*, 123ff.

24. See Macquarrie, *Principles*, 92.

25 Ronald H. Stone, "John Macquarrie at Union Theological Seminary," in Morgan, *In Search of Humanity and Deity*, 71–72.

of human being and religious experience[26] where, in Schleiermacher, *theoria* meets *poiesis*.[27] And in Macquarrie's new style philosophical theology the human being is not at bottom considered from the standpoint of the *ego* but as the communal being: the *we*, not the *I*. Again, his theology is not divided into "natural" and "revealed" as is traditionally the case, but into "philosophical" and "symbolic," which is a new style, suggesting that the old style is *out of style*. This results from his division between "description" (phenomenology) and "interpretation" (hermeneutics), and we have already commented that requires him to collapse any hard distinction between revelation and reason, between special and general revelation. Even among followers of Heidegger, Macquarrie would find resistance for not following the (traditional) division between "faith and philosophy," and among many theologians, he may be accused of confusing "experience and revelation." Such notions of a dated set of concepts in modernism are at the heart of Macquarrie's theology, and this is certainly polemical. As well Macquarrie rejects any notion of the modern, secular view of the self as hostile to the possibility of reception of the Gospel,[28] and with it the kind of certitude that was expected with the immediacy of the coincidence of Reality (Being) with Knowing (consciousness). And in this way, he follows the postmodern rejection of a substantial self, and favors the model of the "self" grounded in temporality. Again, Macquarrie redefines the traditional understanding of truth, *adaequatio intellectus et rei*, where *adaequatio* was taken to mean the "agreement" or "correspondence" of "thought and thing," of "language and reality." Instead, he takes *adaequatio* to mean simply, "adequacy"; "what we say is true to the extent that it is adequate to what we are talking about . . . But its adequacy—or inadequacy—does not depend on its picturing the reality in the way of direct representation."[29] Certainly, this is a more tentative view of truth and language and is in line with the denial of any metaphysics of presence, which typifies modernism. Although, we must hasten to add, that although Macquarrie does allow for a consciousness of the presence and manifestation of Being, this is never in a "totalizing" way: Being always eludes our grasp however powerfully its presence is

---

26 Macquarrie, *On Being a Theologian*, 35.

27. Macquarrie, *Paths in Spirituality*, 1st ed., 67–68 where Macquarrie links religious experience with aesthetic experience.

28. Macquarrie, *In Search of Deity*, 234–36.

29. Macquarrie, *Thinking about God*, 23–24.

felt.[30] And so Macquarrie walks the fine line through the *apophatic* and *cataphatic* traditions where one is compelled to speak about that which cannot be represented.[31] With all this, we need to be reminded that for Macquarrie any new beginning is undertaken in the framework of modernity, which we cannot escape. We are embedded—we might say—in modernism. But is this not one way of understanding *post*modernism? If postmodernity is "the continuation of modernity *by another means*," then can we not say that "postmodernity is the condition under which we today conduct the business of philosophy and theology . . . ?"[32] We now have passed through modernity but we are located within a horizon of thinking defined by the modern.

Macquarrie, for his part, does not dismiss the significance of postmodernism,[33] yet neither does he embrace it. "Postmodernism is unlikely to be either the herald of a glorious new age or an early-warning signal of the final disintegration of western culture". It is not a legitimately *new* movement but merely another manifestation of modernism that Macquarrie says is likely to be exaggerated in its importance. He would accept the statement from Terry Eagleton: "Postmodernism is such a portmanteau phenomenon that anything you assert of one piece of it is almost bound to be untrue of another."[34] And yet, Macquarrie does believe there is a *common spirit* functioning through all the *diverse meanings* of postmoder*nism*, while remaining sensitive to the differences between individual thinkers. He finds disturbing trends in postmodern theology, in some cases continuing some of the more negative (and nihilistic) trends of "death of God" theology, where his dialectical theism was offered up as another possibility. Yet, with the legacy of Nietzsche, we have the influence of Kierkegaard. So that postmodernism is both theological and anti-theological having this in common with Macquarrie's existential roots. We do well to remember that Macquarrie's theological pilgrimage and the establishing of his dialectical theism develops within the shared

---

30. Macquarrie follows Schleiermacher in defining feeling in such a way that it is both a cognitive and affective experience.

31. This is biblical. Isaiah tells us that God is a God who not only shows himself but also hides. Paul tells us that the invisible God is made visible (although "darkly") through what is visible. And, it has a long philosophical tradition from Heraclitus, as Heidegger was fond of reminding us.

32. Caputo, *Theology and Philosophy*, 37.

33. Macquarrie, *Twentieth-Century Religious Thought*, 447.

34. Eagleton, *The Illusions of Postmodernism*, viii.

historical context of the beginnings of postmodernism so there cannot be a complete disjunction between these since they share similar formative factors in their thought and language.

Macquarrie's dialectical method recognizes that a consequence of secular thinking is—to borrow a phrase from Derrida—"a block to all theology." So in his review of the "common spirit of postmodernism," we may recognize that this "new" movement which considers itself "post-secular" and a "return to religion" has indications and structures that are familiar to dialectical theism, sharing certain "family resemblances." This being said, Macquarrie would fit more into the correlation approach to theology that comes under attack in postmodernism generally. So from Heidegger, through Derrida and Marion, we find a complaint of the constructive dialogue and shared discourse between philosophy and theology. Macquarrie insists that he does not make theology subservient to philosophy while recognizing that theology needs philosophy for its expression. However, there may be points of contact here as well between Macquarrie and these representative thinkers, who have not escaped the constraints of "Athens" in their return to "Jerusalem." To give just two examples, John Milbank makes the point about Marion that he "effects the most massive *correlation* of his theology with contemporary philosophy."[35] And James Smith has written about the more rational Kantian aspects of Derrida's religious views.[36]

In his review of postmodernism, Macquarrie plays off ten opposites that he feels are not only thematic, but that are key issues for theology emerging out of modernism.[37] In each case of "postmodernism and modernism," "objectivism and subjectivism," "fragmentation and totalization," "particular and universal," "self and others," "relative and absolute," "pluralism and uniformity," "passion and intellect," "ambiguity and clarity," and "truth and opinion" there is a critical stance taken toward any attempt to resolve these opposites and binary pairs by either a reduction to "clear and distinct" concepts or resignation to hermeneutic relativism. Macquarrie's dialectical theism follows the *via media*. In this sense, he avoids resolving the difference between these to either side of the opposition. His philosophical theology always has in view the reality

---

35. Milbank, *The Word Made Strange*, 36.

36. Smith, "Re-Kanting Postmodernism?" and "Determined Violence."

37. Of course, he does not claim that these ten are exhaustive only heuristic and pragmatic representatives. Macquarrie, *Twentieth-Century Religious Thought*, 448.

of the *coincidentia oppositorum*, an ancient precursor to the postmodern conundrum of "undecidability."

His review of postmodernism, however, does not offer a defense of his dialectical theism. So, in our discussion of postmodernism and dialectical theism, we will draw upon several of Macquarrie's writings over his career to fill-out a response. This will allow us to extend the discussion from the previous chapters, which focused on the context of Macquarrie's thought. We can concentrate on a few themes that were of concern during the development of Macquarrie's theology, and have re-emerged in postmodernism. We will not offer any exhaustive discussion of postmodernism, but restrict ourselves to Macquarrie's themes: elaborating along the way to shed light on Macquarrie's dialectical approach. Our overall concern is to witness how postmodernism compares with Macquarrie's theology: still within the orbit of situating Macquarrie's theology.

Macquarrie's ten oppositions are, by his own admittance, arbitrary and contain areas of overlap.[38] Themes such as "fragmentation and totality," "particular and universal," "pluralism and uniformity" contain many of the same concerns related to the structures of modernism and postmodernism. As well, "objectivism and subjectivism," "relativism and absolute," "truth and opinion" have several topics in common, covering similar ground. We will not omit any of Macquarrie's concerns, but we will extend the discussion in certain areas where Macquarrie does not. For example, the relationship between dialectic and deconstruction requires exploration, and Macquarrie does not raise the question of a "postmodern view" of scripture, although the issue of language (and writing) in postmodernism is one he is deeply interested in. But there are similarities with Macquarrie's view of scripture and postmodernism that should not escape our attention. Accordingly, we will search for identity and difference between dialectical theism and postmodern themes.

So, if postmodernism is defined as a reaction to rationalism[39] where theology is determined by systems and totalities of Reason,[40] and instead seeks to be reasonable where reason is "*situated* within particular narratives, traditions, institutions, and practices";[41] then Macquarrie shares

---

38. Ibid., 446.

39. Vanhoozer, "Theology and the Condition of Postmodernity: A Report on Knowledge (of God)," in Vanhoozer, ed., *The Cambridge Companion to Postmodernism*, 10.

40. Ibid., 19.

41. Ibid., 10.

similar views. If postmodern theology is defined as a suspicion toward one universal and over-arching metanarrative, then Macquarrie could be counted among postmoderns who recognize discontinuity in our interpretation of historical existence and not a continuous linear logic of understanding of *all of* existence and reality. If postmodernism is defined as rejecting one single unifying truth—here and now—in favor of an awareness of difference, plurality, and complexity,[42] then Macquarrie may not disagree as long as one does not abandon the *ideal* of unity even if it is only a pragmatic indicator, a "formal indication" that needs its content and details supplied through experience, which may continue to project a "not yet" in an endless deferral of life lived as *homo viator*. If postmodernism is defined through a rejection of the view of language as some form of "transparent medium that enabled consciousness to grasp reality,"[43] and instead sees language through a form of social participation in meaning, then Macquarrie would agree. But there is ambiguity attending each of these comparisons permitting hermeneutic flexibility, and what we recognizes as a theme in Macquarrie's vision for the role of theology is that it has a hermeneutic function; bridging our everyday experience with an interpretation of reality, an interpretation that carries with it a risk of faith. Macquarrie, the proponent of ambiguity, the thinker suspicious of labeling and categorizing thought, is to be located in the space created by the ambiguity of the "modern" and "postmodern" divide, his theism is a dialectical play of what is "modern" and what is "postmodern."

---

42. Ibid., 11.
43. Ibid.

# PART TWO

*Onto-Theology:
Dialectical Theism and Postmodernism*

5

# The Problem with (the Violence of) Natural Theology (I)

WE HAVE ALREADY SEEN that Macquarrie's dialectical theism rejects any complete division of revealed theology from natural theology, and his new style denies any separation of faith from philosophy. Here he appears to differ from his mentor Heidegger. Heidegger had claimed that any marriage of faith and philosophy is impossible, yet there is the view also found in Heidegger and in postmodernism, that philosophy itself has a religious sense.

This is part of the legacy of Nietzsche that carries through Heidegger into postmodernism. In *Beyond Good and Evil*, Nietzsche says, "it appears to me that though the religious instinct is in vigorous growth, it rejects the theistic satisfaction with profound distrust."[1] Macquarrie has no disagreement with this sentiment. Indeed, Macquarrie has argued that through the various phases of secularism and the impact of the secular on theology, there persists a "religious instinct," and it is precisely this persistence that moves him to develop a method for theology that would help the religious regain their trust in God. Against the "death of God" theologians who deny any theistic satisfaction to our religious instinct, Macquarrie calls for a Nietzschean "trans-valuation of all values" that would allow a shift from a hermeneutics of suspicion toward a hermeneutics of faith embracing a "theistic satisfaction" to this "religious instinct" in a new style. A hermeneutic, that is, which would turn the tables

1. Nietzsche, *Beyond Good and Evil*, 44.

on Nietzsche (along with his "death of God" followers) and perhaps (re) turn Heidegger to his Christian origins. To accomplish this he listens to Nietzsche's cry that "god is dead" and to Heidegger's repetition that reiterates the death of Platonic eternal essences, of old style metaphysics. He listens to Heidegger and follows his call to an existential-ontological phenomenology that will be a way for a new style natural theology to speak with renewed vigor to a new generation.

And so following Heidegger, he says philosophy as phenomenology must make room for a generalized type of revelation, that is, non-rational cognition. With no distinction between natural and revealed theology[2] there is no *special* revelation. All revelation is *particular*, revealed through particular phenomena and as such revelation will include, but cannot arbitrarily be restricted to biblical revelation.[3] With the concreteness and particularity of revelation there exists, Macquarrie insists, a "universal possibility of revelation, which is, in turn, the condition that there may be any particular occasions of revelation whatsoever."[4] Revelation, as he says, is merely seeing differently what is always present and manifest: it is an awareness of Being through the phenomena. However, Macquarrie continues to associate revelation with a *reasonable* faith: faith in Being, faith in God, faith in Christianity, faith in Christ as the existential-ontological archetype for human existence. Faith is a commitment to total existence as this is revealed through phenomena and disclosed to reason (philosophy), open to reason where reason is never autonomous but always reasoning from within and through the fore-structure of faith. And here he is at one with Derrida who is "offering another way to think of the relationship between faith and reason . . . because reason is grounded, structurally, in commitments, trust, pledge . . . before questioning there is a commitment; before knowing there is faith."[5]

There is the question also arising within postmodernism whether natural theology is at all possible if the Enlightenment exaltation of

---

2. Macquarrie, *Principles*, 57.

3. Ibid., 89. Against Barth, for example, who, he says, "frequently insists on the particularity of God's self-revelation, telling us that the bible does not permit us to set up the general thought of a being furnished with divine attributes but 'concentrates our attention and thoughts upon one single point and what is to be known at that point.'" Macquarrie will argue that such particularity is only possible because of the generality and universality of revelation.

4. Macquarrie, *Principles*, 53.

5. Smith, *The Fall of Interpretation*, 183.

reason and special revelation are disallowed. If there is no possibility of an ontotheology, what access do we have to any theology at all? Are we stuck with an a/theology? This is a concern that Macquarrie has with Karl Barth, but also with Heidegger, Derrida and with many of the representatives of postmodern philosophy and theology he engages. However, and importantly, here the natural theology that is called in question by Barth, Heidegger, and Derrida is the old style natural theology also rejected by Macquarrie.

Postmodern thinkers are very interested in showing the limits of reason and also the inability of the finite (human thinker) to capture the infinite (God). In this regard there is a similarity between many postmodern thinkers like Derrida, and Marion with Barth,[6] who declared a resounding "No!" to the possibility of natural theology. The similarity is grounded in the shared idea that finitude cannot grasp the infinite: that reason grasps in vain after what can only be known because it is disclosed through a form of revelation: there is no analogy between (infinite) Being and (finite) beings. For Macquarrie to have any success with his new style natural theology he needs to rely on there being some analogy of beings with Being (God). Does this mean that any natural theology will always and only be the work of a constituting ego, a violent reduction to the structures of reason? This was after all the conclusion of Barth, Heidegger, and Derrida. Is there any way to avoid the violence involved in the separation of faith from reason? The violence that pulls beings apart from Being in the name of ontological difference? An infinitely qualitative difference?

And so he asks, what if we take the incarnation seriously? This is what Barth claimed to do and Heidegger's ontology is structured upon. What if consistent with the incarnation, it is the infinite that condescends to the finite and not merely an intellectual ascent to the infinite that is the key to the possibility of natural theology? What if it is the infinite condescending to the finite that allows for any analogical understanding at all? Macquarrie writes:[7]

> But what if the transcendence of God was also dynamic, the energy of the divine love thrusting out beyond, God's *exitus*

---

6. Barth has been variously labelled as a "premodern," "modern" and "postmodern" thinker. See John Webster, "Barth, Modernity and Postmodernity." For a specific connection with Derrida, see Ward, *Barth, Derrida and the Language of Theology*. Also see Macquarrie, *Twentieth-Century Religious Thought*, 468.

7. Macquarrie, *Theology, Church and Ministry*, 58.

into the world of the finite? Some such idea comes to expression in a striking passage in the writings of Denys. He says: "And we must dare to affirm (for it is true) that the Creator of the universe himself, in his beautiful and good yearning towards the universe, is through the excessive yearning of his goodness transported out of himself in his providential activities towards all things that have being, and is touched by the sweet spell of goodness, love and yearning, and so is drawn from the transcendent throne above all things, to dwell in the heart of all things, through an ecstatic power that is above being and whereby he yet stays within himself."

Would this not be a reversal of the typical modern epistemological situation? Macquarrie identifies Barth's epistemological presuppositions to be found in just such a reversal where the Word comes from God to man.[8] For both Heidegger and Barth there is, to borrow a phrase from Kierkegaard, an infinite qualitative difference between Being and beings: an ontological difference: *Finitum non Capax infiniti*. Macquarrie sees this in postmodern thinkers, too, especially in Derrida who carries this Heideggerian-Barthian legacy into deconstruction. Whether we speak of Barth's view of God (*totaliter aliter*), Heidegger's view of Being (*schlechthin andere*), or Derrida's view of *différance* (and *khora*) as the *das ganz andere*, all stand as the origin of all that is, and therefore have a different order of Being-ness from what is brought into play. Macquarrie sees this same theme in postmodern thinkers generally; that is, that human reason is not capable of transcending the distance that separates the constituting ego from that which is infinitely qualitatively *different,* so one must begin from above, one must be receptive to what is given and work with that in order to understand one's relation to what is transcendent and Other.

Are we not speaking about the priority of ontology over epistemology? Where Being seizes us and we are grasped by Being.[9] That there is "a priority of Being over beings; Being is the *transcendens,* it is already thought with every being, it is the condition that there may be any beings whatsoever."[10] This is what is suggested in Macquarrie's new style natural theology, in his dialectical theism, which begins with the grace of Being and is centered around and even grounded in the incarnation.

---

8. Macquarrie, *Twentieth-Century Religious Thought,* 321ff.
9. Macquarrie, *Principles,* 94–95.
10. Ibid., 211.

But is this *natural* theology? Or is it *revelation*? For Macquarrie revelation only ever occurs through phenomena. Being is only known through its letting-be, in its presence and manifestation through all beings. Theologically, God is only known through his acts in and through the world including (especially) human beings, as this has been revealed through the Logos, the Word made flesh, Jesus Christ. So for Macquarrie, these old style distinctions of natural theology or revealed theology are based on a mistake of modernity. Indeed Macquarrie has explicitly stated that there is no pure natural theology, no unaided knowledge of God. Any knowledge of God requires revelation working with reason and reason working through revelation.[11]

Postmodern thinkers, with their reaction to the conditions for knowledge established by the Enlightenment, have generally accepted revelation through phenomena, if only as a trace, whether through the face (Levinas), or the saturated phenomena (Marion), or *différance* (Derrida) and so we see again the close connection between experience and revelation and this requires a way of thinking that allows reason to be permeated and illuminated through revelation. Our engagement with the world of the Other, is an engagement of the infinite meeting the finite. Here we have a correspondence between postmodernism and Macquarrie's dialectical theism, but not agreement. There is correspondence in how experience and revelation have a similar structure,[12] but as was noted in an earlier chapter, there is not agreement on the importance of keeping reason central with revelation.

Coming back to revelation itself, Macquarrie says that it "would seem that almost anything in the world could be an occasion for revelation. Natural phenomena may take on the dimension of a revelatory situation."[13] This revelatory situation is what he identifies as "seeing differently" and "more deeply" what is universally available through experience. It is recognizing transcendence through immanence. Recognizing revelation through natural phenomena requires a form of participatory thinking that has an empathetic character to it, an attunement to the other, which is also discerned in a reasonable way.[14] Macquarrie is not likening this experience to a form of subjectivism. Subject-object

---

11. Macquarrie, *Theology, Church and Ministry*, 62.
12. Macquarrie, *Principles*, 8.
13. Ibid., 7.
14. This will be outlined in more detail in our next chapter.

dualism is part of the old style natural theology grounded in a metaphysics that is not sustainable. Macquarrie agrees with the postmodern rejection of the sufficiency of reason, as well as its rejection of special revelation, but disagrees that this leads only to a method that "blocks the way to all theology" (Derrida). Such a view maintains the hermeneutics of suspicion, furthering a modernist view of skepticism and agnosticism. In this case the only way to theology seems to be an extreme fideism, or mysticism, which only furthers the secularizing of culture: the "privatization of belief."

Macquarrie's new style natural theology is an ontotheology, which is anathema to the theologian Barth and the philosopher Heidegger and their postmodern progeny. Macquarrie's new style, therefore, also requires a resuscitation of *analogia entis*. For it is through the analogy of being that any reasonable discussion of how "talk about particular beings or their properties can ever indirectly refer to Being and be illuminating for it."[15] We might ask, however, is this really anything "new," is it worthy of a "revolutionary theology," as Macquarrie describes his own approach, to stick with such traditional ideas as ontotheology and the analogy of being; especially when in the postmodern era this idea has itself become a scandal? Macquarrie is resolute, however, and he says: "The problem of analogy is a very old one in theological discussion, but it seems to me that it lies very near the center of the current debates, not only about language but about God and the meaning of the basic Christian doctrines. It is probably the case that many of those engaged in these debates *do not explicitly recognize the relevance* of the problem of analogy to their work, and may even think that it belongs to an older way of doing theology."[16]

Can *analogia entis* span the (infinite) ontological difference so central to Heideggerian ontology which Macquarrie wants to (re)turn to Christian (re)sources? Heidegger would protest, but Macquarrie thinks Heidegger protests too much about the difference between his ontology and possibilities for theology through analogy of Being with beings. Even in light of Heidegger's opposition to *analogia entis* Macquarrie feels that to discuss Being in the way of a non-entitative origin of all beings along Heideggerian lines is to revisit the analogy of being in a new way; where what is "totally other" is revealed to us and opens itself up to the possibility of description. More accurately, Macquarrie wants to revisit an

---

15. Macquarrie, *Principles*, 138.
16. Macquarrie, *God Talk*, 212; emphasis added.

incarnational model of the analogy of being that overcomes the distance so central with Barth, Heidegger and their postmodern counterparts. Macquarrie's interpretation of analogy of being will have something to offer to those who have said No! to *analogia entis*. Heidegger's opposition to *analogia entis* is paralleled by Barth's and is carried forward in Derrida (and postmodernism generally). Macquarrie finds a common spirit operating between Heidegger, Derrida, and Barth, a structural similarity in their view of language requiring the necessary silence of any reasonable talk about that which is Wholly Other. Are we to be reduced to poetry, to never ending *aporias*, in our "God-talk'? Macquarrie thinks not.

Barth is the theological nemesis of Macquarrie's natural theology and there is a similarity in focus on absolute transcendence in different ways with Heidegger, Barth, and Derrida. The *totaliter aliter* of Barth, and the *schlechthin andere* of Heidegger, which Macquarrie says was later adopted by Derrida as *différance* and *khora* are all variations of a theme: the narrow understanding of the relationship between ontology and theology, of the order of being and the order of knowing, of the relationship between revelation and reason. So Macquarrie says that with all of these thinkers the "totally other" or "wholly other" is meant to somehow represent that which "is more in being and more beingful (*seiender*) than anything that is, yet is somehow Being."[17] We are speaking of the "the *fons et origo* of all beings."[18] Of course, only Heidegger would acknowledge the use of the word Being (but even he later crossed it out), but whatever we call It (or Him), it is "meant to point to an unknown . . . beyond the realm of existent entities and therefore beyond the range of human thought and language.[19] Barth says that God makes himself known through special revelation, his Word embodied in Jesus Christ; Heidegger speaks of the It Gives (*Es Gibt*) and Derrida of *différance* and *khora*. However we imagine this mystery of transcendence, It (He) is responsible for there being anything at all and It (He) *does come to us*, in the form of Gift, donation, or love: the *exitus* into the world of the finite by Being or God, or *différance*: of this fact Macquarrie, Heidegger, Barth, and Derrida are in agreement.

But according to Barth, Heidegger, and Derrida to speak of *analogia entis* is to speak the language of ontotheology, the reduction of God to a being. This is the god of metaphysics, the *causa sui*, that is nothing

---

17. Macquarrie, *Twentieth-Century Religious Thought*, 468.
18. Macquarrie, *Principles*, 211.
19. Macquarrie, *Twentieth-Century Religious Thought*, 468.

but a projection of man himself, the ontotheological god is a philosophical concept that claims God and all beings share properties in common, where "God" is the name given to the highest being of the class of beings, a *summum ens*, where all difference is removed and God is confused with the realm of creatures, or where human reason is elevated to the status of deity allowing for the mistake of creating analogies between Being (God) and beings (creatures). This God is not worth talking about. With the end of metaphysics, we have heard of the death of this god. Macquarrie, of course, would not lament this turn of events.

But how does Macquarrie's appeal to the analogy of being avoid succumbing to the wiles of this god? How does Macquarrie talk about Being (God) to Heidegger who never wants to talk about Being theologically, and if he did speak theologically claims he would never use the word Being? How does he talk about Heidegger's *Es Gibt*, the "It Gives," the Source and self-giving Being Itself, the *Es Gibt* that for Heidegger is a way of recovering the original idea of Being? How could Macquarrie convince Heidegger that there is a possible interpretation of Heidegger in Christian terms that will not fall into an ontotheology where Being becomes humiliated and equated to the *causa sui*? Macquarrie maintains: "In Christian theology, God is love. In Heidegger, "It gives" is an act of giving or donation, and since he has told us that the "It" which gives Being is Being itself, then the act of giving is also an act of self-giving, and so not different in any major respect from love."[20] There can be no ontological or epistemological determinacy promised in Heidegger, only room for possible interpretations of the impossible, and so he is cautious to not say that for Heidegger the "It gives" is God, only that there is enough ambiguity and similarity in the idea that it could be and so this leaves space for Macquarrie's appropriation and interpretation.

Do Macquarrie and Derrida have anything to say to one another when Derrida's thought is circumscribed through *différance* and deconstruction where deconstruction is a passion to think the unthinkable through *différance*, which wants to defer all thought about the unthinkable? How would Macquarrie reassure Derrida that Being is not a dangerous idea? Derrida who wants to avoid speaking about Being and wants only to speak about *différance* and *khora*[21] that strange wilderness of a "place" between existence and non-existence where beings receive

---

20. Macquarrie, *Heidegger and Christianity*, 99.
21. More about this below.

their form,²² which for Macquarrie is close to the undoing of creation, more of a chaos than a cosmos. Would there be a way for Macquarrie to interest those like-minded to Derrida that there is a way to do theology that is not locked into an apophatic approach, lost in the impossibility of language? That theology is possible and it can be witnessed through a return of Heideggerian Being to its Hebraic-Greek roots? Is there any point in engaging Derrida, who introduces the idea of *différance* and *khora* in order to move beyond or away from the Heideggerian motif that supplies "the circle of credit and debt . . . all back in debt of father Parmenides and other Greek fathers and creditors, the entire line of a distinctly Heideggerian *patrologia graeca*" where "Thinking now means thankfully-thinking-back on (Greek) Being"?²³ Derrida who wants to direct us in "How to Avoid Speaking" says about Heidegger's approach: "With and without the word *being*, he wrote a theology with and without God."²⁴ Deconstruction is the experience of the impossible possibility of the impossible, but one cannot really speak of that which has yet to come, of that which has yet to be done, of the "Wholly Other" that is both with us and without us. Can one? Maybe it is here, precisely in the dialectic of the given and the hidden (or non-given), that there is room for a conversation between a lapsed and a revisionist Heideggerian.

How does Macquarrie address Barth who says a resounding No! to any talk of God that associates Him with that all too Greek concept of Being? Theology is impossible but necessary Barth says, but do not usher in any *mixophilosophicotheologia* and call it authentic talk of God (theology).²⁵ "Nowhere and never," Barth tells us, "is the *Deus dixit* a reality except in God's own most proper reality . . . everything hinges on his covering his inaccessible divine I-ness with a human I-ness as with a veil so that we can grasp him as a person."²⁶ According to Barth, the possibility for theology is only through the incarnation of Jesus Christ. This is a special revelation; he does not acknowledge the *Deus dixit* through any general revealdness, as Macquarrie thinks is essential. God is Given through the incarnation of Jesus Christ. As Webster tells it:²⁷

22. Macquarrie, *Twentieth-Century Religious Thought*, 469.
23. Caputo, *Prayers and Tears*, 166.
24. Derrida, "How to Avoid Speaking," 128.
25. Barth, *Evangelical Theology*, iii.
26. Quoted in Webster, "Barth, Modernity and Postmodernity," 14.
27. Webster, "Barth, Modernity and Postmodernity," 15.

> Construed through the Trinitarian and incarnational categories as the free, self-manifesting majesty of God's presence, that givenness for Barth made possible a kind of theological activity whose primary concern was not with the question of its own feasibility in a culture in disarray, but with the sheer actuality of God's act of revelation, which as it were has already set theology on its path, thereby requiring the theologian to follow its given-spiritually given, but nevertheless given-presence and movement. The direction of that movement, he came to see, is towards the church, appointed by God as the sphere in which revelation meets the recognition of faith.

There is a great deal of Barthian influence in Macquarrie's theology. But the differences are also pronounced, differences we will return to in relation to his view of *analogia entis* and his view of the Trinity. The general difference we should immediately notice, one that makes all the difference in the world apologetically for Macquarrie and distances him from Barth, is how one answers *"the question of the feasibility of theological activity in a culture in disarray."*

This raises the question of the division between Church and World, between revelation and revealdness; it exposes the difference between Barth and Macquarrie of a perhaps too particular a revelation in Barth and a very general revelation in Macquarrie. As we will see in due course, Macquarrie thinks of Barth as too much a universalist in relation to his theology of salvation through Jesus Christ,[28] and too particular in his view of the revelation of the Logos. Yet, in spite of these divisions, we hear Macquarrie say that Barth was absolutely right when he insists that the living Word, the *incarnate* Word, gives birth to the written word of scripture and the living voice of the Church.[29] However, Macquarrie does not draw a "hard and fast" line between Church and World,[30] there is dialectic of identity and difference, and he rejects the notion of an absolute "antithesis" between "Church" and "World." The relationship between Church and World has to do with the dialectic between creation and

---

28. See Macquarrie, *Theology, Church and Ministry*, 66–67. But see in this connection Macquarrie, *Stubborn Questions*, 139, where Macquarrie writes: "But although men and women still remain alienated from God, we are pointed toward the hope of final universalism, in which through Christ the whole human creation will share with him the divine likeness."

29. Macquarrie, *Principles*, 454.

30. Ibid., 387.

incarnation,[31] where the Church is continuous with both the creation and incarnation: we might say that this is the origin of Macquarrie's view of the identity and difference between general and special revelation. There is a difference of degree only between Creation, Church, and Incarnation, for both the Creation and the Church are extensions of the Incarnation. It is only through the dialectical activity of the transcendence and the immanence of Being (God), symbolized through the Incarnation, that there is Creation or Church.

But what of the dialectic of givenness and non-givenness? This dialectic of givenness and non-givenness is also resolved through the incarnation. It is through this very activity that Macquarrie finds a possibility of not only a positive theology of the hidden God (Being), but a possibility of natural theology. Macquarrie generalizes revelation into a natural theology, but revelation, Barth insists, can only be *exclusively* particular in and through Jesus Christ, for him the incarnation is a specific event and never a philosophical generalization. For Macquarrie, the Logos of Athens and the Logos of Jerusalem meet in the incarnation of Jesus Christ which indeed is a particular focus of Being: the presence and manifestation of God *par excellence*. Not so for Barth (or Heidegger and Derrida). Webster tells us that for Barth "The holy that is obvious, the sacral, is never truly holy. The true holy is spirit, not thing. The *Deus dixit* is revelation, not revealdness."[32] Here Webster contrasts Barth from postmodernism, but we could add, from Macquarrie. But here we find ourselves in a hall of mirrors. For Barth is too often (and too easily?) associated with postmodernism, yet maybe we need to draw a line with Barth's "No" on one side and Macquarrie and the postmodern "Yes" on the other: for is it not the case for Macquarrie that what makes any positive Christianity possible is the real phenomenological possibility exposed in postmodernism that we are always dealing with revealdness through phenomena? Is it possible that followers of Barth perhaps have more in common with dialectical theology than is immediately evident, even in light of postmodern denunciations of correlational theology? How would Macquarrie convince Barthians that although Being (God) is incomparable, we need not be deterred (or deferred), we need only be wary of "any familiar and over-literal talk of God,"[33] that there is both

---

31. Ibid., 388.
32. Webster, "Barth, Modernity and Postmodernity," 14.
33. Macquarrie, *God Talk*, 222.

identity and difference, continuity and discontinuity between creation and creator, beings and Being, revealdness and revelation? "Being" is a verbal-noun. The *I Am* that "was," "is," and "will be" is not the static undifferentiated ahistorical Parmenidean plenum referenced by Derrida and feared by Barth. Biblical "Being," He *Who is* God, could be read—has been read—as a Hebraic correction to the ontology of the Greeks. Analogy, Macquarrie will say, is the bridge between these, where the language of the "Jews" meets the language of the "Greeks." To this meeting of Jerusalem and Athens through analogy and symbol, Macquarrie says "Yes" to Barth's "No"!

Macquarrie is unsure how exactly Barth wants to interpret the *Deus dixit*. On the one hand, we are asked to take the proposition "God Speaks" literally; it is not a symbolic statement.[34] On the other hand, if God does indeed speak then this is not a usual kind of speaking (like "Socrates speaks'), in fact, it would be incomparable to any kind of speaking we know. So, how could it be taken literally?[35] Both Macquarrie and Barth, of course, acknowledge the incomparable language of God, the Word of God, from that of human speech and language. If we say God loves, how does this compare when we say we love? If we say God is good, in what respect does this compare with goodness in humanity? Consider these words from Tim Bradshaw:[36]

> Macquarrie assumes that goodness applied to God and to humanity has no literal commonality of meaning, and one here is reminded of the dialectics of the early Barth in terms of the *ordo cognoscendi*. In speaking of God we have no common ground, no shared field of meaning, to work from. "Good" may be used, but it is not a term which has any necessary application to God, who defines his own meaning for it . . . God is beyond goodness. God is beyond the terms good and evil . . . Being, which is organically immanent, transcends our knowing and perceiving, our categories. Being as present and manifest ought to balance with absent and hidden, if we take Macquarrie's logic consistently. Any knowledge of God can only be analogical, and only that in a dialectical fashion.

Macquarrie likes to remind us that for Barth "during most of his career his stress was upon the distance between the divine and the human,

---

34. Ibid., 45–46.
35. Ibid., 46.
36. Bradshaw, "Macquarrie's Doctrine of God," 14.

and even if he came to modify this and to recognize what he has called the "humanity" of God, he has not relinquished his insistence on the utter inaccessibility of the divine from the human side."[37] Macquarrie sees no other recourse but to work with symbol and analogy, otherwise we will be shut off from theology (God Talk) and driven into a form of *via negationis* "listening to God's language" but in no way able to reproduce it, retreating into silence.[38]

Even those who claim to remain silent about God (Being) have had much to say, so we must find a way to speak of God (Being) and to do so without fear that every reference to an ontotheology is necessarily a reduction to a metaphysics grounded in the all too human projections of the *cogito*. For Macquarrie, to deny any analogy of being "raises difficulties over how we may talk about God."[39] He is quite critical of those who exaggerate the ontological difference between Being (God) and beings (creation), to the point where the ontological difference becomes merely another form of dualism. Here of course, he is at odds not only with Heidegger, but also with Barth and Derrida.[40] For Derrida our thought and language can never coincide with the "wholly other" and his method of deconstruction will not allow for the kind of closure suggested by the analogy of being. Barth has said that the anti-Christ invented the *analogia entis*[41] and any attempt to employ it is blasphemous.[42] Barth was convinced that the *analogia entis* would lead to a reduction of theology to anthropology, of God to man, of Being to beings. As Barth understands the analogy of Being, he is convinced that we ascribe to God our experiences and our understandings of things so our wisdom is used as an analogue for God's relationship toward us. God cannot be captured through or limited to whatever symbols or analogues we ascribe to him. There can be no commonality between the Being of God and the being of human being; it is God's actions that are the models of which our actions are analogues. If we love, it is because he first loved us. If we use the designation father, it is because he was first a father to us, etc. This is the *analogia fidei* and the *analogia gratiae*. There is a way from Christology to

37. Macquarrie, *God Talk*, 46.
38. Ibid., 47.
39. Macquarrie, *Principles*, 138.
40. Macquarrie, *Twentieth-Century Religious Thought*, 468.
41. Betz, "Beyond the Sublime," 3. Barth makes this statement in his *Church Dogmatics* (KD1/1, viii).
42. Macquarrie, *Theology, Church and Ministry*, 50.

anthropology, but never from anthropology to Christology. Both Barth and Macquarrie know that for any natural theology to be possible there must be a way from humanity to God.

But Macquarrie is not thinking of *analogia entis* in this way, as a way of lifting human characteristics up to the level of God in order to describe his Being. His dialectical theism "enables us to interpret the *analogia entis* in a way that will neither assimilate God to man nor yet put an unbridgeable gulf between them."[43] Macquarrie says that it is precisely because the Word is incarnated in Christ, which is so central to Barth's whole theology, that we have a way to natural theology through *analogia entis*. He will say that since Christ is the archetype of humanity and the *arché* and *telos* of history then this makes possible a way from anthropology to Christology. In fact we can recollect the words of Barth, quoted above, "*everything hinges on his covering his inaccessible divine I-ness with a human I-ness as with a veil so that we can grasp him as a person.*" Because of this covering, we have a way from anthropology to Christology. Macquarrie writes:[44]

> I have been moving in the area of natural theology. The whole claim that man is the initial datum for theological reflection is enormously strengthened when we turn to the Christian revelation and specifically the doctrine of the incarnation. For according to this teaching, God has made himself known in and through a human person. We could on the one hand say that in Jesus Christ humanity was brought to that level of transcendence at which the image and likeness of God, obscured in our humanity through sin, has been brought to its full and explicit realization . . . A human being can manifest the being of God only because God himself has descended into the created order. There can be a divinity in man only because there is already a humanity in God. At this point we can pay Karl Barth his just due, but while he was right in affirming the ontological priority of God in this as in everything, and I would have no desire to differ from him on this point, it leaves unchanged my own contention that in the order of knowing, there is a legitimate and indeed compelling way that leads from the knowledge of the human to the knowledge of the divine.

---

43. Macquarrie, *Principles*, 138.
44. Macquarrie, *Theology, Church and Ministry*, 58–59.

And what of Heidegger? Heidegger thought of the *analogia entis* as an error of thinking belonging to metaphysics and ontotheology. For him, it commits the sin of objectifying Being, reducing being to an entity and therefore contributes to the forgetfulness of Being; concealing Being, or reducing Being to beings. Because he uses an incarnational model Macquarrie in no way sees *analogia entis* as a reduction of transcendence to immanence but as a method of dialectic between transcendence and immanence: it is relational. Being (God) is revealed to us through natural phenomena and natural phenomena are revealed to us as part of Being (God). True, for Heidegger Being is incomparable, Wholly Other, only knowable and accessible through beings, so Macquarrie wonders whether with this "new or, rather renewed assertion that God is Being rather than a being . . . a sufficient basis can be found for analogical talking about God."[45] He wonders, too, whether a renewed understanding of ontotheology could be possible through a re-reading of Heidegger's own existential-ontology.

The crux of the matter for Macquarrie is he thinks both Barth and Heidegger are limiting *analogia entis* to a framework of subject-object metaphysics where "God is a kind of super-being who differs from us chiefly in that he is a cause of his own being, but who nevertheless is a distant being."[46] This is the kind of approach that Macquarrie's dialectical theology is a response to, he wants to move beyond this category of modernism. "We are concerned here," Macquarrie writes, "with something that is neither subjective nor objective, to an unbroken unity of subject and object"[47] It is a form of knowing that is not primarily or exclusively analytical, but is also empathetic and intuitive, it is "feeling of absolute dependence."[48] It is quite evident in Macquarrie's new style theology that he is against any kind of analogy of being that sets the subject over against the object of thought, this is where he sees the weakness of Barth's criticism of analogy of being; it is limited to an old style subject-object metaphysics where God is the "Wholly Other" only known through the *analogia fidei or* the *analogia gratiae*, a view Macquarrie considers "arbitrary and unconvincing."[49] Barth's refusal to accept the analogy of

---

45. Macquarrie, *God Talk*, 223.
46. Macquarrie, *Principles*, 138.
47. Ibid., 98.
48. Ibid.
49. Ibid., 138.

being as a way of thinking and speaking about God is a result of his insistence that God is infinitely qualitatively different from human beings and the creation. Macquarrie questions both the biblical veracity and the reasonableness of this "gulf." How can we ever come to know God when separated by such a gulf? As mentioned, Barth himself seems to have adjusted and softened his view of the *total* otherness of God later in his life when he came to more overtly speak of the "humanity" of God. However, Macquarrie believes that even with this modified view, Barth would in no way acknowledge the possibility of natural theology or the value of the analogy of being.[50]

Macquarrie sees an inconsistency in Barth's position. Beginning from the human side, we begin by knowing human relationships and from this beginning we form some analogical concept of what God is like, what God does. The inconsistency is greater when we remember that for Barth the supreme revelation is through Jesus Christ, the incarnate God. If there is such a radical discontinuity between God and the world then it leads to questions about how the Word of God could ever have been incarnate in the world in any real sense. If Jesus Christ is the beginning and end of creation as Barth insists, then why would we not begin with the humanity of God through Christ as a model for our knowledge of God? Begin with human being who is the image and likeness of God? And if Jesus Christ is the beginning and end, in fact, the wisdom of creation as the Logos (Revelation), why cannot creation itself be a vehicle for God's revelation through Christ, a participation of Spirit and Matter, a sacramental-incarnational presence of God in the world (Revealdness)? In a sense, revealed theology *is* natural theology[51] since revelation requires natural phenomenon as a vehicle, whether human phenomenon or that of the wider created order.

Macquarrie is not offering a theory of analogy that argues for the similarity, or resemblance, between Being (God) and beings (creatures), as Barth assumes. It is similarity of relation, in the original sense of analogy "according to a ratio" that is at the center of Macquarrie's view, an analogy of proportionality. It is not a question of the images and concepts in the mind of a person, and then applied to Being (God), but the

---

50. Macquarrie, *Theology, Church and Ministry*, 63–64.
51. Ibid., 54.

situation in which man relates to Being. It is a relational similarity, an analogy of Being as relational. He explains:[52]

> If Being is incomparable with particular beings, it is hard to see how any property of a particular being could be like a property of Being, if indeed one could even talk about a property of Being. It is not, however, inconceivable that I might be related to a being or to a group of beings in a manner which in some regards might resemble my relation to Being. The similarity is not between a being and Being, for although there is affinity between Being and the beings, this affinity is not simple similarity. The similarity is between a relation of beings and a relation of Being to a being.

It is an *analogia proportionalitatis*, in the form of A is to B as C is to D.

We cannot know Being in itself, God in Himself, only as Being (God) is related to us. This is the point of the analogy of being: "These analogues do not indeed disclose to us Being "as it is in itself" (if one may so speak), but being as related to us . . ."[53] Indeed Macquarrie considers selfhood (personal being) to be the most adequate symbol for Being because God (Being) is in some sense personal.[54] Still, Being is present and manifest through the whole range of beings. There is a continuum of beings, from the smallest wave-particle of energy through to human existence and each being participates in Being to a greater or lesser degree. Macquarrie comments: "even the atom of hydrogen has a minimal participation in Being and a tendency, if we may speak, to "imitate" Being, in so far as it plays its part in building up the fabric of the world."[55] And this is why Macquarrie speaks of a sacramental universe. However, Macquarrie believes that it is human being's relation to time, creativity and the incarnation which is most significant for any analogy of being.

We live, love, trust, care, and sin as embodied temporal beings, and we do so creating worlds of relationships that are more or less authentic through time. And as such beings, we relate to Being as these creative, embodied, temporal creatures. We authentically or inauthentically relate to beings proportionally. At its best, Macquarrie's analogy of being is a

---

52. Macquarrie, *Principles*, 140.

53. Ibid., 141.

54. Ibid., 208. Macquarrie views analogy and symbolism as corresponding terms (140).

55. Ibid., 225; Macquarrie, *Stubborn Questions*, 123–33.

description of dwelling sacramentally, at its worse, it is a description of the presence of disorder in creation, the threat of chaos in creation, not dissimilar to Levinas' *Il y a*.

Human beings exist (stand-out) from other beings because of their temporality, human beings do not merely exist from moment to moment, like other creatures: human beings are constituted by their temporality.[56] Macquarrie, following Heidegger, believes that "time offers the horizon for any understanding of Being whatsoever"[57] the more intentionally one lives their life the more one transcends time as mere successiveness, we live our life in the fulfillment of Being (God) by extending ourselves through past (memory), present (judgment), and future (anticipation) with the possibility of building a unified self through transcending beyond the pull of immanence.[58] The innate desire for God pulls us into a transcending attitude. Macquarrie characterizes God as the "God-Who-Lets-Be," in freedom and love we desire this (re)turn to God as a natural aspect of *Imago Dei*. An impassible God or a pure Being would be monolithic and an unchanging immanence, and indistinguishable from Nothing.[59]

Macquarrie pursues a *via eminentiae*, not via *negativa*, because Being who is becoming, this is who God (Being) is for us: known only through his acts as letting-be. Being, however, is not "in" time, but time is "in" Being (God), and as the image of God we are likewise temporal. "It is rather that God too takes time into himself and extends himself in time. He needs time to create, to act, to make history . . . so that the unimaginable vastness of past, present and future are gathered up in the totality of his Being in a manner in which we get some faint hint from the way in which these dimensions of time are brought into the unity of a self."[60] Time is a link between creaturely being and divine Being. Of course, this word "totality" is marked with controversy in postmodern philosophy and theology. It is a word Macquarrie frequently uses in various contexts. However, Macquarrie does not mean by this a reduction of all difference and particularity. A totality is a uniting of what is to remain in difference and particularity. It is a synonym for Macquarrie for "meaning." His

---

56. Macquarrie, *God Talk*, 224.
57. Ibid., 225.
58. Ibid., 224.
59. Ibid., 225.
60. Ibid.

rendering of the opening sentence of the Gospel of John reads "In the beginning was Meaning," where "Meaning" here is not too distant from the idea of *Logos* as gathering together or *alétheia* as revealing. This unity is possible only through transcendence, it is not some Aristotelian metaphysical permanence of Identity;[61] rather it is an identity through difference, unity through a continual creativity and reception to that which is new. An organic gathering together in Meaning.

The analogy between Being (God) and human beings is not to be found in rationality, as in old style natural theology, it is to be found in creativity, in the ability for human beings to participate in a limited way, proportionally, in the shaping of what Macquarrie also sees as the helping to fulfill the potentialities of being, especially in relation to the other, the neighbor, to participate in helping another fulfill his or her own being.[62] The possibility for any being to transcend and to work for the benefit of creation is due to the coming together of God with humanity through creation. This, of course, is the center of Macquarrie's dialectical theology, the participation of God and humanity through immanence and transcendence, through matter and spirit, through the presence and manifestation of Being (God) with beings (creation). The incarnation is the most concrete symbol of this, where a person "becomes a symbol of Being, the revelation of God."[63] But it is with Jesus Christ that "we see the upper reaches of our human nature, transfigured into the divine nature or, if we think of it from the other side, made transparent so that the divine nature is revealed through him."[64]

If Macquarrie names human being as the highest possible symbol for being, it is not because he is reducing theology to anthropology. He says:[65]

> Let me suggest that as one surveys the rising grades of being, the character of Being is itself more clearly manifested. For whereas the lowest or simplest beings are, the higher ones not only are, but let-be, and this becomes peculiarly true at the level of man's personal being, with its limited freedom and creativity. So again, the symbols that are drawn from the level of personal being have the highest adequacy, since they point to the letting-be of Being.

61. Ibid.
62. Macquarrie, *God Talk*, 226.
63. Macquarrie, *Principles*, 143.
64. Macquarrie, *God Talk*, 227.
65. Macquarrie, *Principles*, 144.

Here we may notice Macquarrie is qualifying the use of symbol. He says that the adequacy of a symbol is to be considered in relation to the range of participation in Being:[66]

> An inanimate object exhibits material being, while an animal exhibits not only material being but also organic being. In man, a material body and an animal organism are united with his distinctively personal being. This is the widest range of being that we know, and therefore symbols and images drawn from personal life have the highest degree of adequacy accessible to us.

And,

> Those beings which are able to display in their kind of being the widest diversity of unity are the most adequate symbols of Being, that is to say, are the best able to be the vehicles of Being's self-communication.

Contrary to Barth's focus on the analogy of being, which concentrated on the inadequacy of human concepts for description of God, Macquarrie's concept of analogy of being is one where the whole of creation participates sacramentally, incarnationally, with the most adequate analogy found through the human being as the image and likeness of God, as the particular being where Being is self-consciously manifest. Macquarrie sees this evident from the phenomena itself,[67] evident through empirical studies, evident in our own experience. Since Being (God) is known only through the phenomena then "every being is a clue to Being, indeed we might say that beings are the language of Being . . . beings are to Being as language is to him who speaks."[68]

His view is similar to Augustine, as seen through Erich Przywara, who Macquarrie discusses at some length in his *Twentieth Century Thought*. Augustine's view of the "restless striving of creation towards God, and the assent through the grades of created things to the God in whom they participate"[69] is the unifying principle between God and creatures, this is the *analogia entis*: "the view *towards* God is already essentially the view *from* God hitherward."[70] For Macquarrie, human

---

66. Ibid., 143, 225.
67. Ibid., 224.
68. Ibid., 142.
69. Macquarrie, *Twentieth-Century Religious Thought*, 294.
70. Ibid., 295.

being is on a quest for meaning for himself, but as well, it is Being which confronts us with meaning.[71] However, this ambiguity is built into the dialectical relationship between human being and Being (God), where ontology precedes epistemology, but we begin with our knowledge and experiences as a response to Being and to uncover the meaning of Being for us. Perhaps here, too, we see a break between Macquarrie and postmodernism. Macquarrie wants to return ontology to First Philosophy, whereas with the exception of Levinas (and to some degree Derrida) postmodernism is still under the spell of Descartes for whom First Philosophy is Epistemology.

Contrary to this, Barth insists that it "is God's grace in his revelation that establishes a community between himself and man, so that we can speak of him in human words. Not an analogy of being but an analogy of grace (*analogia gratiae*) makes our talk of God veracious."[72] But, is this really different from Macquarrie's stance? Commenting about Barth's rejection of *analogia entis* Macquarrie writes, "Barth may well be correct in claiming that divine personality, divine fatherhood, and the like, are *ontologically* first, and their human analogues derivative; but must not the human analogues be first *epistemologically*?"[73] Considering Macquarrie's comments as a whole, can we not say that Macquarrie's view of the analogy of being presupposes and is in fact grounded upon the analogy of faith and the analogy of grace? For there would be no order of knowing if it were not for the order of being. And can we not say that Barth's view of the analogy of grace involves an element of appropriation having its beginning in human concepts that were then applied to God?[74] In this respect, Macquarrie's dialectical theology, his new style natural theology can be considered a supplement to Barth's theology, or perhaps a correction to Barth's theology of transcendence. In Macquarrie's estimation, the analogy of being far from reducing God to anthropological subjective projections, guards us against subjectivism and mystical fideism, a danger he finds equally possible in Barth and the postmodern thinkers who function in his shadow.[75]

71. Macquarrie, *Principles*, 87.

72. Macquarrie, *Twentieth-Century Religious Thought*, 324.

73. Macquarrie draws attention to the structural similarity between Heidegger and Barth on this issue. Ibid.

74. Ibid. Macquarrie refers to Reinhold Niebuhr, "Barth himself must have taken the concept of personality from man and then applied it to God."

75. In regards to Barth on this issue, see Macquarrie, *Theology, Church and*

We can continue the outline of Macquarrie's new style natural theology with a transition from the analogy of Being (epistemology) to the structure of Being (ontology), understanding that for Macquarrie these are integral to one another. Macquarrie's dialectical theology is a theology of the incarnation. The incarnation requires a movement from transcendence to immanence. But we need to develop our understanding of Being (God) dialectically, "that is to say, each property is qualified by its opposite, and God himself, in accordance with the logic of the infinite, is understood as *coincidentia oppositorum*."[76] The triune structure of Being (God) is dynamic, it includes becoming and Macquarrie says there is "already an intrinsic connection between the thought of God as triune and the thought of God as Being, as diversity in unity."[77] When we outline the ontological-triune structure of Being (God), we are looking at Macquarrie's natural theology from "above," as it were.

Primordial Being, what is traditionally called the Father is the ultimate act of "letting-be," "the depth of the mystery of God."[78] Primordial Being moves out of itself as "expressive" Being,[79] what in the Christian tradition is known as the Son, but also as the *Logos*: "We could not possibly know anything of him "in himself," Macquarrie writes, "we know him only in so far as he does pour himself out in the dynamics of Being and is revealed in and through the other persons who are joined with him in the unity of Being."[80] It is the *Logos*, the Son, who gives rise to the world of beings in space and time and returns in "unitive" Being, traditionally the Spirit, which gathers beings back to their *arché* or leads them to their *telos*. It returns beings back to the beginning, which is Being (God).

The mystery of Primordial Being is revealed through expressive Being, the mediator, and the one through whom all things are created and re-created. "These beings, as we say, come into being and pass out of being, that is to say, they have a temporal character, so that Being (and certainly any dynamic Being) is understood by us in terms of time."[81] But Macquarrie is quick to ensure that we understand that expressive

---

*Ministry*, 53.

76. Macquarrie, *In Search of Deity*, 228.
77. Macquarrie, *Principles*, 197.
78. Ibid., 199.
79. Ibid., 201.
80. Ibid.
81. Ibid.

Being (the Logos) is not to be identified with the beings of creation, but is co-eternal with primordial Being. The Logos expresses Being in and through beings, from the lowest being that participates in Being to the highest, which Macquarrie identifies as the human being. But it is also this human being who with their responsibility and limited freedom can forget Being and become alienated from Being. Speaking about this possibility within human being, Macquarrie says: "although they have received their being from the letting-be of Being; and having become alienated from Being, they themselves slip back from fuller being to less being, and toward nothing".[82] *Corruptio optimi pessima,* as it were. The unity of Being, therefore, is constantly threatened and it is the role of the third person of the trinity to work to re-unite Being with beings; to preserve the unity of creation, to bring forth reconciliation and a free response of faith, which is possible because "Being itself has grasped us and communicated itself to us . . . so that the beings that belong in the world as are seen not as self-subsistent entities but as beings in which Being is itself present-and-manifest; while correspondingly we know ourselves not as autonomous beings, but as guardians of Being."[83]

Macquarrie considers his description of the triune structure of Being to be a result of the dialectical analysis of Being, from the concept of revelation itself, and not grounded in the content of Christian dogma. Any reflection on the idea of God, he says, will automatically take on a triadic structure. We have here an example of the coherence and dialectic of reason and revelation, which will be discussed in more detail below (and in the subsequent chapter). According to Macquarrie's analysis, the analytic of revelation itself shows the triune structure of revelation. Even Barth, enemy of natural theology as he was, develops his view of revelation from "a formal analysis of the idea of revelation in general,"[84] in Macquarrie's understanding, he and Barth are in agreement that the very concept of revelation will lead one to a Trinity, and Macquarrie understands this as being consistent with a *natural* theology.

This logical unfolding of the concept of revelation is for both Barth and Macquarrie a *demonstratio* of the Being of God, it is not offered merely as a useful *persuasio,* a rhetorical reflection of the Being of God. Here we have a natural theology that attempts through the triune

---

82. Ibid.
83. Ibid., 202.
84. Macquarrie, *In Search of Deity,* 231–33.

structure of Being to account for the origin of all beings in dialectical unity through difference. Creation stands out from nothing, with human beings at the highest point removed from nothing, yet most vulnerable to fall into nothingness. Creation "in the beginning" shows dependence on Being (God) for all things. We have our origin and our sustenance through the work of Primordial, Expressive and the Unity of Being. Human beings can ascend to Being (God) because of the prior descent of Being toward us, and we can descend away from God, become alienated and forget Being (God) because we have the freedom to lose ourselves in the nothingness of the world of beings cut-off from Being.

In Macquarrie's theology, we are called to follow the Logos, the Wisdom of the world, the Son of God, revealed in Jesus, the archetype of humanity, where the dialectic of transcendence and immanence coheres perfectly without distortion. "Jesus Christ may be properly understood as the focus of Being, the particular being in whom the advent and the epiphany take place, so that he is taken up into Being itself and we see in him the coming into one of deity and humanity, or creative and creaturely being."[85] The human reality unfolds where there is a harmony of movement from the world of beings to Being (God) and from the self-giving of Being (God) toward beings. This is possible because we all have the potential, even in our imperfect and "fallen" state, to mirror Christ. "Indeed," Macquarrie says, "the antithesis between adoptionism and incarnationism is a false on. These two are complimentary."[86]

Here we have the analogy of being, the similarity of relation. "A human being can manifest the being of God only because God himself has descended into the created order."[87] Human beings sum up all levels of being that we can observe in the universe, human beings are a microcosm; "a human being mirrors not only the universe but, as gifted with mind and personality, God himself in his relation to the world."[88] The Logos that gives being to the world also is reflected in our being, in our reasoning and in our feeling. It is true, Macquarrie insists that where Christ is sinless, meaning there is no disorder or imbalance in his existence, we still function with the threat of falling away from harmony with Being (God), we struggle with the imbalance in the polarities of

---

85. Macquarrie, *Principles*, 303.
86. Macquarrie, *Theology, Church and Ministry*, 60.
87. Ibid.
88. Ibid., 59.

our existence, which leads to a sense of alienation from the very Being with which we are ontologically united. It is no exaggeration to say that Macquarrie feels the only hope to overcome such disruption between our own being and Being itself is through a viable natural theology. But it is quite clear that for Macquarrie there is no "pure" natural theology, that is, one that is grounded in reason without revelation. Being and nature are united sacramentally, through the incarnation there is no matter without spirit no reason without revelation, there is a way to discuss Being (God) from below, the *ordo cognosendi* through the analogy of being, because this is made possible from above, the *ordo essendi,* through the triune structure and revelation of Being. For Macquarrie there can be no hard distinction between these: no "natural" verses "revealed" theology since these are merely different aspects of the same reality. It is the error of modernism which has divorced these, and he wants them reconciled.

We have spent some time going over the epistemological and ontological structure of this natural theology, through the analogy of being and the triune structure of Being, both grounded in revelation. But is Macquarrie's view of revelation all too reasonable? More needs to be said about the relationship between reason and revelation. We have suggested that there is more to connect Barth with Macquarrie than there is to divide them, and there is more to discuss in relation to dialectical theism and postmodernism. As far as Barth goes, not much more will be said, but it is worth mentioning that both Macquarrie and Barth are arguing for a theology grounded in faith and grace; Macquarrie sees this extending into a natural theology defined through a renewed understanding of Being and a universal possibility of revelation and of the incarnation that pushes Barth farther than he wants to go. But if one wants to be a dialectical theologian of the given and non-given, of the revealed and hidden, following the logic of the incarnation, can Macquarrie's dialectical theology in a new style pave *a way, one* way, that is both reasonable and faithful?

We began our discussion about the possibility of natural theology with a call to think of reason differently from that of modern rationalism and to extend our understanding of reason to include revelation, so we have no separation between "reason" and "revelation" if we do so we have an opening to a renewed understanding of natural theology. It is through the analogy of being that Macquarrie considers any natural theology possible, and he sees the possibility for analogy of being to be the result of the dialectical movement of the triune structure of Being itself centered on the incarnation. Reason is a necessary formative factor for theology. Macquarrie mentions in *Principles* that broadly speaking there has been a positive attitude toward reason in theology. However, he comments "a very influential counter-current has coursed through the Fathers and the Middle Ages, and found its most vigorous spokesman in some of the schools of orthodox Protestant theology. This counter-current either has assigned a very minor role to reason or, in a few extreme cases, has actually denounced reason as the enemy of revelation."[89]

This is why Macquarrie's description of reason as "speculative" and "critical" is central to his dialectical theology. For Macquarrie, it is scarcely possible to think at all unless one is using "critical reason," but he does admit, "a theology addressed to our time would seek to avoid any heavy dependence on speculative reason."[90] Such speculation is what forms the arrogance of Enlightenment philosophy and "blocks the way to all theology" and in this he is of one mind with Barth, Heidegger, Derrida, and postmodernism generally. Reason cannot be the foundation for faith. It is, rather, subsequent to faith offering a critical insight to the content of revelation.[91]

Macquarrie speaks instead of a "constructive reason" necessary to theology. "Constructive reason" is grounded upon imagination, not deductive argument and *apriori* self-evident principles. And here we can think again how Macquarrie avoids remaining in the world of fragmentary experience. He says that by imaginative leaps we "integrate the fragmentary elements in inclusive wholes" and this is the "architectonic" function of reason.[92] Such a function Macquarrie considers more akin to aesthetics than to the "conceptual violence" of rationalism. In relation to revelation, this "imaginative" or "aesthetic" reason allows for coherence to theology, a synoptic view, that is reasonable, open to and dependent upon revelation, disrupting our daily experiences. Critical reason allows us to recognize how revelation is a deeper look at our daily experiences.

---

89. Macquarrie, *Principles*, 15.
90. Ibid., 16.
91. Ibid., 101.
92. Ibid., 16.

# 6

# The Problem with (the Violence of) Natural Theology (II)

MACQUARRIE'S NEW STYLE THEOLOGY focuses on being more fundamental, descriptive and existential, than any traditional natural theology grounded upon reason. The fundamental conditions Macquarrie outlines for any religious experience to be possible remove the distinction between natural and revealed theology. In this way, Macquarrie shows he is free from the confines of modernism, more so in fact than many postmodernists who in their situating *any* philosophical theology under the banner of ontotheology are restricting themselves to the categories of modernism they so radically claim to escape. Postmodern philosophers and theologians willingly follow the later Heidegger in the thinking of Western metaphysics as ontotheological. Indeed, in the divergent projects of postmodernism, some are attempting to redeem metaphysics others to recover theology, but ontology is to be abandoned as a relic of "unenlightened" thought.

Heidegger says, "western metaphysics, however, since its beginning with the Greeks has eminently been both ontology and theology."[1] Ontotheology deals with the question of beings as such (ontology) and beings as a whole (theology).[2] Ontology investigates the unity and ground of the Being of beings, theology, Heidegger tells us, is "the unity of the all that accounts for the ground, that is the All-Highest."[3] Theology, according to

---

1. Macquarrie, *In Search of Deity*, 54.
2. Ibid.
3. Ibid., 58.

Heidegger, encloses beings within its own account of the whole, thereby attempting to account for the whole of being while remaining apart from such enclosure. Theology wants to give a ground to phenomena, to "show" what otherwise is invisible through the phenomena. Heidegger wants to destroy such a metaphysical, ontotheological, approach because it is not allowing the things themselves to show themselves, theology is showing us a construal, a construct of what it is that the phenomena do not show. Heidegger's particular understanding of Christian theology denies any form of natural theology. God, it is assumed, cannot and may not appear through phenomena.

As a biblical and natural theologian, Macquarrie argues that scripture and our daily experience both testify that God is visible through the phenomena. Heidegger's ontotheological reading of the western theological and philosophical tradition enters into postmodernism as a point of departure for any criticism of the question of Being. However, instead of abandoning "Being talk"(ontology) in his "God talk" (theology), Macquarrie reminds us that Heidegger was too "Greek" in his thinking, pagan even (and here his assessment is in agreement with most postmodern thinkers); that he "borrowed" concepts from scripture and interpreted them in a secular way. He reminds us, too, that there is a "Jewish" tradition regarding the revelation of the divine name YHWH, the translation of which is related to the verb "to be," that has been passed down in the Christian tradition through the incarnated "I Am" sayings of Jesus that leads us to consider the classical dialectical character of God through the logic of the incarnation. Macquarrie embraces "Being-talk" (ontology) and "God-talk (theology) through the mystery of transcendence and immanence[4] through a "Jew-Greek" view (to borrow from Derrida), a "Jerusalem meets Athens" dialogue, that seems to have been lost in the "Jewish" response of Derrida and Levinas, who may be attempting a biblical correction of "Greek" thinking, but in their respective ways may lead us "astray," literally, "away from home."

Now there is no question Macquarrie is an "onto-theo-logian," and like postmodernists, he follows a phenomenological method, but he wants to think otherwise not of "Being" but of a certain way of thinking and speaking of Being. Though he never uses these categories, he is not opposed to thinking through *différance* or the *aporetic* (Derrida), thinking God as Love or *invisibility* (Marion), finding a trace of the Infinite in

---

4. Macquarrie, *Principles*, 196–98.

the neighbor or acknowledging the *unsaying of the said* (Levinas), or of thinking seriously of the realities of religion without "God" or a/theology (Taylor), yet in the pursuit of such transcendence Macquarrie wants to be vigilant so the experience of human being as one who is both a creature immanently present to others and yet transcendently directed, who is "in the world, but not of the world," is not renounced to the point of erasure. That all immanence is not diabolical, that there is and can be a dialectic that recognizes the priority of transcendence through immanence, and is hopeful in a Good creation that gets its goodness through a "Being Who Lets-Be" (God), and is not reducible to beings or any schema or ground that is *Causa Sui* in some Cartesian-Heideggerian ontotheological sense.

Macquarrie's ontotheology is one that is *hyper-ontic*, beyond beings (indicating Being), but also in a certain way *hyper-ousia*, beyond Being (indicating the "Holy'). In its dialectic the *apophatic* is a correction to the *cataphatic*, the infinite *in*forms the finite. Yet, he recognizes that no thinker can remain within the tradition of Judaism without recognizing the moving Spirit of God within the world, and no Christian can think of God apart from the triune revelation of God, or more fundamentally the Incarnation. It is the logic of the incarnation that is the engine driving Macquarrie's dialectical theology.

Macquarrie rejects the "all-devouring Absolute" of Hegel[5] and its egoism, as he rejects the Husserlian reduction of the transcendent to the immanence of the ego. Being, in his dialectical theism, is not something that has closure; there is no end that can be reached with Being or with ourselves.[6] Different from postmodernism, he also rejects Heidegger's blanket generalization of all theologies as ontotheological, reducing God and Being to a supreme entity.[7] He thinks within the general and premodern categories of Augustine and Aquinas, where God and Being are inseparable, *Deus est Suum esse*, but he accepts what he considers a more subtle way of thinking of Being. Indeed, as being itself (*esse ipsum*) God is identified with Being where "'being" (*esse*) is understood in an active verbal sense, not as a substantive (*ens*)."[8] He agrees with Eriugena that God is "'He who is more than being" (*Qui plus quam esse est*)"[9] and in

---

5. Ibid., 359.

6. Ibid.

7. Macquarrie, *Heidegger and Christianity*, 55; Macquarrie, *In Search of Deity*, 162–63.

8. Macquarrie, *In Search of Deity*, 162.

9. Ibid., 90.

returning to this tradition, Macquarrie wants to argue that we have here language and thinking that has not succumbed to the ontotheological critique of Heidegger and postmodernism, he speaks of it as an alternative tradition to that which understands God as "a supreme being in the ontotheological metaphysical sense."[10] Macquarrie wants to bring together phenomenology and God, which since Heidegger have been divided. He recognizes in some postmodern thinkers the return to religion, where God and phenomenology are on the road to reconciliation. He wants, as it were, to affirm what is denied in the postmodern return to religion, and within the limits of the apophatic tradition of negative theology to say what can be said within the limits of what cannot be said and must remain unsaid.

The descriptive and existential character of Macquarrie's new style natural theology is a testimony that he is not undertaking a "science of God," an endeavor that horrifies postmodern thinkers as the sin of ontotheology. Such a rationalistic and theoretical approach is distasteful to Macquarrie. What Macquarrie is attempting to do is articulate a philosophical theology that has its *arché* in revelation and is faithful and reasonable in what he calls the "constructive" and "critical" sense, concepts we will discuss in chapter 7 below. Macquarrie's thesis that nature (phenomena) and God (Being) are ambiguous, requiring faith to resolve uncertainties coincides with the postmodern notion of "undecidability." Postmodern thinkers respond to undecidability through a leap that is faith simply because it does not depend upon reason: it does not *know*. John Caputo writes: "No one really knows what they love when they love (their) God, even if they do not lack for words when we ask them. That indeed is the condition of their faith, the reason their faith is faith, not Knowledge, and why religion can be true without Knowledge, why religion is also without religion."[11]

Macquarrie would disagree with the reduction of God in every respect to complete mystery. "Faith is faith in the face of the anonymous," says Caputo,[12] and in various ways, Marion, Levinas, and Derrida would agree. Macquarrie speaks differently, he speaks of faith that is faith in Being, which he names "God" and the "Holy." And, in so doing, he feels

---

10. Ibid., 162.
11. Caputo, *On Religion*, 124–25.
12. Ibid.

he is following the revelation of scripture[13] and Christian philosophical tradition that itself is a destruction of a certain way of doing metaphysics and speaking of Being. Such faith does not remove mystery through the violence of the concept; neither does it resolve ambiguity into "decidability" as in speculative metaphysics. Certainly, there is mystery in relation to God. As we said earlier, God is a God who cannot be imagined (Isaiah 40:18) and is a God who hides (Isaiah 45:15; John16:16). However, God is not only mystery but also a God who reveals and manifests himself through his work Ps. 104, Job 12). God is a God who appears (John 1) and departs, a God who is near and is also far (Jeremiah 23:23; John 14–15). This is one of the fundamental paradoxes surrounding God and the central theme of Macquarrie's dialectical natural theology. As well, when Derrida quotes Augustine's words "I do not know what I love when I love God,"[14] Macquarrie suggests that because of the infinity of God, any believer can say these words. But he asks how can one *love* what is only *Wholly* Other? How can *we love* that which abolishes *any* similarity *any* analogy, *any* relation, which also appears to abolish the Incarnation? Macquarrie writes that the situation of faith implies "at least a minimal awareness through revelation or otherwise, of the one who is loved."[15] Awareness through revelation is a possibility in postmodernism (it is the possibility of the impossible). However, minimal awareness "*otherwise*" than revelation points us traditionally to reason. The condition of faith is trust in Being through the revelation and reception of Being as the initiator of the experience, not as a "clear and distinct" concept but ambiguously, "through a glass, darkly."[16] It is because of this that Macquarrie insists on the need of weighing faith on the scales of critical and constructive reason, "otherwise" than revelation not in place of revelation, but alongside revelation as the "other" side of revelation. This traditional question of the relationship between faith and reason is recontextualized in postmodernism as the relationship between "passion" and "intellect."

In a previous comment about postmodernism we mentioned the danger Macquarrie sees in favoring "passion" over "intellect," and in his analysis of this Macquarrie acknowledges his fear that there is a pervasive anti-intellectualism present in postmodernism leading in many ways to

---

13. Macquarrie, *Principles*, 196–97.
14. Macquarrie, *Twentieth-Century Religious Thought*, 470.
15. Ibid.
16. Ibid.

an inconsistent "negative theology." Macquarrie's preference for Schleiermacher over Hegel, as we will see in more detail later, is partly due to the former having a passion for the infinite that is overly intellectualized in the latter. However, this is where Macquarrie reminds us that we must accept the full impact of pathos while avoiding *not* speaking and thinking reasonably about God. We need a renewed set of concepts to think theologically, to express the passion of Christ and the pathos of God in non-objectifying language.

We have already seen in Caputo, for example, that our relation to God, to meaning, to hope, is left to the passions and not to the intellect, for any such relation is beyond the intellect. Caputo seems to think that especially *deconstruction* has been driven by a passion for God[17] and that *différance* is the God of negative theology. But Macquarrie would see in this dualism of passion and intellect a vestige of modernism that is necessary to overcome. Because of the undecidability and ambiguity of the meaning and experience of "God," Macquarrie wonders what feeds the confidence of postmodern thinkers to assume that one faculty over another is better suited to approach the questioning of God and the undertaking of any theology. For his own approach, Macquarrie will employ the admittedly "modern" concept of "architectonic" reason, which he qualifies as being more "aesthetic" than "speculative," and this "aesthetic" reason articulates the incarnational foundation for the renewed approach he takes to the *analogia entis*, which in his hands is meant to bridge the very modern divide in postmodernism between the passions and the intellect (faith and reason), a gulf which Macquarrie considers is as evident in the anti-intellectualism thematic in postmodernism[18] as it is in the over intellectualization of rational theology. Like postmodernists, Macquarrie rejects a thoroughgoing rationalism, where talk about God tends to resolve itself into a set of deductive statements amounting to a cold and distant ontotheological calculus. However, one could say Macquarrie wants to perform a "Heideggerian *Destruktion*" through dialectic of the aesthetic and the rational, leaving us more open to Being (God). He says, "the exuberant passional life of man cannot be extinguished in the interest of his intellectual capacities, though certainly the extravagances of passions need to be kept in check by rational reflection."[19]

---

17. Ibid., 469.
18. Ibid., 457–58.
19. Macquarrie, *Twentieth-Century Religious Thought*, 457.

Macquarrie acknowledges that the term "passion" is vague, open to a variety of meanings, but it is obvious that he sees it as a postmodern reaction to the rationalism that is prevalent in modernism. In both a postmodern reliance on passions and its prejudice toward reason and any metanarrative, there is a hindrance to theology. In this context[20] he refers to the example of postmodern thinkers who refuse to say anything positive about God, preferring to stay within the mystery of transcendence.

Dialectical theism attempts always to strike a balance between transcendence and immanence, not a balance of symmetry, but of proportionality where there is always "more to" immanence that points us toward transcendence as the *fons et origo* of all phenomena and meaning. He would agree with Aquinas: *Deus est unicuique intimus, sicut esse proprium rei est intimum ipsi rei.*[21]

Such a view Macquarrie calls sacramental. Similarly, a sacramental existence is one that requires proper proportion between passion and intellect, there must be a dynamic interplay between passion and intellect in any liturgical life. It is, as it were, an Aristotelian dialectic of potentiality and actuality grounded in the verbal revelation of Being (*Ehyeh Asher Ehyeh*) through the phenomena. It requires acknowledging that since language cannot express completely the mystery of faith and God in a calculative-ontotheological sense, this does not deny the possibility that language can in its "stretched" form through analogy, symbol and paradox offer up coherent theological statements. If postmodernism (deconstruction) is, as Caputo suggests, a passion for God, a desire for God, then this is a desire that cannot be satisfied since there is always deferral, already with Heidegger there is waiting for a more divine god, and especially with Derrida and Levinas the passion is for the transcendent God who cannot be made present but who leaves traces that are undecidable: i.e., are hermeneutically open to a variety of interpretations, of possibilities for what otherwise is impossible. In postmodern philosophy and theology, there is a fundamental mistrust of any dialectic between immanence and transcendence since it is assumed that dialectic is doomed to be lost in the immanence of the Same: where the Wholly Other trace of God is reduced to an idol of consciousness. Macquarrie thinks this underestimates the power of God (Being) to appear through the phenomena and yet escape our gaze and reductive concepts. It underestimates our desire

20. Ibid., 458.
21. Gilson, *The Spirit of Thomism*, 69.

to renounce our hold on Being (God) and receive that which is (wholly) other than our self.

That there may be traces of the divine in nature through the Other, as "undecidable" as they may be, does not mean reason cannot be brought to attend to these ambiguities through faith. Postmodernism carries the *apophatic* tendency implicit in Heidegger's ontotheology to an extreme. But this raises the question, if in postmodernism reason and knowledge are helpless here, is not their articulation of the very concept of undecidability in vain? Or, is "undecidability" a *reasonable* reaction to the ambiguity of experience, moving us to a certain assent of faith? And, if so, faith in what? Faith in whom? Is the ambiguity a reflection of whether one is unable to decide if there is, in fact, a transcendent God (Being) or merely a Fitchean, Freudian, Sartrean deception of our ego? A trace of One Who is absent, a memory of what once had been, or of One to come but can never be considered present and may never arrive? In the varieties of postmodernism are we necessarily obligated to accept a "Platonic" form of desire (*eros*), that is, an overwhelming intensity that refuses any satisfaction? Is our hope in the possibility of the impossible only ever a desire for desire?[22] This seems to be the case for Derrida and Caputo, and perhaps even for Levinas who calls the desire for God the desire for the Good, "non-erotic par excellence" but which is still a desire without resolution, a Sisyphean task that resolves the desire, perhaps, into more intense desire, a restlessness that can never rest. When Macquarrie speaks of the *possibility* of our articulation of theology he does so with the faith that it is the *impossibility of God* (Holy Being) breaking through immanence, saturating immanence, smashing the narrow categories of modernist ontotheology, that allows us at once to "see" the absence of God through the presence of phenomena. And is this not a resolute faith, a passion for the impossible?

We have a desire *for* Being built into our very constitution Macquarrie argues, and although language of universal *apriori* preconditions would be strange coming from the mouth of any postmodern thinker, the expressed view of (pre)existing desire that presumes to rescue us from the trappings of immanence is inescapable.[23] In Macquarrie's view Being not only discloses itself through phenomena, but our awareness of Being

22. In what follows I follow Wyschogrod and Caputo, "Postmodernism and the Desire for God."

23. Macquarrie, *Heidegger and Christianity*, 20. Human beings are drawn to transcendence.

through affective states is due to our capacity to receive and recognize revelation through phenomena "calling" us toward transcendence. Our desire is rooted in a response to Being which initiates the call and instills the desire. As one might expect, what or how desire for "Desire" or for the "Good" or "Love" or "Justice" is instilled in us, what its origin is, receives various answers among postmodern philosophers and theologians, yet as variable as they may be they have their origin in what Macquarrie has called a form of "existential Angst,"[24] how this connects with Sartre's nihilistic Being, or Levinas' exploration of the *Il y a*, will be discussed below.

We are caught always, Macquarrie says, in the tension of the polarities of anxiety and hope,[25] which are not mere feelings, but are ways we interpret existence both intellectually and passionately. These polarities represent a "totality of the relationships of the human reality to the world."[26] And again, this has nothing to do with the totality that encloses and erases transcendence, it is no rational plenum. Although our desire and quest originates through passion and affective states, this cannot be divided from reason. Macquarrie is convicted that we are pulled more toward the pole of hope, more toward the affirmative mood,[27] toward transcendence, and therefore the "quest for sense, coherence, a meaningful pattern, thus takes its rise from the very constitution of existence."[28] This arises from his view that transcendence takes priority ontologically and epistemologically, it is as he has said "God in search for humanity" and biblically is expressed in the presence of the Spirit in creation, the purpose of the incarnation. We will return to this theme below when we consider whether the "Desire" that has no object to resolve it is one that carries with it the hope that attends the direction from immanence toward transcendence.

---

24. This, of course, is Heidegger's influence. *Angst* is a unifying factor (mood) where distinctions and divisions disappear, "and one is left with a feeling of totality or perhaps of nothingness, it is not quite clear which" (Macquarrie, *Two Worlds Are Ours*, 27–28). Ultimately, what Macquarrie calls for as a resolution of this ambiguity is "Faith." Faith in Nothingness or Grace (the revelation of the holy). The difference between e.g., Sartre and Lyotard, on the one hand, and Derrida, Levinas, and Marion and Macquarrie, on the other hand, is grounded in the ambiguity and mystery and awe of sublime existence, which will be addressed below.

25. Macquarrie, *Principles*, 64.

26. Ibid., 65.

27. Ibid.

28. Ibid., 87.

This desire for God in postmodern thinking is a passion that takes hold of us and transfixes us. It is passion for the impossible, and therefore seems inherently unfulfillable. But still, it is a desire that is a desire for meaning for the future (*telos*) and for the past (*arché*). To desire is to relinquish autonomy and to surrender to the Other. It reminds us of the Augustinian cry *Inquietum est cor nostrum*, where for Augustine this cry gets resolved in the promise of an end to all deferrals when we rest in and through the transcendent Other who is God. Macquarrie agrees, if we speak of desire and passion, we must do so in relation to Being (God) and therefore this is a passion that has a *telos*. It is a desire that can be fulfilled through authentic retrieval of the meaning of Being (God), which includes as part of its meaning the invitation to commune and participate through feeling and understanding while simultaneously being aware that ultimately we are summoned to acknowledge the inexhaustible, incomparability of Being (God) to any concept. In this sense, there is deferral of any absolute meaning without negating possibility and promise of fulfillment. This idea of desire for Being (God), which is a retrieval and repetition of the meaning of Being, is what blocks the way to theology according to postmodernism, such a desire, it is claimed, traps us in the "metaphysics of presence": the reduction of the Other to the Same. But, Macquarrie's dialectical theism as a sacramental theology is no such reduction: in its repetition and retrieval of the meaning of Being (God) it is simultaneously immanence *and* transcendence, presence *and* absence; given *and* non-given. To attempt to see God (Being) through all things, to live in the tension of polarity without deciding for one side over another, to find balance is, Macquarrie says, a *natural theology of sacramentality*.[29]

For postmodern theology in its claims to be *post*-secular the compromise with Enlightenment principles is to have passed. To have passed too, is any metaphysics grounded in Being, Heideggerian or otherwise. Nevertheless, postmodernism is still busy in its post-Heideggerian way with working out the "ontological difference" between Being and beings, where preference for difference between Being and beings as the horizon for meaning allows for an infinite distance between the beings and Being. Of course, such a view is what separated secular theology from Macquarrie's approach, and for both secular and post-secular thinking, religion can have no connection to an ontotheology of any sort. This marginalization of philosophy from theology is a significant concern for Macquarrie.

---

29. See Macquarrie *A Guide to the Sacraments*, chapter 1.

Macquarrie fears that the call from some circles for an "end to metaphysics," of a relegating to the heap of obsolescence any *ontotheology*, is to declare theology strange to any trajectory of thought relevant to our *sitz im leben*. And so his dialectical theology is an apology directed toward those who want a retrieval of metaphysics without ontology, equally it is a rejection of those views that desire transcendence without immanence, or an immanence without transcendence.

Perhaps the desire to recover metaphysics without ontology comes most forcefully and obviously from Levinas. For he considers ontology to be a subordinating exercise, generalizing and totalizing what should be sought through particularity and difference. Ontology is imperialistic, seeking to possess and control through knowledge that which is beyond our abilities to conceive, perhaps even to speak. Levinas' distinction between "metaphysics" and "ontology" creates a disjunction where traditionally there has been coherence. His preferring metaphysics to ontology is determined by his view that the former does not require the elevation of Being, but waits upon the revelation of the Infinite. Metaphysics *is* desire for the Infinite; it is a desire that is not grounded in a lack we discover *a posteriori* in our own nature, but is a desire that is revealed *to us*, it is given *to us* through the Infinite itself: the "Wholly Other." And so, Levinas insists that truth is revealed, it is not grasped. Macquarrie would certainly agree with this much of what Levinas has to say, however in what Macquarrie describes as a natural quest for Being (God) one needs to be aware of what is lacking. One is on a quest for fulfillment, working out one's own salvation with fear and trembling, quite aware that any meaning, any fulfillment is a gift one needs to be receptive to. It is the dialectic of desiring and renouncing, of choosing and receiving, of knowledge and faith. Macquarrie has no quarrel with the idea that our awareness of difference is a gift originating with a Giver and therefore he would agree with Derrida and Levinas that a Giver cannot be reduced to the Gift, but must be recognized through what is given. This is traditional incarnational theology. That the appearance of God is manifest through the created world and disappears too is a reality of the inability of any phenomena to restrain the infinite. The Infinite, for Levinas, is disclosed to us not through the particular but as the transcendent through immanence: not through a generalized and totalizing ontology. Its disclosure is not through ideas, but through ethics. Macquarrie rejects the view that "Being language" means we are ignoring the mystery that attends phenomena, or that we forget that we are grasped by the infinite

Other, that we are grasped by the transcendent Letting-Be of the Giving of Grace. A proper ontotheology allows thought and language of God to be an activity directed toward the non-objectified Infinte without reducing the Infinite to the finite. Macquarrie speaks "Being language," but it is verbal, relational, and oriented always to another or toward the Other. For Macquarrie, Ontology and ethics coincide.

Ethical values for Levinas are anterior to intellectual values; the good is more fundamental than Being,[30] and, in fact, replaces Being. For Macquarrie, this is taking this Platonic idea further than it properly belongs. Of course, Macquarrie agrees that the Infinite is only disclosed through the particular, but he sees a danger in Levinas' gloss on this. For Macquarrie, there can be no proper distinction between Being and the Good in any phenomenological sense. He does not succumb to Heidegger's "neutrality of Being," that Heideggerian ontological anonymity that so offends Derrida and Levinas, while appearing in their metaphysics through another way. To elevate the Other, the Good or Love is itself a forgetfulness of the Difference that both connects and names our responsibility to the other. It results in a structural asymmetrical indifference to the neighbor. Macquarrie draws attention to a saying of Plato in his discussion of Levinas to illustrate this point: "The objects of knowledge not only derive from the good the gift of being known, but are further endowed by it with real and essential existence; the good, far from being identical with real existence, goes beyond being (*epikeinas tes ousia*) in dignity and power."[31] Although Macquarrie himself will speak in this "Platonic" way, of "Being beyond being," and indeed it would be no exaggeration to say that Macquarrie's whole dialectical theology is an exploration of this Platonic theme of "Being beyond being," he nevertheless is concerned over the danger of creating a theology that lives only in absolute dissimilarity and disagreement between beings (existence) and Being (ontology). Macquarrie would remind Levinas that if anything is to *be* good it first must *be*. If anything or anybody is to reveal goodness, there must be a

---

30. It is not insignificant, I think, that Macquarrie and Levinas are in ultimate agreement that the most fundamental category that unites is the "Holy." Derrida reports that Levinas said to him: "You know, one often speaks of ethics to describe what I do, but what really interests me in the end is not ethics, not ethics alone, but the holy, the holiness of the holy" (Derrida, *Adieu to Emmanuel Levinas*, 4). Macquarrie writes in Macquarrie, *Two Worlds Are Ours*, 240: "One advantage of seeing the holy rather than deity as the centre of religion is that it allows for a unifying phenomenon common to all religions..."

31. Macquarrie, *Twentieth-Century Religious Thought*, 462.

coincidence (not identity) of ethics and existence through Being (God), he would respond to Levinas (in a very Augustinian way) that for God to *be* and to *be Good* is the same. Just as he would respond that for God to *be* and to *be Love* is the same.

But isn't this an old story for Macquarrie? Isn't Levinas' elevation of ethics (good) above ontology (being), a variety of thinking found in secular theology and "death of God theology," where the concern for humanity (the Other) overruled quests for a God that subjected humanity to the status of servants? Yes and No.

To reiterate, the emphasis in secular theology was on a rational religion, whereas post-secular theology subjects the intellect to passion. To be post-secular for postmodernism requires an a/theism to recover religion without religion. For secular theology, atheism was a natural outcome of the secular critique of religion and the acknowledgement of the "death of God." But for both, the word "secular" refers to the scandal of particularity, locked up in history and time. But there is difference. The "gospel of liberation" of secular theology is a teaching of humanity coming of age, very much in line to the call of the Enlightenment and the proclamation of Nietzsche that sets the context for so much (post) secular theology. There is an ethical focus on the response to and remedy for injustice and suffering experienced by humanity, at the hands as it were of an angry transcendent god. It is passionate, in protest to the impassable God. Yet, it is grounded in rationality, and liberal theology in general dismissed in many ways the trust in revelation that postmodern theology is emphasizing in order to recover religion. Secular theology was a reduction of transcendence to immanence, the very opposite of the claims of postmodernism's post-secularity. But have postmodern theologians moved beyond rational (secular) religion as they claim?

Postmodernism as post-secularism is a movement of the "*death of the death of God.*" Secular theology declared theology impossible announcing a renunciation of transcendence and a celebration of immanence. Post-secular theology wants to accept the possibility of the *im*possibility of theology. That is to say: the reality of the breaking into experience of a transcendence that exceeds the conditions of thought described by Enlightenment rules of engagement, which defined "secular theology." There is a renunciation of any petrified immanence. However, Macquarrie (similar to Lyotard) will also announce that postmodernism is merely a (radical) extension of modernism, therefore, Macquarrie is suggesting that these various movements—liberal theology, radical theology, postmodern theology—share significant points of contact in a conversation about changing secular culture. For Macquarrie, the swing from modernism to postmodernism, from theologies of immanence to transcendence, is an illustration of the kind of polarities best managed through a dialectical theology and analogical imagination.

For Caputo, as for Derrida, the post-secular is a call to "religion without religion," and one can ask how this compares with the call from Barth, at one extreme, and secular theology, at the other extreme for a "*Christianity* without religion." In the case of Derrida and Caputo, there is a call to move away from messianism (that favors any one faith, dogma, liturgy), to the messianic (a formal structure of justice and deconstruction of all *isms*).[32] But is there not something similar in the case of "secular theology" and "neo-orthodoxy," who articulate different theologies of "Christianity without religion'? There is a call to the messianic Christ and a response to distance oneself from the reduction of the Christian faith to *a* religion. That is, there is a call to a universal ethics grounded in the scandal of the particular, the *kenosis* of the incarnation and the resultant "death of God" through the crucifixion of Christ. In Christianity "without religion," there is a call to the ethical which is a call to a repetition of the sacrifice of Christ, with an emphasis on the uniqueness of Christ. For Macquarrie, this is merely another way to voice the dialectic of the particular with a general or universal possibility of revelation.

It is the ethical life exhibited by Christ toward the neighbor that motivated secular Christianity, even "atheistic Christianity," in its call to a responsibility toward the neighbor. The ethical life of Christ is interpreted to be a radical deconstruction, breaking through the ethos of any "*ism*." But as such, is this any different from proclaiming the way of Christ as a universal structure to be followed by all of humanity in its ethical existence? Is this not similar to the very modern Enlightenment Kantian archetype of humanity which was clearly modeled after Christ? And of which Karl Rahner has said: "Christ has always been involved in

---

32. Macquarrie is not comfortable with thinking a general structure, or abstract idea of ethics and justice that could be shared by all walks of faith (or "unfaith"). Always there is to be the particular revelation (incarnation). In Macquarrie, *Stubborn Questions*, 133, he writes: "But can we say that in Jesus Christ there dwells not the fullness but the essence of God, that essence being love? And, can we say, without overstepping our inescapably human point of view, that if God has revealed himself in other Christs or will reveal himself at other times and in other parts of this vast universe, it will be the same essence, the same eternal Logos, though in forms unimaginable to us?"

the whole of history as its prospective entelechy."³³ Can we not interpret this as possible through the trace of (the image of) God in humanity? If so, then we have something similar in postmodernism, but generalized in a post-*Christ*ian way. It is a gloss on the Old Testament concept of Justice: "He has shown you, O man, what is good. And what does the LORD require of you? To act justly and to love mercy and to walk humbly with your God."³⁴

Postmodernism seems to be moving a step further in its "religion without religion." This is significant, for it appears that in the postmodern claim to be post-secular (and therefore, post-Enlightenment), there is a compromise with rational structures (regulative ideas) in the fashion of Kant, and therefore we see that there remains a trace of Enlightenment rationalism in the question of religion. So whereas secular theology is to be situated within Christianity as a *messianism* but moving toward a reduction to the *messianic*, postmodern theology has moved beyond the particular revelation of Christianity and seeks a universal—perhaps anonymous—justice which is not particularly Jewish or particularly Christian, but a structure generalized from these and is designated the Messianic. This is why postmodernism, which seeks to be post-secular, can be considered to be advancing secularism. And we cannot help but to recognize that there is a parallel between Heidegger (and his followers) "secularizing" of Christian sources and Levinas and Derrida's "secularizing" biblical concepts of the law. We cannot help but ask whether here in this highest concept of "justice" found in postmodernism whether we have a master word beyond deconstruction, and therefore a surrogate ontology.

A universal structure of justice is prevalent in Levinas and Derrida, with no mention of Christ,³⁵ and can be thought not only in the context of their Judaism, but also more broadly in the Judeo-Christian heritage of the messianisms they are responding to. In the face of the other I am confronted with the trace of God. There is a call away from any "inauthentic" "cheap grace" and a call to an engaged "risk of faith" and "trust toward the other": the "man for others," in Bonhoeffer's phrase. Here there is no

---

33. Macquarrie, *Stubborn Questions*, 207.

34. Micah 6:8.

35. Macquarrie mentions in *Principles* that one of the consequences of "death of God" theology is the inevitability of the rejection of Christ and this seems to be fulfilled in the current theory of "religion without religion."

ontological foundation grounding theology, but an asymmetrical absolute disjunction between Gift and giver lost in the *aporia* of ethics.

Macquarrie has sympathies with Levinas' "ethics as first philosophy," however, he sees no way of establishing an ethical approach grounded in *eros* and separate from ontology, and this becomes a point of difference in his approach and the approaches of liberal, radical and postmodern theology.[36] What Macquarrie wants to acknowledge is that there is a general structure that grounds our approach to justice and grace. A ground that nurtures our need and desire to love and the desire to show mercy toward others; toward transcendence. But in a (post-) secular culture where talk of God is too ambiguous to ground anything, ontology is perhaps still the best way. Otherwise are we not lost in the particular? How would I find a trace in every face if the trace were not transcendent in a way that can be thought at least partially through a generalized concept? Such thought means we are in need of a language that captures general structures. Is this not what is meant (partly) by the image of God in both Christianity and Judaism? Is this not what (post-) secular theology is talking about while pretending to not talk about it?

As a Christian theology, Macquarrie's philosophical approach situates ethics in a wider context, even an eschatological one; ethics is a communal activity that points toward the future reconciliation of *all* beings. When Levinas seeks the Infinite only in the trace revealed in the face of the other, Macquarrie sees here a theological anthropology which is reminiscent of teachings within the Hebrew Scriptures and with the Christian teaching of the incarnation. He would not, however, accept the asymmetry of Levinas' ethics. Both Macquarrie and Levinas would agree that I and the other share in the image of God, Macquarrie would say, share a common humanity. However, Levinas' ethics requires absolute alterity, for Macquarrie this would be as problematic as trying to relate to the Absolute alterity of God. If there is absolute otherness, how would I *recognize* the other as my neighbor? If there is no universality, how do I *recognize* my responsibility to any or all others?

Macquarrie would agree with Derrida and Ricoeur that between myself and another, there is a transcendental symmetry: "the other as my likeness and myself as the likeness of the other."[37] Recognizing the other as my neighbor, as another human being allows for a symmetry between

---

36. Levinas rejects ontology because of its association with "ontotheology," but he does use the word "metaphysics."

37. Ricoeur, "Approaching the Human Person," 46.

people, this is the beginning of the recognition that allows me to respect the other in dissymmetry: the "letting-be" of the other. The beginning of how I renounce my Self for the benefit of the Other. "Without reciprocity or without recognition," Ricoeur states, "alterity would not be a matter of one other than myself. But the expression of a distance indistinguishable from absence."[38]

As well, although for apologetic reasons Macquarrie emphasizes "theology from below," an "anthropological" grounding to theology, where God's revelation has a special focus in Christ's humanity, he believes that the Hebrew Scriptures and the Christian teaching of the incarnation show us that God can be known in ways other than through the human being. If we accept that God can be known through the human being—individually and communally—we are also suggesting that God must be capable of being present in the world (however "undecidable" or "ambiguous'), otherwise we are in danger of making God's revelation perhaps too narrow, reducing it to a form of humanism and emphasizing God's discontinuity with nature. In connection with this, Macquarrie finds it questionable whether the experience of meeting other people "inescapably" (Levinas' term) leads to the encounter with "The Other." Macquarrie wonders whether Levinas assumes too much. Doesn't our knowledge of the Other (even the other person) depend upon the willingness of the Other to reveal itself, to open himself or herself through self-giving? Does every face equally offer a trace of God? Has Levinas undermined, *forgotten*, that the "divine image in man, the trace of his origin, has been grievously damaged by sin"?[39]

For Levinas "the idea of the infinite comes from the Infinite itself, encountering us in and through the face of the other . . . In the face of the other, we receive the idea of the Infinite, overflowing the image of the other." The "other" is infinitely "other" escaping any categories. It can be disclosed metaphorically or analogically, however, through the "face." "The face resists possession, resists my powers. In its epiphany, in expression, the sensible, still graspable, turns into total resistance to the grasp."[40] The face is an actual phenomenon that is also a symbol or analogy of the ultimate Other: God. Levinas speaks of "the alterity of the Other and

---

38 Ibid.

39. Macquarrie, *Twentieth-Century Religious Thought*, 464.

40. Levinas, *Totality and Infinity*, 197.

the Most High."⁴¹ God is both near and far for Levinas, and is prior to all relationships with the neighbor, yet "different from every neighbor, transcendent to the point of absence, to a point of a possible confusion with the stirring of the *there is*."⁴²

Macquarrie is impressed with the degree to which Levinas stresses the point that the "idea of infinity is *revealed* in the strong sense of the term."⁴³ And done so through the "face" which is at once phenomenal and yet more than phenomenal, the face is not reducible to an object, yet nevertheless confronts me objectively. Macquarrie's account of how phenomena reveal Being requires one to acknowledge the presence of Being through the phenomena, while not reducing Being to phenomena. There is no rational grasping or intellectual striving after the Infinite; it is disclosed to us in its truth not unlike how Heidegger expressed the idea of truth through the Greek idea of unconcealedness (*alétheia*). This is an experience that breaks through the discrete and fragmentary nature of experience, calling us to a relationship with the other in a strong ethical sense. For Levinas, this is the trace of God, a way of thinking of God that excludes the category of being, since Levinas believes that "being excludes all alterity."⁴⁴ It avoids the idolizing tendency of philosophy to create a world in my image—to reduce the other to the same. Levinas writes: "The ontological event accomplished by philosophy consists in suppressing or transmuting the alterity of all that is Other, in universalizing the immanence of the Same *[le Meme]* or of Freedom, in effacing the boundaries."⁴⁵ This is a glimpse of wholeness and unity of self with others and the Wholly Other, reducing divinity to the knowable, but a non-conceptual knowledge.

Of course, Macquarrie thinks that Levinas's view of the access to the Infinite is too narrow: "For him, God or the Infinite, encounters us in the neighbor, and nowhere else . . . But I think it is wrong to deny that there are other possible ways of being encountered by God."⁴⁶ Macquarrie's natural theology requires all phenomena (although not equally) to be a possible revelation of Being (God). As well, Levinas' project of thinking

---

41. Ibid., 34.

42. Levinas, *Basic Philosophical Writings*, 140.

43. Macquarrie, *Twentieth-Century Religious Thought*, 463. The quotation is from Levinas' *Totality and Infinity*; the italic is Levinas'.

44. Levinas, *Basic Philosophical Writings*, 74.

45. Ibid., 11.

46. Macquarrie, *Twentieth-Century Religious Thought*, 464.

of God "otherwise than Being" ("the God of the Bible signifies the beyond being, transcendence"[47]) is at odds with Macquarrie's whole approach. What we receive through Levinas is a phenomenology—he speaks of it as *another* phenomenology—that allows the phenomena of the face of the neighbor who remains within being, within immanence, to open us up to transcendence, to that which is not limited to that which can be constituted by the finite ego, to that which is otherwise than being.

Macquarrie, however, does not accept the exception Levinas offers: that the encounter with a human "face" can escape the "ontological event" universalizing the immanence of the "Same." Of course, Macquarrie refuses the idea that ontology inescapably involves a reduction to immanence. Whereas for Macquarrie the ontological question of the relationship between Being and beings is still one requiring further investigation, still an inquiry with deep philosophical and theological import, Levinas rejects this. Instead, Levinas thinks through the categories of Same and Other. These categories are the more fundamental, more fundamental than Being. Macquarrie and Levinas are following Plato here. Macquarrie concerns himself with the battle for the meaning of Being, Levinas over the non-reducible relation of the Same and the Other.

Plato, of course, had argued that *tauton* and *to heteron* are irreducible, even to being or non-being. For Levinas, *to heteron* is infinite. However, when Levinas adopts Plato's use of the categories of "same" and "other" he is not necessarily cutting himself off from a reading of revelation that is fundamental to Macquarrie's project of ontotheology. As Michael Morgan has stated "things called "the other" are not new entities as much as they are or represent unnoticed or repressed perspectives, dimensions, or aspects of the world as we already experience and think about it. The divine, on this reading, represents a perspective on nature . . . that we might regularly ignore but that, with greater attention and direction, we might better notice and appreciate."[48] We see the same phenomena in a deeper way: "otherwise" than in our typical "everyday" experience. Indeed, although Macquarrie does not use this category of expression he does admit that we can "totalize" our empirical and rational encounters with the world, reducing the world to a mythologizing ego: to the "Same." However, it is through revelation that we become aware of the need to

---

47. Levinas, Basic *Philosophical Writings*, 130.
48. Morgan, *Cambridge Introduction to Levinas*, 90.

deconstruct the Same and see phenomena in their radical Otherness: to break out of the "everyday."

Levinas emphasizes that we are drawn toward that which it cannot grasp. This is an intentional aim, but it is an "intentionality of a wholly different type."[49] This is an intentional relation that "overflows," is overwhelmed, it is beyond immanence and transcends to infinity even though infinity "is reflected *within* the totality and history, *within* experience."[50] Transcendence through immanence, only to point (back) toward transcendence. So although reason cannot grasp the infinite because of its own finitude and methods of reduction; we have the finite phenomena revealing the Infinite: or the infinite revealing through the finite: and for Macquarrie this would include a revelation of the infinite through the finitude of human reason. Macquarrie, of course, would accept that although we cannot constitute Being (God) in Its (His) wholeness, Being (God) can seize us through an experience that overwhelms us, much like the "face" in Levinas' approach to phenomenology. Such experience (or experiences) comes through the beings (phenomena) themselves. Therefore, although Macquarrie considers Levinas' allowance of what can reveal the infinite too narrow; the method of revelation of the Infinite through the finite is structurally similar in Macquarie and Levinas. This is God's O*utrance*.[51]

There is, I believe, also a similarity in this regard with Marion. Macquarrie is not in any way impressed by Marion's stance on natural theology. Without ignoring the important differences between these two thinkers, there is a significant point of contact with Marion's and Macquarrie's own phenomenology. This point of contact has to do with a shared idea that there is a possibility of experiencing phenomena as religious, and through such an experience lays the possibility of theology—a universal possibility of revelation—at the heart of natural theology.

Marion's theology centers on the role of Being, and similar to Levinas he wants to think God *without* Being. His resistance to the philosophical concept of Being is due to "the human tendency to project our own all-too-human imaginings and to call them "God."[52] For Marion conceiving of God as Being is to create a conceptual idol and therefore he

---

49. Levinas, *Totality and Infinity*, 23.
50. Ibid., 23, 25; italics in the original.
51. Macquarrie, *Stubborn Questions*, 117
52. Macquarrie, *Twentieth-Century Religious Thought*, 474.

rejects Being as a Name for God, replacing Being with Love as the only proper Divine Name. Love according to Marion is the only possible way of thinking of God otherwise than Being. God as the one Who loves, Who *is* love,[53] and loves in such an excess that it overwhelms any naming or predication. Macquarrie thinks it a mistake to oppose love and being[54] in this way, it leads, Macquarrie will insist, to an absolute qualitative difference between God and creation. It is love that saturates, God "gives himself in an excess that crosses out our (mis-) understandings of him as *causa sui*, necessary being, etc."[55] Through "saturated phenomena" we are to find our way through phenomenology to God, without reducing God to the ego, without constituting God in an immanent intentionality.

Marion finds the phenomenology of both Husserl and Heidegger to be guilty of a reduction of phenomena in its transcendent "otherness" to an immanence of the Same (the horizon of the "I," or "ego," to "finite concepts'). Here he follows Levinas. But whereas Levinas speaks of the "face of the other" as the way to experience the trace of God, Marion includes other possibilities where phenomena are saturated, exploding our interiority.[56] He writes: "Can we not envisage a type of phenomenon that would reverse the condition of a horizon (by surpassing it, instead of being inscribed within it) and that would reverse the reduction (by leading the *I* back to itself, instead of being reduced to the *I*)?"[57] This is similar to what Macquarrie has described as the reverse of the typical epistemological situation, in his view when we are seized by the phenomena itself, where it reveals itself while remaining itself for us to see. This is what he refers to as revelation.

---

53. Ibid., 475.

54. In an interesting essay of Macquarrie's entitled "The Cosmic Christ," Macquarrie, reflecting on the self-giving love of God, asks in rhetorical mood: "If Jesus Christ is taken to be the icon or image of God, and at the same time he is characterised above all by self-giving love, then must not the confession that God is love (1 John 4.16) be at the heart of Christian doctrine, and the love of God as we have learned it in Jesus Christ is no less than the ontological principle through which all things hold together?" (Macquarrie, *Stubborn Questions*, 128). Here Macquarrie has a similar conclusion with Marion, namely *Love* is central, but he aligns love *as* an ontological principle. More will be made of this below.

55. Macquarrie, *Twentieth-Century Religious Thought*, 475.

56. Marion, "The Saturated Phenomenon," 103–24. Also, Marion, *In Excess*. And, Marion, *Being Given*. See the very helpful analysis of Horner, *Jean-Luc Marion*.

57. Marion, "The Saturated Phenomenon," 107.

Like Macquarrie, Marion acknowledges that all phenomena are potentially religious, that is, when they appear as "saturated phenomena" their appearance exceeds our ability to constitute them objectively. So, like Macquarrie, our experience has the potential to be a religious experience. However, Marion argues, such experience is open only to philosophy (the "god" of the philosophers; ontotheology; idolatry); it is at best an *indication* of a true and proper revelation of God. Macquarrie would see Christian theology as a particular (but perfected[58]) manifestation of religious experience; where transcendence and immanence are held in perfect tension. Marion would see Christian theology as the corrective interpretation of any generalized religious experience. Is the difference between Macquarrie and Marion one of degree only?

Faces, flesh, historical events, paintings, are all examples of phenomena that can be saturated so that our experience of them is such that we are overwhelmed, unable to conceptualize them. Phenomena can be saturated so we are confronted with "invisibility," a term Marion uses to indicate the failure of our intentional aim, being confronted with amazement.[59] For Marion a saturated phenomenon is given without limit, therefore it has certain "unbearability" overwhelming our perceptions creating in us an experience of "bedazzlement,"[60] and an inability to conceive the experience. He refers to such an experience as a "pure event"; it is singular and absolute. In a way we cannot look at a saturated phenomenon because it "refuses to let itself be looked at as an object, precisely because it appears with multiple and indescribable excess that suspends any effort at constitution."[61] He does not mean nothing appears, only that we are overwhelmed by the perception of the givennes of the phenomenon. This approach to phenomenology is not meant to be a mystical experience, but a deeper look at phenomena as appearing as itself, not according to the limits of our own consciousness. Marion is trying to move beyond Kant and Husserl and Heidegger and offer a phenomenology that is more radical: appearance that overcomes, or overwhelms subjective structures of consciousness, which presents phenomena as revelation. It is God who gives himself perfectly, more so than any other phenomena. These other phenomena are ambiguous, provisional in their revelation.

---

58. Macquarrie, *Principles*, see chapter 7, "Religion and Religions."
59. Marion, "The Saturated Phenomenon," 113–14.
60. Ibid., 114.
61. Ibid., 119.

However, God (and Christ) as the paradigm of revelation has a force that exceeds any other: "The revealed does not thus define an extreme stratum or a particular region of phenomenality, but rather the universal mode of phenomenalization of what gives *itself* in what shows *itself*... philosophy has neither the authority nor the competence to say more."[62] It is up to theology to determine saturated phenomena that is a Revelation (Marion uses the upper case in the context of God) and not merely revelation of a more general type. This raises the question of the interpretation of what is *theological* and not merely *philosophical*; put another way, of what is *natural* and what is *super*-natural. Marion functions within a hermeneutic of ambiguity (undecidability). "The capital R Revelatory aspect of the phenomenon could still only be one range of possibilities of the small r revelatory phenomenon."[63] It seems that this is not dissimilar to Macquarrie's view that Christian theology is a particular manifestation of religious experience, requiring a hermeneutic of engagement with the phenomena of experience (revelation).

Although Macquarrie observes that similar to Barth Marion denies any natural theology, we see here the conditions for a natural theology not dissimilar to Macquarrie's new style. What would separate Marion from Macquarrie is Marion's own theological hermeneutic as a supplement to philosophy (phenomenology) grounded in the (Heideggerian) distinction between philosophy and faith. For Marion (and Heidegger) Being can never have a place in faith. However, in a hermeneutical theology can one really argue that the phenomenon that is interpreted as religious (saturated) is better explicated through the idea of Love and not Being? Although Macquarrie discusses none of the details of Marion's saturated phenomena, he does deal with the questionable distinction in Marion's theology between metaphysics, or ontology, and Love. Referring to Bradley who said that metaphysics is a way of experiencing God, Macquarrie says: "I wonder if there is any fundamental difference between Bradley's experience and Marion's. Both are experiences of the "sublime," a moment when, at the limits of thought and experience, there breaks into the mind as a "revelation" the truly great that lies beyond."[64]

The criticism of modernism and the reduction to immanence is met with a counter indication that is a desire toward transcendence. With the

62. Quoted in Horner, *Jean-Luc Marion*, 133.
63. Horner, *Jean-Luc Marion*, 133.
64. Macquarrie, *Twentieth-Century Religious Thought*, 475.

mistrust in reason and its "violent" tendencies of reduction, other avenues to transcendence need to be pursued. Phenomenology in this new style opens a discussion about the possibility of a revelatory experience through phenomena itself. But here we have the interesting situation that what emerges is an overwhelming presence through phenomena of what is interpreted as the "transcending other," or "transcendent Other"; that which is Wholly Other" than any of our concepts. With the discussion of Marion—and this is true in general of Heidegger, Macquarrie, Lyotard, and Levinas—we are left with an ambiguous hermeneutical situation: the phenomena requires interpretation, it is not a purely given concept or idea or experience. The hermeneutical situation oscillates in all cases between a "Kantian" idea of the sublime and a "biblical" notion of revelation.

Lyotard, for example, does not allow for any epistemological foundationalism as a guide to the truth of any idea or experience, but he embraces the Kantian notion of the sublime because the sublime "disrupts the flow of rational thought" affirming certain ideas and experiences. Since Lyotard does not attempt to legitimate his views (since this would require rational proof) he reads the Kantian idea of the sublime as trying "not to supply reality but to invent allusions to (that) which cannot be presented."[65] Macquarrie accepts the reference to the sublime for what it is; a possible opening for the presence of religious experience.[66] But, this can be an allusion to Being or to Nothing. In Macquarrie's discussion of the character of Being he states that it is possible that one can experience Being as either gracious or as nihilistic, as we find in Sartre for example, or as monstrous as in Levinas and Lyotard. Possible, that is, because the sublime is itself an ambiguity. Macquarrie never allows for dismissing the experience of another. He shudders at the idea of anonymous Christians or the view that there are no real atheists. There is, to be sure, equivocation in Being and there is, in the turn to the religious, phenomena open to interpretation either as revelation or as sublime. Macquarrie's own use of the Heideggerian *Es Gibt* is a form of hermeneutics put to use to avoid the "*tohu bohu* of the *il y a*."[67] It is a hermeneutic choice in face of the ambiguity of reality, and, Macquarrie would perhaps suggest, the confrontation between "faith" and "unfaith."[68]

65. Lyotard, *The Postmodern Condition*, 79ff.
66. Macquarrie, *Twentieth-Century Religious Thought*, 466.
67. Kearney, *Poetics of the Imagining*, 165.
68. Macquarrie, *Principles*, 81.

Macquarrie's preference for the unity of reality as a natural attitude of the human condition is resolved through his choice for "faith in Being," which favors singular and unifying "ideas" inherent to our thinking, like the transcendence of Good, Beauty, Truth and also Love (*agapé*). His is an existential commitment to a desire that has a transcendent origin. The Nietzschean legacy found in certain postmodern thinkers resists this, but in other thinkers one finds an apophatic neo-Platonic influence. So faith in a "unifying idea" remains in thinkers like Levinas, Marion, and Derrida.[69] This being the case (and accepting the ambiguity of the meaning of such an assertion), is this still not a shadow of a desire for the One—a unifying desire? A Desire above all desires? Is this not also a vestige of ontology? Even if it is a negative ontology, *via negativa*, embracing non-Being rather than a positive ontology, *via eminentiae*, embracing Being? Macquarrie argues we experience the particular in their particularity, but inescapably through the particular transcendence is indicated, we are pointed toward a unity. We have such an experience because as beings we have a capacity to receive the idea of the unity of phenomena. Macquarrie resolves the ambiguity of difference and identity through the influence of Schleiermacher, an interpretation of Kierkegaard's theory of repetition, and Heidegger's rethinking of Being. This is the foundation of his natural theology, his phenomenological-ontology.

However, how are we to read Macquarrie here? Is he not trying to "save the phenomena" in its unity by assuming that which does not appear? Does not the whole of Macquarrie's dialectical theism depend upon an ontology that requires "more than" the phenomena themselves, through a general structure (of Being)? Can he show that the unity of experience through repetition is really an indication for Being (God)? And can we say, unambiguously, that phenomena indeed point toward Being and not Nothing? This is, of course, a main concern that postmodernists have with any ontological-phenomenology. For postmodernist thinkers, like Levinas, Heidegger's Being is as much of a totality as is Hegel's Spirit (or any ontological surrogate). In Marion, Being is nothing less or more than idolatry and one of the great errors of thinking. But Macquarrie wonders: are the projects of Heidegger and Hegel so similar?[70] Does this not assume that all ontological visions are the same: locked-up in univocity? No! Macquarrie believes that an incarnational interpretation of

---

69. Macquarrie, *Twentieth-Century Religious Thought*, 470.
70. Ibid., 463.

Heidegger's ontology is more beneficial to maintaining respect for the plurality of phenomena (beings) than Hegel's all-embracing system. Further, he insists that it is the very *idea* of Being which acts as a guard against idolatry. And, indeed, Macquarrie can see no way of grounding a true and proper ethics *without* Being, or a true and proper theology *without* Being. We are on the razor edge of ontology. For the path to a proper understanding of Being is paved through the dangerous territory of reason, experience, and revelation.

7

# Reason, Experience, and Revelation

WE HAVE SEVERAL TIMES mentioned the relationship Macquarrie's dialectical theism has with postmodernism, entering him into conversation with several representative thinkers. But his differences with these interlocutors is what allows Macquarrie to proceed with an *ontotheology* that is also a *natural* theology. We will pick up themes touched upon previously, with the hope of continuing our conversation and performing a *repetition* worthy of the idea: namely not a mere going over but a retrieving with the hope of finding more depth and new insights.

Postmodernism rejects outright the role of reason to form systems and unities. His method of bringing together ontology and natural theology is another way of indicating the role *phenomenological-ontology* plays in Macquarrie's search for unity in experience and in creation; Macquarrie's search is for a dialectical unity between reason and revelation that is not content with rational systems and in this regard he stands with the majority of postmodern thinkers. Therefore, we will begin with his argument for the unity of reality and experience, which will involve us in a discussion with Lyotard and his famous definition of postmodernism as incredulity toward metanarratives. This will bring us back to the relationship between ethics and ontology discussed in the previous chapter. For, it is our contention that a fundamental disagreement Macquarrie has with postmodernism is over the issue of ethics and ontology: the relation of the Good with Being. From here we will move on to his view of reason and imagination, which proposes a non-objectifying, non-rationalistic concept of the unity of reality. This will naturally lead us to a discussion of experience and revelation which is central to reason and thinking. And revelation, in a way, brings us back to the beginning: *phenomenological-ontology*. For Being is revealed only through the phenomena, and the phenomena only have their meaning through the revelation of Being.

When discussing Macquarrie's view of unity, it is good to remind ourselves that he stands in a long line of Christian thinkers, who sees "things in their unity and interconnectedness and who have found this to be a situation in which God is present and self-disclosing. Being and oneness are both by definition incomparable, unique, *sui generis*. Indeed, in a long tradition of reflection from Plotinus to Heidegger, being (difference) and oneness (Identity) have been found to be two sides of the same concept."[1] But we must be reminded that Macquarrie is rejecting a unity and coherence grounded upon system and old style Enlightenment metaphysics.

To illustrate this, we can return to Macquarrie's criticism of Lyotard's view of metanarrative, which is a way of seeing things "in their unity and interconnectedness." For Macquarrie, metanarratives are certainly possible as a natural outcome of imagination, and the use of reason. However, since he rejects the idea of a "neutral" reason, in the Enlightenment sense of rationalism without prejudice, then we are led to assume that the metanarrative would not be a pure description of experience, but an interpretation of experience, a "likely story" that contains values of great importance. Therefore one cannot say it is presented as a self-evident universal state of affairs. The legitimacy of any metanarrative, therefore, rests in its persuasiveness, in its rhetorical and pragmatic value: in the sense that it is an adequate representation of the phenomena.[2] Here, one needs to *show* the value of the constructed narrative and evaluate whether it fits with one's overall commitments and experiences in the world. And this is fundamental to the distinction Macquarrie draws between old style natural theology and his new style natural theology.

Lyotard considers modernism to be "'nostalgia for the whole and the one."[3] Whereas, the postmodern imagination "renounces the demand to totalize the plurality of narratives into so-called "real unity"—a demand which is nothing other than a transcendental illusion . . . The postmodern imagination—be it that of the writer, the artist or the thinking citizen—is one which invents and reinvents narratives without recourse to unifying

---

1. Morgan, *In Search of Humanity and Deity*, 180.
2. Macquarrie, *Thinking about God*, 4; Macquarrie, *Principles*, 36, 56.
3. Kearney, *Poetics of the Imagining*, 209.

strategies of preordained systems."⁴ Of course, this rejection of universal prescriptions is itself a universal prescription,⁵ which moves beyond the particular and seems to be a gathering together of experience in a form of unity. Lyotard otherwise seems to offer no middle ground: one is either after a unity and therefore "'Modern" or after radical pluralities and therefore "Postmodern."

Macquarrie criticizes Lyotard's application of the term metanarrative to *ahistorical* theories of reality, those "ambitious theories that try to assemble in a unitary system all the phenomena of human life and sometimes of nature as well."⁶ Macquarrie insists that any unity of the particular, any narrative, needs to be historically and temporally constituted, not only are these formative factors for theology; they are constitutive of Being itself. He also allows for a construction of systems of reality, indeed even a variety of these, each of which may have a distinctive rhetorical force corresponding to particular historical and existential circumstances. This, indeed, is the possibility afforded through the role of imagination in concordance with reason. But, this may not be completely dissimilar to Lyotard's argument and the difference with Macquarrie is subtle,⁷ but this does not mean the difference is not also enormous: an absolute qualitative difference of the transvaluation of all values.

Lyotard's concern regarding metanarratives is not with their scope but with their ground or legitimacy.⁸ It is not with the unity but with how we claim this unity is founded or grounded. The distinction is important. Macquarrie is critical of Lyotard's boasting of "not seeking to "legitimate" his opinions,"⁹ but the legitimacy Lyotard is speaking of is primarily concerned with a rationalistic deduction found in any systematic and speculative metaphysics. Is this not similar to Macquarrie's criticism of old style metaphysics? Is this criticism not the very reason Macquarrie rejected "speculative reason" as a ground to philosophical theology? Lyotard's criticism of totalizing metanarratives is due to their rational closure, their "absolutist schemes."¹⁰ His criticism is of the evaluation of

---

4. Ibid.
5. Ibid., 210.
6. Macquarrie, *Twentieth-Century Religious Thought*, 465.
7. Smith, "A Little Story About Metanarratives," 261–76. See also his *Speech and Theology*.
8. Smith, "A Little Story about Metanarratives."
9. Macquarrie, *Twentieth-Century Religious Thought*, 466.
10. Ibid.

the metanarrative from the perspective of rational metaphysics itself: *sub specie aeternitatis*. So far, Macquarrie would be in agreement. But Lyotard offers no concern for another way of legitimacy.

Macquarrie[11] complains that Lyotard would reject theology as a totalizing system of creation and eschatology, insisting that he is not sensitive to the "variety of ways theories can be interpreted,"[12] how they can be legitimated. Any theology, therefore, can be a theology only if it attempts to privilege its point of view at the expense of all others; otherwise it will be reduced to a story of scope that is merely one mythology in relation to other mythologies: a theology, in relation to other theologies grounded in an agreed upon language game of a community; it is reduced to relativism. The error in Lyotard's type of criticism is that he is, in fact, holding up Enlightenment ideas as the only way of legitimizing truth claims: where the possibility of theology requires accepting the ground motive of rationalism. That is, if legitimacy is limited to the rules of Rationalism, any rejection of Rationalism becomes a rejection of the legitimacy of other possibilities of narrating truth claims and therefore reduces these claims to subjectivism and relativism. What if the legitimacy can be found through the experience of the individual and the Other, the community and not in a deductive rationalism? What if through phenomenology we can legitimate a way to theology through ontology? This will be the path Macquarrie takes. He will argue for the unity of experience and also for the unity through reason. We will return to these two themes below.

Macquarrie would see in his dialectical approach a way of offering a grand-narrative that aspires to having a claim to being "true" (adequate) while not being reduced to a deductive system or calculus of logic. It is, as we mentioned in a previous chapter[13] a view of truth that is more tentative, it is not a form of truth that demands closure. It claims truth but not in any exhaustive sense; truth claims are adequate to our experience, not pure coherence of thought and object, neither are they direct correspondences with experiences even though as true they indicate, *point*, to the unity and truth of Being that is unveiled. That is, he would accept both theories of great scope and a form of legitimization that is open to a plurality of interpretations of truth. For truth as adequacy is always open to progress and in this regard we see a move away from Lyotard who

11. Macquarrie, *Twentieth-Century Religious Thought*, 466. Following the criticism of Gary Browning.

12. Ibid.

13. See chapter 1 above.

claims relativism because the criteria for truth based on Enlightenment principles is not met. But more, as David Naugle discusses,[14] *adaequatio* is related to a way of knowing and truth that implies that human beings receive truth, it is given by God in epistemic grace to enable them to know and apprehend the diversity of beings that constitute the cosmos, both spiritual and physical. Truth is disclosed, unveiled. It is an idea that gathers together sensation and reason with imagination, with empathy, with feeling, a sense and taste for the infinite. It involves the whole of the person. It is enough that truth is adequate because as finite beings we cannot apprehend the Infinitely True.

In Lyotard's pluralism, there cannot be legitimacy of one truth-claim over another; all claims are interpretations *of interpretations*. This is the kind of subjectivism that Macquarrie finds so damaging in postmodernism, leading to utopian self-aggrandizement or negative and even nihilistic views of existence. For it seeks no value beyond its own valuation. Macquarrie is not impressed with Lyotard's destructive nihilism.[15] It is a form of irrationalism. It is the difference of "faith" and "unfaith,"[16] with significant ethical consequences. Macquarrie is aware that reality can be disclosed in a negative sense. As one who lived and moved in the world of existentialism, Macquarrie was always confronted with the tension within existentialism between atheism and theism, this tension has reappeared in postmodernism. Richard Kearney says that for Lyotard "the monstrosity of horror is just as "ineffable" as the vertical transcendence of God . . . There is, in short, an apophasis of the monstrous as there is an apophasis of the divine."[17] Kearney continues, "Lyotard relates explicitly to a postmodern version of the Kantian aesthetics of the sublime." Again: "In the realm of the sublime, the upwardly transcendent finds its mirror image in the downwardly monstrous—or what Kant called "radical evil." Both extremes transgress the limits of representation . . . the two are indistinguishable." Lyotard's view reminds us of Sartre's experience of Being as Nothingness and Levinas's *Il y a*. And, as we previously mentioned in Macquarrie's view this is tantamount to admitting that the universe is unintelligible,[18] lacking a reasonable structure a *tohu wa bohu*. Sartre says

14. Naugle, *Worldview*, 334.
15. Macquarrie, *Twentieth-Century Religious Thought*, 465.
16. Macquarrie, *Principles*, 81.
17. Richard Kearney, "The God Who May Be," in Captuo, *Questioning God*, 164–65.
18. See chapter 3 above.

that such a view is a way of existence, a certain way of apprehending the world signifying "the totality of the relationships of the human reality to the world."[19]

This is true. However, it suggests that regardless of postmodern attempts to avoid metaphysics, a grand-narrative, there is a tendency in human existence to seek unity of some sort. But in Macquarrie's view, *this* type of unifying experience would be a projection, and not a unity of reality as properly understood. It is a projection of an ego lost in its inauthenticity. It is the very idea of closure that Lyotard complains about, for it is not open to creativity and to growth, but to destruction and consummation. For Macquarrie this is a threat to the unity of creation, of reality and Being.

Macquarrie takes the reality and influence of evil very seriously, and this has led some to claim he is too focused on evil.[20] He agrees with Kant, Levinas, and Lyotard that evil is a radical reality in the world: a pull toward chaos, with the power of the "Nothing" or "Abyss" or *tohu wa bohu* to absorb us. This can be a way of interpreting the Kantian "sublime." "Kant himself," Kearney writes, "stopped short of the "abyss of the monstrous," realizing that to suspend the limit separating good and evil would be to embrace a form of amoral nihilism."[21] Kearney comes to a conclusion which would also represent Macquarrie's concern. "For as soon as the human subject dissolves into the void of the Monstrous "real," it seems to me we no longer have a stay against regression to the radical indifferentiation of pure drive—the chilling indifference of the There is (*il y a*). Do we not thus regress to the traumatism of the *tohu wa bohu*, the condition of the Real before the ethical God spoke the symbolic Word and the world divided into good and evil?"[22] This is a reversal of the work of creation, a risk Macquarrie finds central to the act of creation itself.[23] It is an act of disunity, of dismantling, of deconstruction which plays at undoing metanarratives, and installs chaos as an over-arching narrative.

In Macquarrie's dialectical theism, evil is the "reversal of the very creative act of letting-be . . . Evil is essentially negative and destructive

---

19. Macquarrie, *Principles*, 65.
20. Kee, *The Way of Transcendence*, 50.
21. Kearney, "The God Who May Be," 166.
22. Ibid., 167.
23. Macquarrie, *Principles*, 255–56.

and thus the enemy of beings."[24] It is the irrational. It tries to cover up the truth of Being with a lie. It creates disorder and allows dark forces to rule in our view of existence.[25] Macquarrie follows a neo-Platonic view that evil is *privatio boni*. It is, as in St. Athanasius's view, the "'lapsing into nothing" or "ceasing to be."[26] The position taken by Sartre and Lyotard perpetuate the ontological possibility of evil, of nihilism (nothingness) as an equal force with Creative Being. Granted, there is no empirical evidence to decide between a view like Sartre's and Lyotard's[27] whether creation is good and not evil. We are locked in a Kantian antinomy. Therefore if one is to employ reason, we cannot rely upon reason alone, we must make use of another method along with reason, and for Macquarrie this starting point is faith.[28] Faith is presupposed by reason, and faith operates phenomenologically, disclosed through our experience and interpretation of the things themselves. The view whether ultimate Reality is gracious or not is the limiting case for the meaning and value of human existence,[29] and Macquarrie says the only way to decide the issue is to "describe the human existence known to us as carefully as we can, and we ask others to look at the description and see if they recognize it as a true picture of the existence that is ours."[30] It gets down to the rhetorical power of phenomenological description.[31] Rhetoric as the other side of dialectic. It is an apologetic grounded in rhetoric and dialectic. This is rhetoric that is ethically driven, grounded in faith in the love that *is letting-be,* one that sees the inseparability of ethics and ontology at the heart and center of creation (existence). An ethical conversation between Self and Other in order to light up the infinitely Other disclosed through dialectical theology.

For Macquarrie, the description of ultimate reality we have in Lyotard, is a form of sinfulness, of being lost in the imbalance of human existence, of living alienated from holy Being: "in traditional theological language, this *aversio Deo* is understood as at the same time a *conversio*

---

24. Ibid., 254.
25. Ibid., 63.
26. Ibid., 255.
27. Ibid., 257.
28. Ibid., 80; also see chapter 5 above.
29. Ibid., 81.
30. Ibid., 82.
31. Ibid., 88.

*ad creaturam*. This means that in his quest for meaning and strengthening of his existence—a quest which we have seen to arise out of the very constitution of existence itself—man turns away from Being to the beings (from God to creatures). Ontologically expressed, this is the 'forgetting of Being'..."[32] Ethically expressed it is the division of the *Good* from *Being*. Lyotard has become lost in the world of beings and has elevated Nothingness and Angst as a unifying factor of existence. Macquarrie reminds us that theologically the "forgetting of Being" is the basic sin of idolatry, "the effort to found life upon beings, perhaps on man himself, to understand life and give it meaning in terms of finite entities alone..."[33]

Macquarrie's faith takes us beyond the plurality of beings, beyond the denial of legitimacy to metanarratives, to where there is a transcendent unity and truth and meaning to human existence. He wants to argue for this phenomenologically, his apologetic method opens phenomena to us "showing" the things themselves in the unity of their aspect. The first stage of Macquarrie's argument for the unity of reality is through our experience of the phenomena themselves.

Macquarrie has never been a proponent of the view that unities are *merely* subjective projections held together in a unity of apperception, for he believes that the unity must somehow also be found in the (objective) phenomena. Therefore, he rejects the subjectivism that has characterized postmodernism.[34] For example he says, "to a human experience there belongs also from the beginning a unity, which allows the manifold items in it to be ordered and related among themselves, and if this did not happen, there would be no properly human experience, but only at most a chaotic flux of impressions... it would be impossible for the mind to impose a unity on the manifold of sensations unless the conditions for such a unity were already in the sensations themselves."[35] He distances himself from any view that the mind creates the order, stating categorically that unity is not "a creation of the human mind, but a discovery."[36]

Macquarrie's position is that awareness of unity is equiprimordial with the awareness of plurality and this is the case whether we deal with

---

32. Ibid., 259–60.
33. Ibid., 260.
34. Macquarrie, *Twentieth-Century Religious Thought*, 449–50.
35. Macquarrie, *Theology, Church and Ministry*, 134–35.
36. Ibid., 135.

experience in science or with religion.[37] "It is repetition, the recurrence of what has been, that makes possible the construction of a unified experience, and this repetition lies in the given, the raw data of experience."[38] Repetition is formative, it is the dialectic of experience. Identity with difference, Same with Other: two sides of the same coin.

It is clear, however, that this allows for the possibility that although reality or the regularity of reality is not created by the mind, the mind orders reality in a *particular* way. That is, it interprets reality from a perspective influenced by the "existentialia," articulated as formative factors. So when Macquarrie writes that postmodernism lays great stress on creations of the human mind "and may even seem to be saying that there is no objective reality independent of our minds, or that, if there is any such reality, it is inaccessible," he is attempting to recover a way to objectivity that he finds lacking in postmodern thinking while remaining sensitive to their criteria for truth and the limits of reason. Yet, we have been saying, it is through this mediated view to objective reality and *only* through a mediated view of objective reality that unity can be "seen" since Being, Unity, the One, can only ever be experienced through things, through creation, through phenomena. If in Macquarrie's view we are a part of the reality we are attempting to unify, then it is not unreasonable to assume that the capacity for unity in human thinking is merely a special case of what is found in nature generally. This, of course, came out in our discussion of Macquarrie's natural theology. That is, the human being (*Dasein*) is the "place" where nature (*physis*) discloses itself; the human being (*Dasein*) is the "place" where the whole evolutionary process is conscious of itself.[39] Human being is the microcosm reflecting the macrocosm of the created universe.

This, however, is not something that can be discovered merely through a calculus of scientific thinking. Macquarrie (following Heidegger) refers to "essential thinking" or "primordial thinking" as a deeper kind of thinking that receives revelation. This is a form of meditative thinking that is rigorous but nevertheless receptive. Thinking as a *received* grace where we escape the destructive power of evil, of reduction to chaos, and see the order and beauty of creation. "This primordial thinking is a philosophical thinking, but it is described as a thinking which responds to the address of being . . . This kind of thinking, then,

37. Ibid., 136.
38. Ibid., 135.
39. Macquarrie, *Principles*, 223–32.

provides a kind of paradigm for the understanding of what is meant by revelation and shows where revelation is to be located in the range of man's cognitive experience."[40] Macquarrie, it appears, would take the view that postmodern thinkers who reject Enlightenment principles are still lost in the modernist paradigm of reduction and deconstruction, to a rational approach of reversal of what is given in the unity of experience.

In this thinking, we are in fact receiving Being through particular beings. It is a form of knowledge that has "a gift-like" character.[41] It is unlike the "calculative thinking" of the sciences, which objectifies phenomena seeking "objective knowledge" or theoretical knowledge of nature and humanity.[42] Calculative thinking is a way of thinking through cause and effect, it is an instrumental thinking, and has been elevated to our detriment during the Enlightenment as a deductive form of rationalism. Through "essential" or "primordial thinking," we are open to receiving Being, "not least through the depth of our own being, for we too are participants in being and indeed the only participants to which being opens itself, so that we not only are but we exist."[43] Such thinking is what comes to us through transcendence, our standing out from existence. It allows us to articulate ontology even though we stand existentially between being and nothing. It allows us to be aware that we are part of the unity of Being. At the level of calculative thinking we are lost in ambiguity, whereas "essential thinking" is open to *physis* in a special way since *physis* expresses being.[44] As Macquarrie tells us *physis* "expresses being in such a way to include "becoming" as well as "being" . . . Nature then is the emergence of the beings . . ."[45]

Yet, Macquarrie is arguing that in an ambiguous universe, in an undecidable epistemological situation, it appears equally as reasonable to assume unity in reality as it is to assume reality is fragmented. However, against modern and postmodern suspicions that may deny any objective unity or rational structure to the cosmos,[46] Macquarrie suggests that the reception of unified experience explains the success of modern science,

40. Ibid., 94.
41. Ibid., 95.
42. Ibid., 91.
43. Ibid., 94.
44. Ibid., 223.
45. Ibid.
46. Macquarrie, *Twentieth-Century Religious Thought*, 451.

which seems unlikely if unity is merely a projection of human thought and not part of the phenomena experienced. There needs to be a correlation between natural events and our understanding of them.[47] The *logos* of thought *is* an expression of the *Logos* in nature (creation). He believes this correlation to be also true of religious experience generally: that the content of such experience must originate from revelation through phenomena and not merely result as a projection from the human mind. The content of such a revelation would be of a general kind, communicated through awe and respect for existence, which would be an experience that is supra-rational (Bradley) or non-rational (Otto). This experience has a religious flavor, a religious experience disclosed through metaphysics (Bradley) or phenomenology (Marion). For Macquarrie, these views are not at odds, since in their various ways they each bring us up against an experience of the unity of the infinite.[48]

Macquarrie wants to find a way that preserves the tension, (i.e., the dialectic) between the universal and the particular. Between (for example), the totalizing methods of Hegel, with its consequential self-annihilation of the individual and the "death of God" into world history, and (for example) Kierkegaard, who gets lost in the scandal of particularity and champions an abandonment of reason for faith. And, perhaps, this is why Macquarrie favors Schleiermacher, who is a way between these two extremes. Schleiermacher offers a method that promises a theology of the possible in light of the impossibility of theology. He will be a bridge between the modern and the postmodern, the rational and the romantic; he will offer a diversity of logics that merge reason and imagination. Macquarrie recognizes both the benefits and the limitations of Enlightenment thinking and the struggles present in postmodern attempts to rethink tradition *against* tradition. He is aware that "we remain inevitably children of the Enlightenment,"[49] in spite of those "who talk about an ill-defined postmodernism."[50] Even in light of the differences between postmodern skepticism and dialectical theism, we have already seen there is space for fruitful dialogue between Macquarrie's theism and postmodern thinking. That reason, in its speculative sense of developing a *rational* metaphysics of a *deductive* universal system, is more of a hindrance

---

47. Ibid.
48. Ibid., 475.
49. Macquarrie, *Jesus Christ in Modern Thought*, 26.
50. Macquarrie, *Stubborn Questions*, 196.

to theology than a benefit is a common theme in postmodernism and Macquarrie's dialectical theism.[51] Indeed, Macquarrie's whole program of new style natural theology is an indictment against these characteristics of old style natural theology. With this, we move on to the second stage of Macquarrie's argument for the unity of reality, through reason.

We might ask: have not both Enlightenment thought and postmodern thought narrowed the idea of reason too much? Are there not nuances to reason that get overlooked? Is it possible that one can have a *reasonable* theology that works with unities and wholeness while escaping the grasp of deductive metaphysical speculation? Is it possible to have a *reasonable* theology that is *grounded in* and at once is *anchored by* revelation? Macquarrie suggests a connection between *imagination* and *reason* to open up possibilities of renewing a fundamental relationship between reason and revelation and to answer concerns about rationalism without surrendering the goal of reason as a unifying principle of experience and thought.

Unfortunately, Macquarrie says very little about imagination in his writings. Nevertheless, what he does say shows it is quite clearly central to his views on the dialectic of reason and revelation; it is central to his view of knowledge and understanding. We will investigate this in some detail as the key to his ontotheology.

There is a genealogy that connects Macquarrie's view of imagination and reason back to Kant. However, it does so through Heidegger, Otto, and Schleiermacher. Understanding this genealogy allows us to see that Macquarrie's dialectical theism is a *via media* between the extreme views of postmodernism (as we discussed with Lyotard), on the one hand, and the extreme views of moderns (in Enlightenment rationalism) on the other. But also, it allows us to establish that Macquarrie's dialectical theology is at heart a dialect between reason and revelation and only through this dialectic is there a possibility for a view of the unity of reality through the phenomena. Therefore, at the heart of Macquarrie's phenomenological method is a "Kantian" view of imagination, as the *apriori* possibility for the experience and thinking of unity. We begin with some general comments on imagination.

In his book *Existentialism*, Macquarrie discusses the importance of the role of imagination for Kant, as this has been interpreted and

---

51. Macquarrie is always careful to show what we should retain in the old style arguments for the existence of God, while making it clear that as arguments they are not overly effective and their view of God is to be overcome.

appropriated by Heidegger. He says, "It is clear that any kind of projecting of possibilities involves the imagination. In everyday understanding, the imagination is motivated by practical needs. In scientific understanding, the imagination also plays a major role, for instance in framing hypotheses; but here it is motivated not by practical needs but for the desire to know."[52] The imagination has the role of bridging the particular with the general. It is not a projection *sui generis* but a project of possibility allowing for hermeneutic understanding.

Similarly, the search for meaning, which we have seen is constitutive to human existence according to Macquarrie, is grounded in the role of the imagination to give direction and purpose to thought and action. Referring to Heidegger's reading of Kant, Macquarrie writes: "the imagination and the temporal nature of man are the fundamental conditions that make understanding possible; of course temporality and imagination are precisely what we see in the activity of projecting possibilities and meanings and even the world itself."[53] The projecting of possibilities and the quest for meaning and understanding require an imaginative synthesis of experience. And therefore—like the idea of unity itself—Macquarrie is sensitive to the question of meaning and of how far it "originates from a reality beyond ourselves, and how far it arises out of the constitution of our own humanity."[54] It is not merely one or the other, it not merely a projection nor is it to be found in a naïve realism. Macquarrie's longest reference to the role of imagination and reason comes from *Principles*:[55]

> It may be noticed however that there would seem to be a function of reason somewhat akin to its speculative exercise, yet in some respects quite distinct from it. I have in mind a constructive use of reason in which we build up rational wholes, theories, or interlocking systems of ideas, but do so not by deductive argument but rather by imaginative leaps which, so to speak, integrate the fragmentary elements in inclusive wholes ... This might be called the "architectonic" function of reason, and it would have something in common with esthetic sensibility. Clearly a well-constructed theology aiming at coherent expression, even if it eschews the speculative reason, will owe

---

52. Macquarrie, *Existentialism*, 131.
53. Ibid.
54. Macquarrie, *Stubborn Questions*, 206.
55. Macquarrie, *Principles*, 16.

> something of its shape and general structure to the architectonic reason.

And later,

> Reason is not opposed to the use of imagination[56] and indeed demands it. Both reason and imagination have their place in the intellectual quest for understanding and each needs the other. In theology . . . the central doctrines themselves may come to be better understood through the deployment of imaginative metaphors, analogues, and symbols which point us beyond the range of rational concepts.

The context of this passage has Macquarrie speaking about reason as a formative factor for theology. As we have already indicated in a different place, Macquarrie divides reason into speculative and critical functions. Speculative reason "endeavors to construct a metaphysic or theory of reality"[57] and proceeds through "pure reason alone and on the concepts which belong to it apart from any experience of the world."[58] It is this form of reasoning and its role in the history of philosophical theology that Macquarrie rejects. Differently, critical reason has an elucidatory function necessary for any thinking whatsoever; it sifts, analyses "and brings into the light the content of revelation."[59] Critical reason has a "descriptive" and "corrective" function necessary for any theological development. This critical or corrective use of reason scrutinizes revelation and brings it into line with other knowledge and understanding derived from experience.

When he speaks of "constructive reason," however, Macquarrie seems to be thinking of a third kind of reasoning that falls between "speculative" and "critical" reason. This is a non-objectifying reason that has both an analytical and synthetic role, structured through an aestheticism "giving rise to imaginative metaphors, analogues, and symbols." We call this activity "imaginative-reason," it is architectonic but not through overriding logical constructs and concepts, instead it is an aesthetic

---

56. In a different place, Macquarrie says, "conjectures and imaginative hypotheses (even, and perhaps especially, improbable ones!) may be more fruitful than inductive generalizations" (*In Search of Humanity*, 67), and we can add "deductive generalizations." This is true in all forms of knowledge (scientific and religious).

57. Macquarrie, *Principles*, 15.

58. Ibid., 16.

59. Ibid., 17.

architecture.[60] Aestheticism is linked to the faculty of imagination. It is the aesthetic reference that is so intriguing. Further, in Macquarrie aestheticism and revelation are structurally identified. In what follows we will tease out the various layers of meaning connected to the association of revelation, aestheticism, imagination, and reason.

Macquarrie describes revelation in a specifically religious sense as that which can remove fragmentariness and the distortions of our existence; that is, restore *unity and truth*. But generally in our experience he describes its role for an individual as "the cognitive element in experience," in so far "as it brings him a new understanding both of himself and of the wider being within which he has his being (for the understanding of these is correlative)."[61] Revelation is a form of thinking (cognition) that allows us to fulfill our quest for meaning, which is constitutive of human existence. Revelation is not merely believed, but experienced through phenomena itself.

With revelation we are concerned with an *affective state* of experience that has a *cognitive structure*, we are concerned "with something that is neither subjective nor objective, to an unbroken unity of subject and object or structure that is known from within. This unbroken unity is experienced on the level of feeling . . . In feeling we intuit the situations in which we find ourselves just as in sense perception we intuit objects in our environment."[62] Macquarrie prefers to speak of moods and says a mood is that which has a revelatory character. A mood "is something like an attunement to the environment, an awareness and response to the total situation in which one finds oneself and in which one participates." It is an experience given to us and received by us and cannot be disclosed through "objective perceiving."[63] No doubt more needs to be said about this, however, with what we have said so far we can see that reason must work with revelation in order to enter fully into any experiences we have. It makes sense then in Macquarrie's view that a thoroughgoing rationalism will cut itself off from depth experiences: from revelation.

Let us return to the relationship between reason and revelation. Constructive reason (imaginative-reason) works with critical reason (with its elucidatory and corrective functions). Macquarrie emphasizes

60. Ibid., 16.
61. Ibid., 84.
62. Ibid., 98.
63. Ibid.

that he supports the use of critical reason, and in doing so he is aware of the controversy surrounding his position. It is *this* form of reasoning that is often opposed to revelation. Any thinker must use elucidatory reason to think critically about anything. But to speak of reason *correcting* revelation is to speak in the way of rational theology. It is important to emphasize, however, that for Macquarrie the corrective role for reason does not assume that revelation is erroneous. Revelation is not opposed to reason. Revelation opens us to phenomena that are *saturated*, which must then accommodate and line up with our other experiences of the world; otherwise a revelatory experience has the danger of remaining purely mystical, *other-worldly*. Reason corrects by *aligning* revelation with our other knowledge and *interpreting* our other knowledge *in light of* and *through* the depths of revelation. It is where the various forms of "logics," of discourses, are brought together in relation to a deeper understanding of the world we live in, removing fragmentariness and distortions. It is a guide in the world of varied discourse and (calculative) thought. Reason, in fact, cannot afford to ignore revelation and therefore get lost in abstract speculation and revelation cannot be cut-off from reason, otherwise it gets lost in its own mythologizing tendency, that is, "it lacks an ordered systematic approach that is characteristic of an intellectual discipline."[64] So reason needs the content of revelation and revelation needs the ordering function of reason.

Macquarrie is indicating that reason must be critical of its own activity and correct its own path with the help of revelation. Reason must function with a set of concepts and language that communicates to the times. We can think of critical reason, in a way, as having both a constructive and demythologizing ability and function.[65] It deconstructs any attempt at an abstract metaphysics and it demythologizes by interpreting the content of revelation in relation to our existence and experience in an orderly coherent fashion. In this way the function of reason is hermeneutical and it is dialectical.[66]

For some thinkers revelation is subject to an objectifying reason, which has been the dominant case in the philosophical tradition

---

64. Ibid., 131.

65. In "Mystery and Truth," in Macquarrie, *Thinking about God*, chapter 3, Macquarrie distinguishes between mythology and mysticism. Mythology must be overcome and new language found to express the truths buried within the myth. Mysticism is some way of thinking that moves beyond the limits of reason in pursuit of the truth.

66. Macquarrie, *Principles*, 133.

of modernity. In this case faith and revelation are subjective points of view, not objective certainties or experiences. For others, reason would be "subject to revelation itself and perhaps even to divine illumination, so that reason here is entirely ancillary to revelation . . ."[67] These views maintain a dualism between faith and reason, a modern project that Macquarrie cannot be linked to, he does not allow a "neutral" "secular" reason to exist along-side revelation. There can be no dualism between revelation and reason in this sense. So, if in Macquarrie's theology the role of reason is to remove or reinterpret any content from revelation that conflicts with and is irreconcilable to other well-founded convictions,[68] in this sense Macquarrie's theology is deconstructive, but it deconstructs mythologizing tendencies in order to maintain theology as *reasonable*:[69] it is not Rational in the old style. In this new style theology, reason allows a constructing role for revelation to supply real content. Reason does not only deconstruct, but constructs through the faculty of imagination, allowing for the reception of revelation through phenomena: imagination brings together revealed and natural theology.

The imaginative-leap Macquarrie speaks of is still a *reasonable* leap, it is the alliance of imagination and reason, and it is the recognition within reason of its own finite limit. Imaginative-reason is the *dialectic* between the non-rational and the rational. We cannot be too hasty and say that Macquarrie favors one side of the dialectic of reason-revelation over the other; he is, as we have said, avoiding either a rationalistic or a fideistic approach that might be typical of modernity. But he has also said that a dialectic, which seeks a balance, does not mean both sides play an equal role: one side of the dialectic might be more fundamental than the other. This, we are saying, in spite of his criticism of Kierkegaard's "knight of faith" and Barth's attack against natural theology is the role of revelation: revelation is the source for imaginative-reason, indeed revelation is the source for any experience whatsoever.

Reason can only operate with the content of experience and revelation, and revelation and experience can only ever be articulated if they are subjected to the ordering and constructing possibilities found in imaginative-reason. Macquarrie speaks of a *reasonable* theology, but any commitment to the expression of theology is grounded in faith; which is

---

67. Ibid., 17.
68. Ibid.
69. Ibid.

the operation of the whole person and an affective state that requires a fundamental trust in experience and revelation. And the very idea that it is a reasonable *theology* suggests first there is an *experience* of God, of Holy Being, which takes the initiative in communicating with us: a Holy Being who reveals and is the source for this fundamental trust.

There is a very close relationship between revelation and experience, and Macquarrie says we cannot make a hard and fast division between them.[70] Nevertheless, it is pragmatic to do so. At one point Macquarrie says, it "would seem that almost anything in the world can be an occasion for revelation" and this includes natural phenomena and history.[71] In its strongest sense, however, revelation *is* Jesus Christ:[72] the sublime made manifest. The sublime is that which breaks open any rational structure while manifestation requires some reasonable structure to be employed in order to recognize an experience as meaningful. "Revelation," Macquarrie writes, "suggests some kind of unveiling . . ."[73] *through* phenomena itself, "that which is known comes into the light, or, better still, provides the light by which it is known . . ."[74] Reason on its own does not allow us to access the unity of phenomena and the meaning that lies behind phenomena. So to penetrate deeper into reality in a *reasonable* way requires access from other sources: this is revelation. In order to bring these ideas together, we need to investigate further Macquarrie's understanding of (what we have called) imaginative-reason.

Macquarrie's understanding of imaginative-reason is "Kantian." Kant declared that without the transcendental imagination there could be no unity to experiences or concepts whatsoever.[75] But to see how this registers with Macquarrie, we need to return to Heidegger:[76]

> As a faculty of intuition, imagination is formative in the sense that it produces an image. As a faculty not dependent on objects of intuition, it produces i.e., forms and provides images. This "formative power" is at one and the same time receptive and productive (spontaneous). In this "at one and the same time" is to be found the true essence of the structure of imagination.

70. Ibid., 8.
71. Ibid., 7.
72. Ibid.
73. Ibid., 85.
74. Ibid., 86.
75. Kant, *Critique of Pure Reason*, 146.
76. Heidegger, *Kant and the Problem of Metaphysics*, 135.

> However, if receptivity is identified with sensibility, and spontaneity with understanding, then imagination falls in a peculiar way between the two.

Heidegger tells us that for Kant, the imagination is presupposed by both sensation (intuition) and understanding (cognition) as an original power, it is *a priori*, and therefore there can be no pure description of phenomena, but only description informed by the imagination. To the understanding the imagination gives the ability to "compare, shape, differentiate and connect"[77] creating a synthesis, or totality, or generality, or universality of the particular "fragmented" phenomena. Kant says: "Synthesis in general is the mere result of the power of the imagination, a blind but indispensable function of the soul, without which we should have no knowledge whatsoever, but of the existence of which we are scarce ever conscious."[78]

We understand phenomena as unified because of the role of imagination. But in Macquarrie, the imagination is not "blind" as it is in Kant. It carries with it affective states, so we do not merely experience unity but unity with feeling that influences our understanding of existence.

Heidegger exchanged the Kantian "categories" which described universal properties of beings with his own "existentialia," which described possible ways of experiencing and existing in the world.[79] Our being-in-the-world is disclosed through these "existentialia" "in two basic and equally primordial ways—through affective states and through understanding."[80] These affective states "color our experience" and "reveals how we are attuned to our environment" and the apprehension of such states (moods) "comes before separation of subject and object."[81] In Macquarrie's theology, this is constitutive of human beings' factical existence in light of possibilities of existence, what he considers as part of the polarities of human existence: "possibilities of existence are always conditioned by the facticity of existence. The existent is never pure possibility, but always factical possibility."[82] This facticity is disclosed through affective states, our possibilities are disclosed through understanding:

77. Ibid.
78. Kant, *Critique of Pure Reason*, 112.
79. Macquarrie, *Martin Heidegger*, 13.
80. Ibid., 20.
81. Ibid.
82. Ibid., 21.

"the characteristic structure of understanding is projection . . . Indeed this is how the world gets built up . . . Understanding also implies interpretation . . . Whatever he encounters gets related to the totality of understanding that he already has. But this is an act of interpretation."[83] The affective states are expressed not primarily rationally *but aesthetically.* This returns us to a previous discussion, the connection between *poiesis* and *theoria,* passion and intellect, the non-rational and the rational. In Kant the aesthetic and the rational were separate, but for Macquarrie they are intermingled and necessary for one another.

When we turn to references to aesthetic sensibility in Macquarrie's writing we find connections to the experience of revelation that further shed light on the association of imagination and revelation. Revelation, Macquarrie tells us, is the experience of seeing the things (phenomena) in a different way, with a depth beyond the ordinary.[84] Aesthetic experience is a type of "experience that touches upon the whole existence, strongly involving feelings, yet certainly not without its cognitive aspect. Again, what is known in the aesthetic experience *is not some additional thing* beyond what is open to universal inspection, but *rather the depth* of what confronts us, a structure or a *Gestalt* that is noticed in the experience. This awareness, moreover, has a kind of gift-like character, and can have levels of intensity that may be experienced as joy or boredom or anxiety but that can come to overwhelm us, for the "beautiful" or the "sublime" like the "holy" or the "numinous," seems to take possession of us." And he concludes that this is "what we call 'revelation.'" Affective states are expressed aesthetically, and aesthetic experience has a structure similar to revelation.

References to the "beautiful" and "sublime" as well as to "holy" and "numinous" connect us to Kant's *Critique of Judgment.* It is this work that Macquarrie refers to as the "most neglected of his *Critiques,*"[85] raising the question as to the real meaning of the "sublime," defined ambiguously by Kant as "'the name given to that which is absolutely great, beyond all comparison great."[86] It is this work where Macquarrie sees a connection with the thought of Otto and his analysis of the *numinous,* which is at the heart of religious experience. Otto reworked Kantian ideas in the service of his

---

83. Ibid., 22, 23.
84. Macquarrie, *Principles,* 89.
85 Macquarrie, *Stubborn Questions,* 206.
86. Ibid.

phenomenology of religion,[87] and as Macquarrie observes, was "praised by Husserl for having made a masterly phenomenological analysis of the religious consciousness."[88] Many of the central categories of Macquarrie's view of revelation are borrowed from Otto, and so we have a genealogy of a Kantian "sublime" aesthetic through the "numinous" into the phenomenology of religion.[89] The "sublime" is that experience that overwhelms the imagination and reason, pointing to something that cannot be contained within the concepts of the understanding: it is an experience of transcendence. Macquarrie's analysis of this, we will see, clearly places him within the gap between modern and postmodern thinkers.

That this rendering of the role of imagination, which is both a cognitive and affective *apriori structure*, is what Macquarrie intends is reinforced through his reliance on Otto. Central to religious consciousness is the key word "holy," which has both rational and non-rational characteristics. The word "holy" in this context is an indicator. "The Christian," Macquarrie writes, "thinks of God in terms of goodness, personality, purpose, and so on, and although—as Otto recognizes—these ideas are applied to God analogically, they are nevertheless rational characteristics in the sense that we have definite concepts of them."[90] Macquarrie follows Otto, declaring both that this rational side is essential for religious experience in general and yet, this rational side "has tended to overshadow the deeper non-rational core."[91] For Otto, Macquarrie reminds us, the holy begins as an *apriori* "non-rational category or numinous element," which retains its foundation in a "cognitive apprehension"[92] and is a religious value *sui generis*. Relying on Kant to show how the *apriori* category of the numinous becomes a rational category we call "holy," Otto tries to show how the non-rational becomes rational, and therefore a cognitive function. Although Macquarrie considers Otto's use of Kant specious at

---

87. Macquarrie, *Twentieth-Century Religious Thought*, 211.

88. Ibid., 213. It is interesting, too, that Heidegger prepared a series of lectures between 1920 and 1921 called "The Phenomenology of the Religious Life," where he explores the contributions to religion of Schleiermacher and Otto. See his *The Phenomenology of the Religious Life*.

89. Macquarrie, *Stubborn Questions*, 206. This carries over to postmodernism as well. In fact Macquarrie distinguishes experiencing Being as gracious or alien, and we have the same in postmodern discussions of the sublime.

90. Macquarrie, *Twentieth-Century Religious Thought*, 214.

91. Ibid.

92. Ibid., 215.

times, perhaps having Kant say more than he intended in his *Critiques*, he does not consider this devastating to Otto's theory. We cannot say about Otto "that his general position is a mistaken one,"[93] indeed, Macquarrie endorses Otto, accepting that the adjective "holy" points to that which is inconceivable, suprarational, sublime, an experience that overwhelms us and is a pre-conceptual knowing requiring a different mode of cognition. It requires the use of analogue, symbols and metaphors all generated through imagination. This is the source of Macquarrie's use of "holy," the adjective Macquarrie attaches to Being, the highest existential-ontological experience in his philosophical theology.

It is true, "that which first falls under our apprehension is being, the understanding of which is included in all things whatsoever a man apprehends."[94] Yet, Being cannot be grasped in itself. Rationally, cognitively, we conceive Being only with our conception of the world (with and through *beings*). But with this conception, we have said, there is a remainder; a transcendence revealed through experience of phenomena that is *supra*rational, *in*conceivable: sublime. Our understanding of Being requires more than reason, it requires imagination. It is imagination that gives us access to categories of thought to at least *point* to the *ens realissimum*, which is "holy" Being; that is, the *unity and meaning of reality*. "Our final analysis of being as the *incomparable*, that *lets-be* and is *present-and-manifest*, is strikingly parallel to the analysis of the numinous as *mysterium tremendum et fascinans*."[95]

The sublime is an experience that exhausts, overwhelms, and transcends the category of understanding. Macquarrie writes: ". . . Kant himself opened up this possibility. His words about the starry heavens and the moral law as awe-producing seem to look very much like an experience of the sublime, of that which "overwhelms" the recipient of the experience and yet "draws" him to itself. Kant's analysis has a close resemblance to Otto's analysis of the numinous, which he resolves into the *mysterium tremendum fascinans* as the heart of religious experience." Macquarrie goes farther and connects the experience of the sublime with the understanding of the historical Christ. "Could we say that Jesus Christ is an instance of the sublime, by which I mean that the historical figure proclaimed in the Christian gospel is identifiable with the archetype of

---

93. Ibid., 224.

94 Macquarrie, *Principles*, 110.

95. Ibid., 115.

humanity which we already find within the human mind? If so, we may be coming into view of a reconciliation between the type of religion and theology which claims to depend on the human mind itself and the type which appeals predominately to a revelation given in history by God."[96] The appeal through "the human mind" to revelation is a reconciliation that is possible through imaginative-reason. And we should not lose track of the depth and breadth of this faculty of constructive reason. It allows for the thinking of the unity of reality, it allows for the possibility of thinking (however limited) of holy Being, the sublime, and it allows for a relationship with Jesus Christ, as the *Logos* made manifest in history and continuing through an *apriori* archetype. This would not only bridge reason and revelation, imaginative-reason seems for Macquarrie to be the way we synthesize our experience of the unity of phenomena and the saturation of phenomena by Being, it is the way we experience the ongoing work of Christ who is the beginning and end of Creation of which we are a part and through whom the meaning of Being is disclosed.

Macquarrie attempts to give a phenomenological explanation of the dialectic of the sublime, of the non-rational, or suprarational, in relation to the rational content of religious consciousness, and he does so through the vocabulary of Otto. We have just made reference to the *mysterium tremendum fascinans*. The *mysterium* is the "wholly otherness" of the experience of that which is utterly transcendent, escaping any conceptual grasp. The *tremendum* indicates the awe or dread that accompanies this experience. The meaning of *fascinans* has to do with the power of the experience of the phenomena to capture and attract our full attention, moving us to "see" more "deeply." Otto believed there was an *apriori* category a faculty, of whatever sort it may be, of genuinely cognizing and recognizing the holy in its appearance.[97] This takes us back to the questions raised previously about the possibility of the appearance of the invisible (holy Being) through the visible (phenomena). Yet, the *mysterium tremendum fascinans* also points to the ambiguity of the goodness or the horror of existence. An ambiguity we have alluded to and will discuss again later. To further fill-out Macquarrie's view of reason and revelation we turn to Schleiermacher, a major influence on Macquarrie's thinking.

Schleiermacher's revival of religion maintains that the *essence* of religion is to be found in the "feeling of absolute dependence" and the "sense

---

96. Macquarrie, *Stubborn Questions*, 206.
97. Macquarrie, *Twentieth-Century Religious Thought*, 215.

and taste for the infinite."[98] In his *Jesus Christ in Modern Thought, Studies in Christian Existentialism*,[99] and *Thinking about God*,[100] Macquarrie has written of the need to reconsider the value of Schleiermacher. More recently Graham Ward has argued that we should think again about the value of Schleiermacher's thought for our understanding of religion in a postmodern world.[101] The renewed view of the phenomenology of religious experience in postmodernism wants to locate an "other," a "holy," or even "dreadful" and "monstrous" presence at the limits of thought that nevertheless penetrates deeply into our experience.

For Schleiermacher, religion is not a rational or moral system, as is the case with Kant and the Enlightenment generally;[102] religion is the ground upon which reason and morality is to be built. Ward comments, "True religion was being conceived now as that which is the experiential condition for the possibility of both speculative thought and community action, the perception of the infinite in the finite. The essence of true religion lay in feeling and intuition."[103] All existence is religious existence. Schleiermacher says:[104]

> The universe is uninterruptedly active and reveals itself to us at every moment. Every form which is produced, every being to which it gives a separate life in accordance with the fullness of life, every occurrence which it pours out of its rich, ever-fruitful womb, is an action of the universe upon us; and in this way, to accept everything individual as a part of the whole, everything limited as a presentation of the infinite, is religion.

For Schleiermacher, the "uninterrupted revelation of the universe" saturates the intuition. For Kant, intuition mediates the world to consciousness, *maintaining a distinction*, a dualism, between the ontological and the epistemological. Ward draws our attention to the fact that in Kant's analysis the ontological is endlessly differentiated through intuition.[105] The ontological remains a mystery inaccessible. In the *Critique*

---

98. Ibid., 210.
99. Macquarrie, *Studies in Christian Existentialism*, 31–42.
100. Macquarrie, *Thinking about God*, 157–66.
101. Ward, *True Religion*, 81–106.
102. Ibid., 81–82.
103. Ibid., 82.
104. Ibid., 84.
105. Ibid., 82.

*of Judgment* Kant outlines how intuition is connected to feeling. Intuition receives the "world," Ward comments, and "feeling spontaneously arises on this reception. Even so, the feelings cannot be *directly* related to the object *since they arise* subsequently in the cognizing subject: there is a division of subject and object. We cannot therefore know that it is the object as such which is giving the pleasure or pain, only the effect of the object upon the subjective consciousness."[106] Are values the result of subjective reaction, or are they somehow part of the things themselves?

With Schleiermacher, however, the imagination receives a freedom of its own. Imagination, feeling and intuition are modified in such a way to "favor an immediate apprehension of a primary unity between mind and world."[107] It is an immediacy of *unity*, not an immediacy of the *object in itself*. Such immediacy of unity does not require purity, like Kant's "pure reason" or any "unprejudiced apprehension" of the world. We saw this in Heidegger, through the "existentialia": we receive the world immediately yet *colored* through affective states and this is prior to any subjective objective division. Macquarrie makes a direct connection between Heidegger's "existentialia" and Schleiermacher's "feeling."[108]

This argument for unity takes on the additional factor that this unity also discloses a presence that saturates the phenomena overwhelming it. Also, unlike the argument from experience, which can be made somewhat "objectively," here the immediacy of unity through the imagination and intuition is heavily value-laden; we receive the world *with feeling* prior to any subject-object division. We can experience the world negatively or positively: through anxiety and dread or through joy and hope.[109] Macquarrie sees these as two sides of the same experience: one reveals the difference between finite being and ultimate reality, the other the *belonging* to the unity of Being.[110] So, here we see one possible source for experiences like Sartre's, Levinas', or Lyotard's, a real possibility of reality itself, of creation itself, a creation with risk, which has always the risk of falling into nothing. In fact, here we are at the crux of the possibilities of human experience: the fact that existence can be so radically put in question: the struggle, ultimately we may say, between anxiety and hope as unifying

---

106. Ibid., 83.
107. Ibid.
108. Macquarrie, *Studies in Christian Existentialism*, 30–42.
109. Macquarrie, *Principles*, 65.
110. Ibid., 65.

factors of experience and reality.[111] Although the situation is ambiguous this does not reduce it to absurdity. As we have seen, Macquarrie considers the experience of hope and belonging to the created universe as more fundamental, and the experience of Angst, of alienation, to be a distortion and an inauthentic interpretation of existence (reality).[112]

This is no facile optimism. It is faith. It is eschatological: dependent upon "how we cooperate now with God's work, for this cooperation is not a matter of indifference but something on which God counts, so to speak, in taking the risk of creation and in laying the being that he pours out open to the threat of dissolution into nothing."[113] In his teaching of the *analogia entis* and the triune structure of Being, described above, we saw how Macquarrie connects the temporal structure of Being with the temporal structure of human being—stretching of human existence through past, present, and future—in transcendence of any moment. This is hope, the gathering together of all things (and experiences) in God (Unitive Being), and the hope is that human beings will overcome the polarities of existence, of anxiety and hope, into a unity of self, and creation itself will overcome the possibility of sinking into Nothing and be built up into a commonwealth of rich and full being. Macquarrie insists that this hope is possible and real, but is a possibility only through the grace of Being (God).[114] Yet, it is not the only possibility.

For those who have faith, the experience of Nothing does not have to have the dread that it carries in Sartre and Lyotard. Lyotard and Sartre, Macquarrie seems to argue, are examples of those who have become lost in the nothingness of existence cut-off from Being, demonstrating that the fall into sin is a reality that can consume us. At the level of holy Being, Being and Nothing merge in a unity that allows for the diversity of experience of beings. The experience of Being requires the experience of Nothingness.[115] When Macquarrie speaks of nothingness he does not mean sheer negativity.[116] Nothingness is *an experience*, not merely an abstract idea. It is indeed what bridges a universal generalized idea

---

111. Ibid., 64.
112. Ibid., 65.
113. Ibid., 348.
114. Ibid., 360.
115. Macquarrie, *Studies in Christian Existentialism*, 88.
116. Ibid., 84.

and existential awareness of being-in-the world.[117] Nothingness is what guards against any subjectivism by connecting existence with the ontological. Nothingness is at the heart of our awareness of our finitude, the "nullity" of our existence.[118] There is an empirical aspect to this, "'Nothing" stands for the disclosure in our experience as existence of this possibility of ceasing to be."[119] This is disclosed through the mood of anxiety. Anxiety is the resulting affective state when we realize that our own life and all other finite entities shrink to nothing, "the wilting away of the familiar world"[120] resulting from the "transvaluation of values" with our awareness of the finitude of all existence. This transvaluation of values is evident when we become aware of the wonder of existence, "why there is something rather than nothing." When seen against the background of nothingness we see things as they really are as entities, as contingent.[121]

"Nothing" in this sense has a positive operation, it is a unifying factor in that it functions as a horizon to our factical existence. Indeed, is this sense of "Nothing" not a synonym for Being, the transcendent pure and simple, that which Lets-be? Being is not another entity, Macquarrie insists, and "Nothing" is precisely *nothing*. Macquarrie speaks of "nothing" "as paradoxically equated with Being itself," which is contrary to the way of speaking in the old style metaphysics, which has contributed to the forgetting of Being.[122] But in the new style of doing philosophical theology equating Being and Nothing is no dualism, but a method that also opens the way to an existential-ontology that is not devoid of mystery and the mystical.

Yet, as we have already noted Macquarrie's is a language adopted to show *positively* the possibility of articulating our experience. It is our experience of nothingness through phenomena that Macquarrie speaks of as implying empirical knowledge. For, it is not as a general logical category, but through our involvement with entities that we are led to an experience of nothingness: an experience Macquarrie states is both rare yet inevitable and universal. Schleiermacher explicitly associates the

---

117. Ibid.
118. Ibid.
119. Ibid.
120. Ibid.
121. Ibid.
122. Ibid., 85–86.

religious "negativity" with the sublime.[123] Macquarrie speaks of this as an experience of the infinite through the finite. In describing the meaning of "infinite" he says: "The word points to the deeply felt contrast between man's own limited, fragile existence and what has in the revelatory moment touched his life—overwhelming Being; or again, to the contrast between those objects in the world which man can exploit and manipulate (and in this scientific age we recognize that measurement is the way to mastery) and the presence of Being, which we can never have at our disposal and which masters us."[124]

Neither Schleiermacher nor Macquarrie want to retrieve a form of mystical monism. For Macquarrie, this is an aberration of religious experience.[125] Reason and intuition may be overwhelmed and saturated by the imagination, but they are not extinguished by it. The imagination allows for an experience or awareness of wholeness of the infinite manifold, without losing awareness of the reality of becoming, of dynamism. Such awareness is pre-reflective, pre-rational, but nevertheless immediately self-conscious. Therefore, we are led to wonder how one begins to speak about such experiences. Is this not the perennial theological issue: the impossibility of theology due to the inability to articulate how the finite can express the infinite? Macquarrie's dialectic is structured around the possibility of (onto) theology, of discourse as the way of sharing experiences and contributing to the retrieval of Being and repetition of the theological tradition. Therefore we move on to the question of the language and logic, the structure of discourse; for ultimately this is what theology is: "God Talk."

---

123. Ward, *True Religion*, 86.
124. Macquarrie, *Principles*, 205.
125. Ibid., 111.

# 8

# Truth, Language, and Scripture

ACCORDING TO MACQUARRIE THE most "distinctive characteristic of man is his use of language. He has been defined as *zoon logon echon*—"the living being that has the word." Whatever man does beyond the most elementary biological reactions, he makes use of language. Even when he is doing nothing overtly, his thoughts are formed by language."[1] Written or spoken language with its systems of symbols and signs points beyond the words used to the things themselves, to phenomena. The word is not identical with the thing but signifies it and is intimately connected to it as the bearer for the meaning of the thing signified.

It is through language that any idea, or mood, or experience is communicated. Language is the way in which our private individual experiences can become public and communal, directed beyond our self and towards an Other. Ultimately, what gives words meaning is "the life and experience of the beings that use the language; or, perhaps better, that language (words and sentences) has to be understood as the bearer of discourse (the conversing of intelligent, personal beings)."[2] And Macquarrie makes clear that even though misunderstanding and ambiguity are inherent to communication, what unites those in any discourse situation is fidelity and loyalty to express as clearly as possible a matter of concern. Macquarrie says that this situation of fidelity and loyalty in communication is best expressed through the biblical ideas of *'emeth* and *alḗtheia*, where the focus is not on a clear and distinct understanding of

---

1. Macquarrie, *Thinking about God*, 3.
2. Macquarrie, *Principles*, 125.

what is communicated between people, but on entering into a discourse situation with trust that you are receiving as far as is possible a true reflection of another's thoughts, feelings, and experiences. Indeed Macquarrie takes the view that language, especially about God can be ambiguous, it does not need to be clear to be true. In fact, in his view, we can expect that language about God will be illogical to our typical understanding. Language will need to be stretched beyond typical use and applied to God symbolically, analogically, in order to move us as close as we can to an adequate discourse.

The incarnation is an appropriate symbol for Macquarrie's view of language. Any speaking and any writing are worldly activities. Language lives and dwells within a worldly context and yet transcends it. The incarnation is a symbol of what is transcendent becoming immanent, a sign is immanent and points to that which is signified, that is to that which is transcendent. The incarnation symbolizes what is both present and absent. As we have stated previously, this is how Macquarrie understands Being as present and manifest within beings, and yet is absent and hidden as well. Being is never fully or purely present. So too with language. Language allows for a bringing into the light what otherwise would remain private, and yet because of the limitation of language through ambiguity and instability in the semantic range of words, language can just as equally hide meaning and understanding between conversation partners. Again, the incarnation is a symbol of mediation between the Infinite and the finite, and language very much is a mediator between thought and expression, between historical and present understandings, between individuals and communities. However, although Macquarrie believes ambiguity is inescapable and words have limited power to capture fully and completely absolute meaning, he takes a very optimistic approach to the ability of language to communicate adequately even the most difficult concepts and emotions.

Language, Macquarrie insists, is a communal activity, socially and culturally conditioned (there are no private languages). As such, it requires repetition, the returning again and again to texts or ideas to find more meaning or to translate into more relevant discourse the meaning that has been carried forward through tradition, history, and culture. What we previously identified as formative factors for philosophical theology, what is always already present in any context of communication. One of the many thematic connections Macquarrie has with postmodernism has to do with how repetition is key to any experience at all and the possibility of communicating experience. A comparison with Derrida can illustrate this.³

Macquarrie, we have stated, takes the view that we have no ahistorical, "god-like," perspective since we find ourselves already in a world of meaning, "thrown" into existence historically and culturally conditioned. This is true of our experience and our reasoning, and in this way he is at one with a post-Enlightenment view of the world. Yet, he sees unity and the possibility of stability to meaning in our understanding our world. This is witnessed, for example, in the successes of science and technology, or in the continuity of recognized relevance and understanding of historical, philosophical, and theological texts. He is also of the view that any and all meaning is open to revision, to which these same above mentioned disciplines are also a witness. This is true, says Macquarrie, because repetition is the key to our understanding of anything. We have said enough about this in the previous chapter that it is not necessary for us to go over the details again. However, in that chapter we quoted Macquarrie saying: "It is repetition, the recurrence of what has been, that makes possible the construction of a unified experience, and this repetition lies in the given, the raw data of experience."⁴ It is not unity or the Ideal that is first, but repetition. As well, repetition as the beginning of constructing (or deconstructing) meaning is an inevitable structure of experience. Derrida takes a similar view (certainly not an identical one) with very different conclusions.

Derrida, states, for example, that "the presence—of the present—is derived from repetition and not the reverse."⁵ All experience begins with repetition, not unity or identity. And, he considers the present as the universal form of all experience and all life.⁶ In this presence, which is also the universal form of transcendental life, lurks the past and the future, "this determination of being as presence, ideality, the absolute possibility of repetition."⁷ Through repetition lies the possibility of meaning, and herein lies the connection with language. Presence, as being itself, has to be re-presented, repeated, in order to continue and have meaning, and it has to be repeated in the absence of any pure origin, or author.

---

3. See the very helpful works by Shakespeare, *Derrida and Theology*, and Smith *Speech and Theology*.

4. Macquarrie, *Theology, Church and Ministry*, 135.

5. Derrida, *Speech and Phenomena*, 52.

6. Ibid., 53.

7. Ibid., 54.

Fundamental to language is that the signs and the signified can be repeated through time, at once "in" time and locked in finitude and yet only meaningful through transcendence, the continuation beyond themselves "here—and—now" to further as yet unknown contexts and situations. Repetition allows for identity of meaning, it allows for the possibility of unity, of Ideality. "For there is no word," writes Derrida, "nor in general a sign, which is not constituted by the possibility of repeating itself. A sign which does not repeat itself, which is not already divided by repetition in its 'first time,' is not a sign. The signifying referral therefore must be ideal—and ideality is but the assured power of repetition—in order to refer to the same thing each time."[8] It is in precisely this idea of repetition where Derrida sees a paradox. For repetition is structured by time and *différance*, that is, constitutive of any repetition of experience, through the repeating of anything, words become destabilized and unreliable as the source of ideality or unity. Importantly, in Derrida's perspective, language which is structured through difference and temporality assures us that there can be no pure presence, no stable meaning, and this is true not only for language but for all and any experience of any kind. Since we are always already in time and difference, any and all experience and language which is meant to communicate these experiences are merely chains of differential marks.[9]

His strange and difficult language notwithstanding, Derrida must of course assume that his ideas are being communicated and therefore have stability and a unity of meaning. But his view of repetition which destabilizes and deconstructs experience and language has theological implications, for whether in the old style ontotheology, or in Macquarrie's new style ontotheology, God (Holy Being) is the origin and focus of meaning, the Creator of Meaning through his Word. But if, as Derrida suggests, there is no origin, no center of meaning, then any God talk is derivative since there can be no "in the beginning was the word" or "in the beginning was Meaning," as Macquarrie likes to render it. But, for Macquarrie, when we speak of God (Holy Being) we are speaking of the very possibility of stability to meaning. Later in this chapter we will consider how to resolve this disagreement between Macquarrie and Derrida as to the role repetition has in stabilizing and constructing meaning, not a resolution ending with agreement, but a resolution that exposes

---

8. Derrida, *Writing and Difference*, 246.
9. Derrida, *Limited Inc.*,10.

the phenomenological and ontological distance between Derrida's and Macquarrie's views of repetition.

Of course, Macquarrie is ultimately interested in theological language, "God-Talk" as talk of the highest kind, talk of the relationship between (Holy) Being (God) and beings, the wider being of nature, but especially human being, who is the being that (Holy) Being (God) opens up to. Macquarrie says, "These are the experiences of the community of faith, in which men move from the questioning of their own being to the search for meaning and to the revelatory experience in which they are grasped by the grace of Being. The language in which they express this has its intelligible logic in the pattern of experience through which they move."[10] This experience is always renewing and repeating as we continue through our life searching and delving further into truth and meaning. In a theological context, we are speaking about the church in the world, expressing a particular form of life. There are many other forms of life, which find this type of language alienating or meaningless. In a world that has forgotten Being, lost in a world of beings and entities, all kinds of language has developed specific to different interests. This is especially language related to different disciplines. Macquarrie abandoned old style philosophical theology for his new style because the language of old style theology had become incommensurate with these other language games and a new style was required to help bridge the gap between theology and other styles of discourse. However, it should not escape our attention that the very project of a new style is in a sense both a deconstruction of the old style, and a repetition of the perennial philosophical and theological themes.

The language of theology has to communicate with other forms of life and discourse. "Its business is to explain and interpret, to make intelligible and credible, and these are characteristics that it has in common with all other intellectual disciplines."[11] Following Wittgenstein and his postmodern beneficiaries, Macquarrie speaks of a variety of language games and discourse situations, each with their own logic. Different disciplines use different logics appropriate for their situation. Nevertheless, these different logics and kinds of language share the "same basic vocabulary and they employ the same basic syntax."[12] Macquarrie's at-

---

10. Macquarrie, *Principles*, 125.
11. Macquarrie, *Thinking about God*, 8.
12. Ibid., 8.

tempt to ground theology on secular philosophical language involves him in a different but very specialized discourse. He considers his efforts to be continuous with the work of early creeds and classical theology that used Greek philosophical vocabulary—*homoousios, hypostasis, physeis, anhypostasia, enhypostasia*—to demythologize biblical concepts. And yet, he is highly critical of the old style classical theism founded on this vocabulary with its substance metaphysics and Monarchical view of God.

And, Macquarrie indeed asks whether anyone can speak of Being or of God through any vocabulary, in any language. Is discourse about God too destabilized through ambiguity, through temporality and finitude, through fragmentation of language? Again, is discourse about God, or to God, perhaps only a conversation to our self, about our own pursuit and desire for transcendence we happen to name Being or God? In Macquarrie's philosophical natural theology, is our experience of God and the presence and manifestation of God through the phenomena really two separate things? He does seem to agree with Bultmann, after all, that talk about God and talk about our self are inseparable. He is not insensitive to those like Derrida who confess difficulty, maybe even the impossibility, of escaping the *aporias* of "God-Talk" inherent to Biblical hermeneutics and philosophical theology. But this would be only part of the story. Macquarrie moves beyond the existential to the ontological *because* he wants to pass through the paradoxical *aporia* of theology and speak of God as Being, who although inseparable from beings is "the *fons et origo* of all beings and the meaning of beings."[13]

And so, as has been a theme in this conversation with Macquarrie's philosophical theology, we restate that we can only ever know Being (God) through our experiences as beings-in-the-world and therefore, we are always speaking through our thrownness into a world, always already in a world of pre-text and context, of understanding and interpretation. Given this, Macquarrie will attempt to escape any narrow subjectivism through his articulation of a faith life grounded in an immanent experience of transcendence that is also shared communally. He attempts to escape the subjectivism of existentialism and postmodernism. Yet, he does so only to move us not to objectivity but to an inter-subjectivity historically and culturally constituted.

Existence in its most meaningful disclosures receives, through revelation, content that draws one closer to Being (God) or alienates one

---

13 Macquarrie, *Principles*, 211.

from Being *(Il y a, khora)*. A faith commitment is a great risk, greater than what might be involved in any calculated certainty, and it takes seriously that when we speak about the content of our faith, we speak the truth to further and deepen our quest as this is experienced in-the-world. There is an ethical dimension to speaking connecting language to truth which reminds us of the ethical dimension of ontology discussed in the previous chapter. Macquarrie takes issue with the way language has developed in postmodernism generally. He is troubled by the idea that language provides the ultimate context for all meaning, where meaning is limited to the values held by the speaker. This is a species of the narrow subjectivism Macquarrie rejected in Bultmann. As we discussed above, there is a relativism and skepticism, even the danger of nihilism that exists as a real possibility in postmodernism that Macquarrie sees as a fundamental threat to truth.

Macquarrie insists that any "saying" of anything implies that what is being said *is* true, a presumed fidelity and loyalty in dialogue. There is, attending any assertion, at least the claim that what is being said is true: this is the case even when deception is intentional, for in this case the speaker at least wants what he says to be received as true. In a culture of "hermeneutics of suspicion" there is perhaps always projected onto what is said question as to veracity. But Macquarrie refuses to be so pessimistic. Even such suspicion, it would seem, assumes the possibility of truth. He wants to make clear that the idea of truth is one that functions as a kind of "regulative idea"; he says for example that "all communication through language is based on a respect for truth."[14] And he aligns himself with Levinas, who maintains that the use of language requires an act of trust "anterior to and implicit in every act of speaking and hearing."[15] An ethical dimension to truth through language precedes values of correspondence to or coherence with any perceived "reality." Macquarrie comments that in postmodernism there are some who through a spirit of "relativism, the absence of foundations, the deficiencies of language, do seem to come close to abolishing truth, but if they do, they cut themselves off from the world of serious discourse."[16]

But, what is truth? "As soon as we begin to think about it," Macquarrie observes, "we see that truth is a polysemous concept. There are many

14. Ibid., 461.
15. Ibid.
16. Ibid.

kinds of truth, many definitions of truth . . ."[17] Macquarrie considers that with a postmodern response to the perennial question "What is truth?" we enter difficult territory since postmodernism "challenges access to "objective facts," it gives rise to the appearance of suggesting that once we get away from the simplest facts, everything is a matter of opinion."[18] Because of the limits to language, there really is no way to escape views of truth and claims to knowledge that are not riddled with ambiguity.[19] This will be one reason one needs to make room for faith. But at the most basic level, the understanding of truth that postmoderns hold in question are those truths grounded in or guaranteed through Enlightenment epistemologies, such as "correspondence theory" and "coherence theory." Macquarrie rejects these as well. Not through a form of skepticism or denial of unity of thought and experience, but because they operate with an epistemology he rejects, one that does not allow fully for a phenomenological analysis of experience. He does not say these views are wrong, as theories correspondence and coherence have a value; however they limit us to a world of beings as entities. And so he develops a view of truth as adequacy.

Macquarrie's view of truth as adequacy suggests a way to work through skepticism because it is a more tentative view, ready and willing to be revised. Much of what we have investigated through Macquarrie's analysis shows that there is an attempt to reveal what lies behind phenomena. In this way, we once again come up against the fact that Macquarrie will seek the truth behind any phenomena and name it according to his faith—as Levinas, Marion, Derrida, and Lyotard each name the *noumena* through their own surrogate ontology, their *meta*-physics, saying to us what is other-than-being, even *beyond* the phenomena. And so we have said that although Macquarrie rejects the dominance of a single language game and accepts the reality of a diversity of language games he refuses to resolve these into relativism, a denial of meaning, a settling for nihilism: which is the opposite of Being's truth. He argues for the truth of his view of Being, while engaging the tradition with a rigorous rhetoric which always leaves open the possibility because of ambiguity that some will "see" through the phenomena the possibility of ontology that he describes as

---

17. Macquarrie, *Twentieth-Century Religious Thought*, 460.
18. Ibid.
19. Ibid., 460–61.

a way to theology. That is, transcendence as a living option to reductive materialism, relativism, or nihilism.

Although Macquarrie thinks language can be opaque, being aware of its fallibility, he believes that it is equally capable of a high degree of clarity in communication. He accepts Wittgenstein's view that whatever can be said, can be said clearly, and laments at the delight many postmodern thinkers take in the ambiguity of language and the "obscure and convoluted ways of expressing themselves."[20] For Macquarrie, ambiguity is part of the fabric of our experience, however, in the search for truth language with all its limits and shortcomings can be a valuable aid in clarifying ambiguity. Since language is a social phenomenon, and meaning is communal, we have an ethical responsibility to strive for clarity, which is key to Macquarrie's reliance on the biblical idea of *'emeth*, of loyalty and fidelity in any use of language. A mutual search for significance requires more clarity so as not to further distortion and perhaps cause alienation and separation among conversation partners. The recognition of ambiguity in experience, however, is not an invitation to subjectivism and relativism.

Because of the social and participatory nature of meaning in language, postmodernists have loosened the rigor in language use and this leads Macquarrie to ask: "What kind of discourse do they use?" He finds fragments of specialized vocabulary from philosophy, psychology, sociology, anthropology, and mythology used without clear demarcation.[21] This eclectic use of discourse creates an atmosphere of equivocation. As well, he laments that the "rather pointless" playing with etymologies furthers this confusion.[22] Is it not the case, then, that such a view of the ambiguity and equivocal nature of language undermines the possibility of clarity in any discourse? Macquarrie believes this to be a real danger, and his view can be expressed in the words of Kevin Hart who writes: "The enterprise of deconstruction always in a certain way falls prey to its own work."[23]

Macquarrie comments that there is "a distinctively negative strain in postmodernism,"[24] founded largely on the influence Nietzsche plays in

20. Ibid., 458.
21. Ibid., 459.
22. Ibid.
23. Ibid., 460.
24. Ibid., 454.

postmodern thinking. Although, Nietzsche's proclamation of the "death of God" was to offer hope for an emancipated humanity, Macquarrie is quick to remind us of the tragic words Nietzsche included in his discourse about the "death of God": "Who gave us the sponge to wipe away the entire horizon? What were we doing when we unchained this earth from its sun? Whither is it moving now? Whither are we moving? Away from all suns? Is there still any up or down? Are we not wandering as through an infinite nothing? Do we not feel the breath of empty space? Has it not become colder? Is not night continually closing in on us?"[25] Of course, it would be too much of a generalization to say all postmodern thinkers are in danger of promoting nihilism, as suggested in Nietzsche's lament. However, Macquarrie sees this as a common danger that accompanies postmodern trends of speaking. It is in their "rebellion against authorities and traditions (shared, of course, with the modernism of the Enlightenment),"[26] which grounds any claims made by postmodern thinkers.

Is everything a linguistic construal? Is there only interpretation of interpretation of interpretation? Macquarrie asks: if there is no "rational ground for the universe is there then only an infinite flux of contingent events, like the waves of an endless ocean? Are we plunged into complete relativism?"[27] We are back to the question of the unity of reality Macquarrie thinks is equiprimordial with plurality. Postmoderns are deconstructing these unities but to what end? For Macquarrie language is the best way we have to explore the ontological foundations to help escape an infinite contingency. Language, with its acknowledged limits, is still our best hope to open us to the truth of reality and allow us to share with one another our deepest and most powerful thoughts and feelings. It is the way we promote the goodness of creation, promoting the truth and spreading the possibility of flourishing through existence. And, still language can be destructive, as we have seen, cutting us off from existence, destroying and deconstructing reality endlessly, settling into ambiguity and paradox and perhaps falling into pessimism and even nihilism. Macquarrie sees this as a dominant theme in postmodernism, where its prophets argue with affective rhetorical force of the "death of God" and all that entails. He observes this while recognizing that there is a parallel

---

25. Ibid., 455.
26. Ibid., 454.
27. Ibid., 454–55.

movement in postmodernism where many reject such negative rhetoric; many who want to usher in the *death* of the "death of God."

In order to bring these points together, we will explore the relationship between dialectic, theological quest, and discourse. This will be an exploration of Macquarrie's view of language use and we will outline the structure of the discourse-situation as Macquarrie understands it in relation to some themes we have already investigated. This is very much a conversational model at the center of Macquarrie's use of hermeneutics. Conversation requires that the participants not only speak but also listen,[28] and the matter of concern in the conversation is what holds the partners together as this is mediated through language. I will hook onto the word "conversation" for heuristic purposes to argue my final point, that the process of conversation is also the process of working out one's salvation.[29] This is a conversation grounded in the experience of transcendence, of faith, and revelation. We will outline how Macquarrie connects discourse and hermeneutics structurally, for interpretation has "the same triadic character that we have come to recognize as basic to the whole discourse situation."[30]

We recall that Macquarrie believes that theology must both be reasonable and comprehensive,[31] and always be on the way, since we can never possess absolute truth.[32] This requires that we do not become entrenched in a dogmatic totality. Always an effective witness for this position, he is vehemently opposed to positions that argue for one way only as the privileged disclosure of God's revelation. His openness to a variety of proposals as well as his defense of a particular way through theology merely supports his position that theology is a discipline which is healthiest when conversing[33] with opposing views, which are held in ten-

---

28. Human existence is not only distinguished through the ability to speak, but to listen: we are, as Rahner has aptly put it, "hearers of the word."

29. Here, I think, we see an interesting connection between scripture and philosophy, where in Socratic dialogue one works out their salvation through conversation, through dialectic in the conversational attempt—through hearing and receiving the word—at recovery.

30 Macquarrie, *God Talk*, 74.

31. Macquarrie, *Twentieth-Century Religious Thought*, 479–80.

32. Ibid., 480.

33. Conversation, dialogue and dialectic can function as synonyms in much of what follows. There are, of course, differences between these and as already stated, I will revert to conversation to amplify Macquarrie's view of discourse in order to thematically connect this with Macquarrie's view of "thinking" and "language."

sion; that is, in dialectical relation. This is well represented by Gadamer. "As the art of conducting a conversation, dialectic is also the art of seeing things in the unity of an aspect . . . i.e., it is the art of forming concepts through working out the common meaning."[34]

Macquarrie is engaged in a hermeneutical-conversation with scripture and tradition. But, as a hermeneutical approach, an interpretation in alternative language is taking place. Therefore, Macquarrie has undertaken in existential-ontological language a hermeneutical conversation with the theological tradition. A hermeneutical-conversation requires sensitivity to other points of view. If the goal is truth then not only commitment to one's own view is required, but also openness to other ways and interpretations is needed. This is possible through Macquarrie's dialectical method, which breaks through the attempt to fix opinions into dogma and rational totalities, and is at once grounded in revelation and an ever-continuing quest for the authentic life. "Dialectic," Gadamer reminds us, "consists not in trying to discover the weakness of what is said, but in bringing out its real strength. It is not the art of arguing (which can make a strong case out of a weak one) but the art of thinking (which can strengthen objections by referring to the subject matter)."[35] And, indeed, this is also the concern of Macquarrie, to look again at the phenomena—however this is disclosed—and let the matter reveal itself. But, also it shows that the goal is unity not disunity: and in Macquarrie this will take us along the way to the community of faith. For one needs the strength of community to work through the (im)possibility of theology, and Macquarrie's whole approach finds itself grounded in the (historical) communal quest for truth.

His dialectical method is a conversational movement. What ties conversation partners together is the matter of concern, the issue at hand. And this is the purpose of dialectic: to hold in tension opposing views in order to advance in the pursuit of truth, to leave behind what is no longer applicable but carrying forward toward whatever is needful. Here the purpose is not dogmatic, arguing for who is right and who is wrong, but the matter under discussion steers the conversation, where partners in discussion seek understanding. The question of God is, of course, central to theology; but Macquarrie is interested in not only clarifying what "God" means in a secular environment, but also how theology—as

---

34. Gadamer, *Truth and Method*, 368.
35. Ibid., 367.

thinking and speaking about God—is possible. How is theology possible? How is "religious experience" possible? That is, what is the logic (*logos*) of religious experience and theology? Such fundamental questions form the beginning of Macquarrie's theological quest. Answering these allow us to form a foundation for all other questions of theology regardless of their "stubborn" nature.[36] However, they also form the beginning of everyone's quest, for the search for an authentic life is a quest and this has its *arché in* an experience that moves us to look for answers we believe exist for us.

In the conclusion to his book, *Twentieth-Century Religious Thought*,[37] Macquarrie quotes Santayana to summarize his own opinion: "I do not ask anyone to think in my terms if he prefers others. Let him clean better, if he can, the windows of his soul, that the variety and beauty of the prospect may spread more brightly before him."[38] Here we have the acknowledgment that the truth of Holy Being, as Macquarrie refers to ultimate reality, to God, is never capable of expression in one view. The pluriformity of experience requires a variety of expressions, and each of these should seek to be as comprehensive and as reasonable as possible. Their validity depends not merely on the conviction of belief but on their intelligibility and coherence expressed in language. Regardless of the time we live, we are not likely "to come to the end of this voyage in quest for truth of religion, or to stand on a firm shore, for then they would no longer be human beings in this world, human beings as we know them, human beings as you and I are, *homo viator*. But the important thing is that the voyage goes on and will go on."[39]

This metaphor of a "voyage" reminds us that in Macquarrie's reckoning theology is grounded in the idea of a quest, where each of us must find our way, although we do this communally. This quest is not to be mistaken for the promotion of individualism, where "subjectivism" or, perhaps, "relativism" are assumed. No, instead, Macquarrie promotes a similar model of unity through diversity mentioned earlier in this book. The individual pursues the truth to be found in theology, which for the Christian is Christ embodied in Jesus as the Truth. The theological life is a communal quest, where the community as the body of Christ is an

---

36. Allusion to Macquarrie's book *Stubborn Questions of Theology*.
37. Macquarrie, *Twentieth-Century Religious Thought*, 481.
38. Ibid.
39. Ibid., 482.

extension of the incarnation. The quest is on-going, just as the presence of Christ is embodied in and through the fellowship of the Spirit.[40]

Macquarrie's approach emphasizes that in the theological quest we need to be personally committed to the truth. However, the quest is complicated because of the fact that in theology we are combining the limits of finite humanity with the preponderance of "paradox": where the infinite inexpressible Being who is God is present in the finite world, and at one time in the flesh through Jesus Christ. This is the Gospel of faith. It is the crux of the *coincidentia oppositorum*.

And so the logic of the language of theology will have a peculiar nature, its own *logos*, which sets it apart from any average discourse or other specialized discourses, as one might find in the natural or social sciences. For there can be no reductionism: either in the form of naturalism, which restricts language to the physical world[41] or idealism, since both "fall into a one-sidedness of their own through the preoccupation with the thinking subject."[42] Theological language must have a *logos* that allows for expression of the "concrete reality of being-in-the-world";[43] speaking about the reality of worldly existence referring to individual beings and yet pointing us to Being, to God.[44] Language is always in tension between these two oppositions of transcendence and immanence. Again, this is why we may speak of the (im)possibility of theology, where the prefix "im-" holds in tension the positive assertions about that which always transcends words and concepts. One can speak of the possibility of the impossible in this context since it suggests a way in which one does not need to remain silent about God, or take a reductionist approach. Again, it is this (im)possibility of theology which has caused so much disturbance in theology, either leading to compromise and secularization, or a rigid orthodoxy. Macquarrie argues, in effect, that the whole idea of theology being impossible because of the centrality of paradox, of the infinite located within the finite, is due to an overemphasis on rationalism or empiricism, and a limiting of our imagination and receptivity to revelation. This, in turn, limits our sense of logic; and so theology requires and alternative logic (*logos*).

---

40. Macquarrie, *Principles*, 550.
41. Macquarrie, *God Talk*, 59.
42. Ibid., 62.
43. Ibid.
44. Macquarrie, *Principles*, 128.

Macquarrie says, "I do not agree with those theologians who have gloried in the "paradoxes" of Christianity, but one can admit that they were correct in recognizing that there can never be one tidy final interpretation."[45] In many ways Macquarrie accepts Kierkegaard's assessment that "paradox" will have a central place in theology, he quotes Kierkegaard: "That God existed in human form has been born, grown up and so forth, is surely the paradox *sensu strictissimo*, the absolute paradox.[46] It is the desire to accept the standards of interpretation and communication of modernity that led to the movement of secular theology, where theology communicates values that are expressible in terms established by a particular logic itself validated through the anti-metaphysical rules of science and empiricism. Macquarrie argues for an alternative logic of God-talk; one that does not require the "death of God," but the "death" of a certain way of thinking about God. This is the death of a rational metaphysical God, what Macquarrie refers to as Monarchical. Macquarrie announces the death of one ontotheology to make room for ontotheology in a new way, a new natural theology that is possible only dialectically as a play between creator and creature, between Being and beings. Theology *must* communicate to a secular culture, it must communicate a paradox; it must communicate the Gospel. Therefore, it must make possible in language that which is impossible to conceive.[47] So what needs consideration is the appropriate way to talk about God and this consideration is intimately connected to a model of thinking that although violent[48] strives to avoid the destruction of reducing transcendence to immanence. This is why Macquarrie speaks of theology always being "on the way," it cannot become a totality in the sense Levinas taught us to avoid: that is, putting a closure on any further development.

45. Ibid., 38.

46. Kierkegaard, *Concluding Unscientific Postscript*, 194–95. Macquarrie, *Principles*, 306.

47. By way of an example, Macquarrie says, in Macquarrie, *Thinking about God*, 38: "A striking illustration of this is provided by the Chalcedonian definition. The great symbol of the God-man is developed with almost metaphysical precision. But breaking into the talk about *ousia, phusis* and *hupostasis*, there appear four negative adverbs: *asugchutos, atreptos, adiairetos, achoristos*. These negatives make it clear that this is no exhaustive description that is being offered."

48. There is always a certain violence to hermeneutics, since one is shaping into a view taking what could be pluriform and making it uniform in expression. Macquarrie inherits this from Heidegger. However, this has to do with the finite perspective of any being.

Commenting on Levinas, Macquarrie writes: "These totalizing concepts, he alleges, are guilty of a kind of conceptual imperialism. The very word "concept" derives from the Latin *capere* "to take," and, likewise the German *Begriff* comes from *greifen* "to seize." The other is not recognized as other in its particularity but is subordinated to a generalizing concept. If one could possess and know the other, that other would have ceased to be other. It is the other, not (as Kierkegaard thought) myself, that rejects the system."[49] Macquarrie is at one with Levinas that we must at all costs avoid the reductionism of the constituting ego. In this way, there is always a deconstruction of our image of God, a continual killing of "gods" without a destruction of the absolute paradox.

Macquarrie celebrates plurality in unity, where unity is a goal, a quest, and the hope of the future: it is eschatological. Macquarrie insists that interpretations cannot be final, neither can there be one interpretation, but interpret one must, because to communicate *is* to interpret.[50] The place of interpretation, therefore, will embrace the reality of paradox. Since paradoxicality is a feature of God-talk that cannot be dispensed with, Macquarrie recognizes that the "discourse-situation" in which God-talk occurs must be grounded in the dialectic of dialogue and interpretation. But here we say again that Macquarrie's criticism of postmodernism being lost in "interpretations of interpretations of interpretations "is fundamentally different from his own view of interpretation embracing paradox. The difference, we have argued, is that Macquarrie grounds all that he says in the dialectic method, which for him is a philosophical expression of the incarnation: the fundamental concrete revelation in history that nevertheless has on-going universal significance. In short, it is in his faith in the meaning of the incarnation where the difference lies.

For Macquarrie, "dialectic," "dialogue," "interpretation," go together since it is through these that we discover meaning, whether communicated in the present through dialogue or through the interpretation of texts, recorded in the tradition and in scripture. "Dialogue" as "discourse" as "conversation"—they are synonyms here—takes us back to the original Judeao-Christian tradition, "In the beginning was the Word." Faith accepts there is "talk" between God and believers, between Church communities, between the Church and the world. Here it is foundational. "Dialogue" as "discourse" as "conversation" keeps us not only open to

---

49. Macquarrie, *Twentieth-Century Religious Thought*, 463.
50. Macquarrie, *God Talk*, 74.

the views and needs of others, it binds us together, it shapes and forms community, and it is the way we witness and confess our own view. "Interpretation" takes into the present what has been said. "Interpretation" is the lynchpin of communication, of understanding, allowing us to cross barriers and to disclose and reveal what is meaningful. All of this comes together in what Macquarrie calls a "discourse-situation."

A "discourse-situation" has a particular structure, what it refers to is the situation in which language expresses the dialectic of one's being-in-the-world; giving expression to one's existence.[51] The discourse-situation is a relational structure. Human beings are beings-in-the-world, and are temporally self-related. Human beings are social and are always beings-with-others. God, too, in Macquarrie's theology is a relational deity: there is no meaningful way to think God without world. All communication and interpretation in a discourse-situation must occur in this wider sense of being which covers the whole range of existing in a world,[52] covering the "totality of existence," tacitly as well as on overt levels. Always remembering that for Macquarrie "totality" is a synonym not for conceptual imperialism, but for the pursuit of possibility of meaning, a totality does not eliminate paradox it incorporates paradox as paradox. The pursuit for meaning, therefore is no Edenic existence. In fact, Macquarrie insists, existence is in danger of always being in the act of falling, stuck in the grasp of inauthenticity, and confronted with "nothingness."

In Macquarrie's philosophical theology existence is riddled with tensions and oppositions, what he connects both with the "sin" of human beings and with paradox, which is central to the Gospel of reconciliation, overcoming the consequences of the "fall."[53] The logic of theological thinking and speaking demand a dialectical approach because of its unique task of having to allow paradox to exist; all communication of existence will be indirect, it will be approximate, it will be oblique and deflected from its true object, and therefore it will be symbolic in the sense that whatever is said can merely indicate what is the case and never conceive it, that is, grasp it in a totality. Therefore dialogue and interpretation are central in conversation with those who are on a quest to come to terms with the paradox of existence, and in theology of the ultimate paradox of the Gospel. But theological language will also be informed

51. Ibid., 75.
52. Macquarrie, *Principles*, 60.
53. Ibid., 306.

by the experience of the Infinite, the sublime, (Holy) Being (God) as this is reflected through the imagination, through passion and aesthetic categories of thought. We find in theological language liturgy, which takes over to give expression to those experiences that lean more toward the non-rational, the passionate.

A theological conversation involves the simultaneity of desiring to draw near to God feeling his presence, and yet remaining at a distance as "beings-in-the-world." Even here we have the dialectic of the presence-and-absence of Holy Being, of God who is present-and-absent, revealed-and-hidden. In any dialogue about God, we are conversing regarding the One who is at times closer to us and who is at times farther from us. And here, we can see where Derrida and Macquarrie glance off of one another. Derrida's "hauntology" where he hears rumors of ontological meaning, "perhaps" deity, always a possibility to come, is stabilized through Macquarrie's paradoxical dialectic. Where one is in the presence of the trace of Being (God) who is not absent in his presence, but ahead of us, passing us by and allowing a glimpse. Faith converts this from a haunting specter to participation through the Spirit.

The Spirit, in Macquarrie's theology, sighs, whispers, moans, howls, and blusters around us.[54] But we are not merely haunted by this presence, we are lead forward as *homo viator*, there is a *nisus*, a striving toward a goal which is to be in the presence of the true deity who is always ahead of us.

For Derrida, "Being must be conceived as presence or absence on the basis of play and not the other way round."[55] In Derrida's phenomenology, "trace" is primordial. Difference and time are the structure of the trace. The trace crosses out any stabilizing Being, and so Derrida wants to say that the trace is nothing, and therefore not absolute. Nevertheless the trace behaves as an ontological structure, it is both originary and not originary. "The trace is in fact the absolute origin of sense in general. Which amounts to saying once again there is no absolute origin of sense in general."[56] One can see why it is that Derrida has been linked both with nonsense and with negative theology. Because, for Derrida, the trace is not an entity, pure trace is difference, it is not visible, audible,

---

54. Macquarrie, *Thinking about God*, 124.
55. Derrida, *Writing and Difference*, 292.
56. Derrida, *Of Grammmatology*, 65.

phonic, graphic, but the anterior condition for all things.[57] Derrida's trace would play the role of Being in Macquarrie's ontology, both are the *fons et origo* of any possible experience. Derrida, like Macquarrie, plays with binary pairs, he sees the world through opposites. Both Derrida and Macquarrie reject a Hegelian dialectic. Yet, Derrida is often interrogating the relationships between presence and absence, self and the other, through the play of being in a dialectical fashion. Each side of a polarity is deconstructed in an on-going repetition. For Macquarrie this leaves us in an all too Niezschean cosmos with no center, no horizon, only the play of interpretations of interpretation, what he laments is the infinite flux of an endless ocean of contingent events. Still, Derrida waits for what may come, and is haunted not unlike Heidegger for a god (who may be) yet to come.

The dialectic found in Derrida's deconstruction is countered in Macquarrie with a dialectic that although non-Hegelian, is attempting to construct meaning, through the play of opposites without smoothing over and harmonizing opposites in a totality as Levinas and Derrida characterize it.

Again, Macquarrie would be in agreement with Gadamer on the role of questioning and dialectic. Dialectic is the art of asking questions. For an individual, asking questions "involves being able to preserve his orientation toward openness. The art of questioning is the art of questioning ever further—i.e., of thinking."[58] Again, "It is called dialectic because it is the art of conducting a conversation."[59] To question is to bring to light a matter of concern, and the art of conversation is allowing oneself to be conducted by the subject matter itself.[60] This is the discourse-situation, the search for meaning and being on the way to meaning with others, which is paramount in Macquarrie's theology. This subject matter that ties us together is the concern for expressing the relatedness of existence-in-the-world, and as we have already said, in Macquarrie's theology this relates us to ourselves, to others, and to God.

When commenting on Heidegger's philosophy of interpretation, Macquarrie writes: "It is violence in the realm of interpretation, but a

---

57. Ibid., 62.
58. Gadamer, *Truth and Method*, 367.
59. Ibid.
60. Ibid.

creative violence, so to speak that breaks open a new level of meaning."[61] And Macquarrie's "discourse-situation" is meant to show how this dynamic aspect of experience that breaks open new levels of meaning is kept alive. For the role of hermeneutics is here the work of dialectic, which is always the move between opposing ideas and therefore is always moving beyond fixity into the unknown, opening up and creating possibilities of understanding. Unlike some postmodern concerns, Macquarrie's dialectic does not lead to the reduction to the Same, but the desire to honor that which is Other. The centrality of paradox guarantees that we cannot reduce theology to a rational calculus of meaning.

Of the relation of paradox to language, Macquarrie says; "when we place it in its discourse-situation and see what it is trying to express in the indirect language of symbols, then we must accord it its right."[62] In theology this is especially true; one cannot directly express the fullness of God, for God involves an inexhaustibility that saturates any ordinary logic. So, because of the inescapable element of paradox, Macquarrie says that the dialectical method is central since it "allows for the possibility that every statement made may need to be corrected by a statement of apparently opposite tendency."[63] The issue is, as in much postmodern thought, the (im)possibility of theology and Macquarrie focuses on overcoming limits placed on logic to find a way to speak of the "possibility of theology." Again, Macquarrie emphasizes, "we have a duty to reflect as deeply as possible and to show, so far as we can, that the paradox is a dialectical conjunction of opposites and not sheer nonsense or irreconcilable contradiction."[64] Theology is always going to involve more than we can say at any one time, it will require a plurality of possible expressions and will always be on the way, hopefully to ever deeper meaning. However, this does not mean that in theology anything is possible, or that nothing is possible. Macquarrie believes the goal of unity is necessary in the pursuit of truth. The Gospel in presenting its truth does so with a logic that although oriented toward unity, is not reducible to a concept or a dogmatic calculation. Macquarrie favors neither reductive rationalism nor a renunciation of reasonableness; rather he is pursuing a dynamic unity of plurality, an organic and reciprocal symphony of truth.

61. Macquarrie, *God Talk*, 161.
62. Macquarrie, *Principles*, 145.
63. Ibid., 306.
64 Ibid.

Macquarrie's method of theology follows a model of discourse, which includes not only dialogue but also interpretation, and as such we called it "conversational," a conversation with both a present community of shared interest and faith, and a long theological tradition stretching back to the original revelation of scripture that founded the community. But also a present community of opposition and criticism that has a genealogy of its own stretching back through the tradition. This is a cultural and historical structure necessary for dialectic to function. Indeed such a structure is built into creation. Macquarrie's view of experience and revelation involve very deeply the repetition of the teaching of scripture, as the repository of primordial revelation, and the engagement with the Christian tradition. Our access to this is primarily through texts that have been handed down to us. We again appeal to Gadamer on Macquarrie's behalf: "Hence it is more than a metaphor; it is a memory of what originally was the case, to describe the task of hermeneutics as entering into dialogue with the text . . . When it is interpreted, written tradition is brought back out of the alienation in which it finds itself and into the living present of conversation."[65] The idea of "conversation" is grounded in the idea of possibility, which is fundamental to Macquarrie's view of humanity always in relation to the communal pursuit of truth and meaning.

Macquarrie outlines the root of the word "saying" in order to illustrate an important point; all saying is an attempt to show or bring to light meaning. In fact, "one can hardly fail to be impressed," he says, "on noticing how many verbs of saying can be traced back to roots signifying "light," so to "say" something seems originally to have meant "to bring into the light." This is true for both philosophical Greek, and biblical Hebrew.[66] A discourse-situation is meant to uncover, bring into the open, what otherwise remains hidden. In this respect it is a social activity. For Macquarrie any discourse-situation, and language generally, is never private, it is always relational. The structure of a discourse-situation as Macquarrie presents it is four-fold,[67] and these four are existential characteristics rooted in the being of humanity making language ontologically possible.[68]

65. Gadamer, *Truth and Method*, 368.
66. Macquarrie, *God Talk*, 63–64.
67. Heidegger also distinguishes four characteristics of the discourse-situation, which Macquarrie follows. However, they are not identical to one another. See Heidegger, *Being and Time*, 206.
68. Ibid.

The discourse-situation is described as follows: There is "the person who says something, the matter about which he says it, and the person or persons to whom he says it."[69] Thus saying is not a direct act, like seeing, for example, and this prompts Macquarrie to take account of a fourth factor, that of language: that is, the words and sentences employed in saying anything at all. Words and sentences must mediate meaning. This indirectness means that interpretation is also inevitable. To understand more clearly the discourse situation, we need to consider the important distinction between "discourse" and "language"; and here again, Macquarrie follows Heidegger very closely.

Language (*Sprache*) is the medium of discourse, it is constituted of the words and sentences tied together in coherent meaningful ways, to allow for the communication of a matter of concern. Language, however, is tied to the existential constitution of being human-in-the-world. Language is rooted in discourse, where there is an attempt to express that which is disclosed to us through our world. Discourse is a worldly activity, expressed through Language. There is no Platonic realm of eternal essences to words and language. However, Macquarrie says that language may be described "as the precipitate of the discourse-situation."[70] (It is interesting that Macquarie uses the word "precipitate," which has a built-in ambiguity of meaning depending on context, both to create a fluid reaction, but also to perhaps result in a negative outcome). This again suggests that relational situation that Macquarrie finds constitutive of all existence. Although it is true that language only has its life in the discourse-situation, so language abstracted from the discourse-situation is not likely to survive,[71] without language the discourse-situation cannot communicate since it is language that is the mediator and bearer of meaning.[72] However, there is transcendence to language itself, a transcendence that ensures we do not merely reduce language to discourse. Languages "are a historical phenomena, they transcend all particular discourse-situations and could be said to have a life of their own."[73]

---

69. Macquarrie, *God Talk*, 64. Heidegger seems to divide this last point into to separate ones, the communication of an assertion, and the making-known of experience. Heidegger, *Being and Time*, 206.

70. Macquarrie, *God Talk*, 66.

71. Ibid. Though Macquarrie is cautious here since there are certain languages that function best in abstraction.

72. Ibid.

73. Ibid.

Discourse (*Rede*) is required for human existence because we are creatures through whom existence is revealed, revealed in that sense of "unhiddenness," originating in the concept of truth Macquarrie adopts, *alétheia*. "To put it another way," Macquarrie writes, "that which is talked about is manifested and made unhidden; and as Heidegger never tires of pointing out, "unhiddenness" or *alétheia* is precisely the expression the Greeks used to convey the idea of "truth." We speak truly if we make what we are talking about unhidden."[74] Macquarrie sees this Greek philosophical view of *alétheia* clarified and deepened in the New Testament use of it and its relation to the Hebrew idea of *'emeth*. Because we are communal beings, and because for Macquarrie there can be no private language, it is the case that not only is discourse a potentiality, but also an inherent desire of existence: both God and humans are constituted to speak. For God, as Creator, reveals himself through the Word. Human beings are not only hearers of the word, but as the image of God are constituted as such to reveal their "world" through their words.

Meaning in any discourse conveyed through language is possible only through the situation in which it is spoken. That is to say, in order to understand religious language and the language of faith, we need to participate in the experiences and community of faith. As we have had occasion to point out, this communal aspect is meant to prevent the fall into subjectivism. Communal existence promotes the dialectic relation of being-with others and God. The "situation" of discourse, therefore, is the life situation of the speakers who share a matter of concern. One can say that ultimately this matter of concern is the meaning of existence.

Previously we quoted Macquarrie as saying that all communication is interpretation. We will now briefly indicate how the structure of a discourse situation involves this. Discourse is "expression"[75] the existential dimension is disclosed through expression, highlighting the creative character of language, giving shape to our world.[76] Language is, then, "world-creating" and one cannot help but feel the tension between the biblical reverberations of this and that of postmodern views of language. Macquarrie states the situation thus: "The existent is already being-in-the-world; it is always self and world together, and these, though distinguishable, are not separable. So we must say that when someone speaks,

74. Ibid., 64.
75. Ibid., 68.
76. Ibid.

what expresses itself is existence in the world, or being-in-the-world."[77] This is what is meant when Macquarrie stresses that the discourse-situation expresses "total existence."

However, it appears to be part of our freedom and creativity to focus our attention and expression on some aspects of existence so that our expression is not always an expression of *total* existence, but can involve a range of possibilities; some more trivial some more significant. With all this, the danger that presents itself is getting trapped in trivial modes of existence and avoiding the more significant. Trivial modes find expression in mundane gossip, in questionable etymologies masking as erudition, or in scientific reductionism, for example. We find this tension between living an inauthentic or an authentic existence. Expression through emotions and value-judgments require modification through what Macquarrie refers to as a "dimming down" of trivial concerns in order to "light-up" other more significant matters of concern.[78]

Such "dimming down" does allows for abstraction in language, making scientific expression possible, for example,[79] and this way, it would appear that Macquarrie is saying that we can contain the more imaginative ways for expressing our thinking in order to work within the limits of the rational. This is valuable, there is always a threat, however, attending abstract rational expression, or scientific reductionism, when for example these views get confused for the totality of existence. So Macquarrie wants to be on guard for the reductionism of naturalism (positivism) and idealism.

Here we see Macquarrie's attention to the Heideggerian notion of the forgetfulness of Being, where "what we have called "total existence" is forgotten."[80] The failure to remember that language is the way we are meant to express the "totality of existence" is a legacy of the Enlightenment. Or better, the desire to limit this totality through alternative logics is a legacy of the Enlightenment. This is especially found in scientific discourse, which has contributed to the "forgetfulness of Being" through technology and the advent of secular thinking and atheism. Science is necessary, of course, and so is its language, "if we are to organize our knowledge of the world and learn how to predict and manage the phenomena

---

77. Ibid.
78. Ibid., 69.
79. Ibid., 70.
80. Ibid.

that we meet within it."[81] However, Macquarrie argues the world created through a reduction to a scientific-technological world view is ever in danger of eliminating the person to the point of erasure. The exclusivity of a scientific-technological discourse dims down to the point of vanishing the transcendent nature of human existence.[82] It would be true too, I think, that Macquarrie would find the postmodern understanding of "totality" a form of "dimming down," in that it wants to smooth-off the rough edges of that concept into a harmonious idealism. If total existence is meant to capture the reality of actual lived-existence—as Macquarrie would have it—totality must include the reality of paradox, *aporia*, of stubborn questions (though not undecidable), of evil, and of angst.

Whereas the discourse of science and technology tries to manage phenomena and eliminate mystery, reducing mystery to a problem to be solved, theology is confronted with what is inexpressible in its totality; theology is confronted with mystery and not merely scientific problems.[83] Macquarrie embraces the distinction between "mystery" and "problem" as a way of indicating the different focus between theology and science.[84] For Macquarrie, we live in an ambiguous world, and so one that is wrought through mystery. Yet, it cannot be denied that at a very practical level we need to solve certain problems in life, as found through our engagement with the material world, scientifically, politically, and socially. There are techniques available for engaging the world as problematic. However, the totality of existence cannot be expressed through any of these techniques and the language that accompanies them. Problems are solved through a reductionist approach, which limits the phenomena through its concept and gives the (false) impression of complete explanation. Theological language, which participates in mystery, will need to limit itself merely to indications of what is inexpressible in totality. The former stresses reason over imagination, the latter imagination over reason; but neither scientific reductionist problem solving techniques nor theological imaginative expression of the mystery of total existence can live without the other. Said another way, theology needs to open up

81. Ibid.

82. Ibid., 71.

83. Think of the distinction between "mystery" and "problem" as Marcel has it. Macquarrie offers a version of this in his essay "Mystery and Truth," in *Thinking about God*.

84. But see Macquarrie, *Two Worlds Are Ours*, 2, where he says the distinction is not absolute.

possibilities of experience and meaning in a world that is defined primarily through science and technology.

"Expression," as one aspect of the discourse-situation, is attended by "referring." How do we relate "talk" to what is "talked about'? Macquarrie says that the subject matter of a discourse-situation is referred to in our talk. Or, we can say that the subject matter is represented in our talk. Language as a medium of discourse points beyond itself through its *referring* or its *representing* "so that the language stands for that about which something is said."[85] Language is empty, Macquarrie states, "unless it has some content that links it to a reality beyond the language."[86] And there is a saturation of content available through the imagination if only language can access it. Language appears to function as a "formal indication." In Heidegger something is "formal" in the sense of being empty of content, it is a structure, not de-fined or conceptual, but pointing and indicating something other than itself. Heidegger, in his early lectures, spoke of phenomenology as "formal indication," where the phenomena show themselves waiting for meaning (interpretation) to be supplied. Macquarrie holds that Being (God) is the initiator of any quest for truth; any quest for God. It is the "grace of Being" that wakes us out of our (dogmatic) slumbers sending us on the quest for truth. Being initiates the desire to express the truth of Being, which is mediated through language. Language functions akin to an *apriori* category—we are constituted as linguistic beings—that gets filled with the content of words and meaning of the varieties of experiences attempting to communicate Being. Language is empty until filled with content.

For Macquarrie theological language refers ultimately to Being, but always of Being as it relates to us, as it embraces us and reveals its holiness to us as Being-in-the-world.[87] And for Macquarrie, as we already know, this Being is God. He quotes Calvin with approval, "our mind cannot conceive of God without rendering some worship to him."[88] In this way, we can say that existence is sacramental, for God is present in and through the world, Being is always with beings, and it is up to language to open-up and light-up this presence and make it manifest. In theology, as

---

85. Macquarrie, *God Talk*, 71.
86. Ibid., 73.
87. Macquarrie, *Principles*, 128.
88. Ibid., 128. Calvin, *Institutes of the Christian Religion* I,ii,1.

we have seen, one is involved in conversation with the tradition and with others, albeit by proxy: and by proxy within a community of discourse.

Perhaps Macquarrie has only deferred the problem, for language seems to be adapted to talking of beings, not of Being that is incomparable, and therefore how does language gain proximity to Being? "The language of religion and of theology abounds in modes of discourse in which language has been stretched beyond normal usages . . . the participation of beings in Being, justifies the logic of a language of beings that has been stretched to serve as a language of Being."[89] Therefore, referring is not direct, as in a reference to some empirical fact, "the reference of this language is rather to be understood as oblique, perhaps ostensibly pointing to some particular being, yet opening a way into an understanding of being."[90] A fundamental claim of Macquarrie's relational theology, is that Being is present and manifest in every being.[91] Therefore, language can refer to Being (God) through beings-in-the-world. And this is central to Macquarrie's natural theology, as we have noted through the *analogia entis*. Said alternatively, Being (God) is represented in language because of the participation of Being (God) in creaturely beings. This is not merely a repetition of Platonic participation, here we are to see again the sacramental and incarnational element of Macquarrie's view of referring and representing through language. Reference to Being (God) through language is possible only because there is a trace of God in the created order and the creativity of human beings is able to give expression to this representation. The person who speaks initiates expression, referring to a subject matter that is a matter of concern as this is said to another person. In this last place in the discourse-situation, we speak of language "communicating." "Communication" is not merely transference of ideas from one person to another person; it is participatory.[92] "Just as the person who expresses himself in language does so as an existent self-in-the-world, so the person who hears and understandingly appropriates the language does so as a self-in-a-world; furthermore, it is in each case the same world, a commonly shared world. Communication takes place

---

89. Macquarrie, *Principles*, 129.
90. Ibid.
91. Ibid.
92. Macquarrie, *God Talk*, 74.

when some aspect of the shared world is lit up and made accessible to both parties in the discourse."[93]

The discourse-situation is meant to allow people to share experiences, and the purpose of theology is the sharing of the experience of God. We immediately recognize that such sharing presupposes frames of reference, horizons of understanding, however, the language of scripture is not a shared horizon of understanding in a secular culture. Therefore, Macquarrie has undertaken to express theology—as a systematic expression of scripture—in existential-ontological language.[94]

With the postmodern rejection of privileged ways of knowing included is the incredulity toward the propositional revelation of scripture as *the* Word of God. For Macquarrie, the authority of scripture does not lie in the *Word of scripture itself*, but in the acceptance and commitment to scripture by the Christian community. Where scripture is a repetition of primordial revelation, where authority is not found in the words but as these words are lived and "are set in the context of the whole life of faith in the community."[95] So revelation is not contained in the text but received by the community as readers of the text. Perhaps this moves away from the "scripture principle" of the Reformers, while maintaining a view of the "priesthood of all believers." Macquarrie's view can be compared to Stanley Fish's argument in *Is There a Text in This Class?* Fish declares that meaning is not an objective property of the text, but neither is it a subjective projection onto the text. Meaning is produced by readers, but any individual reading is guarded by the interpretive community in which the text belongs.[96] Such a view is coincident with some postmodern approaches and their turn to the authority of interpretive traditions.[97] Vanhoozer writes: "For many postmodern interpreters, there is no "the meaning," no "the past"; instead there is "my interpretation" or "our interpretation of these things." Here Macquarrie would feel right at home in recognizing the necessity of receiving "the past" and whatever meaning it carries forward only through our interpretation of things while one is still digging for the "meaning" of scripture. There are obvious connections with Macquarrie's view and postmodernism. When dealing with

---

93. Ibid., 74.
94. Macquarrie, *Principles*, 130.
95. Ibid., 9.
96. Fish, *Is There a Text in This Class?*
97. Vanhoozer, *The Cambridge Companion to Postmodern Theology*, 157.

the opposition of subjectivism and objectivism in postmodernism, for example. Macquarrie writes: "It is often said that postmodernism has a strong tendency toward subjectivism, while modernism prizes the objective. There are good reasons for accepting this statement, but we have to be careful in assessing it . . . We are still a long way short of being able to judge whether postmodernism leads inevitably to skepticism or whether we can discover in it some affirmative tendencies that will unblock the way to theology."[98]

In the context of theology, if we consider Derrida's repeated reminder that we live after the Tower of Babel, this places scripture in question. There is no common language, certainly no primordial or divine Word, whether Biblical, Platonic or Heideggerian. Yet, Macquarrie would insist on an original, primordial revelation expressed through scripture but in a way that aligns him with Derrida in some respects. That is to say, what is primordial or original for Macquarrie is that which is already in time, caught in the play (letting-be) of Being (God). Scripture is itself not revelation, but an on-going primordial record of communal experiences recorded for posterity. Primordial, in Macquarrie's philosophical theology, points to the source of inspiration, a foundation as condition of possibility for the continuation of a community or of ideas. As text, scriptures contain a plurality of sources, of meanings and interpretive possibilities. The received text is already an interpreted and redacted text. Further, even if we were to allow for the possibility that God speaks through the text, as Macquarrie would, such language could never coincide with the text, since language always has both an excess and scarcity of meaning. Here Macquarrie sees something positive in Derrida's view.[99]

If we venture a comparison with Macquarrie it would be that the historic and present community is always (re)interpreting the text of scripture as received, digging through the mythological language to its existential and ontological significance. Macquarrie would, perhaps, not be uncomfortable with speaking of an indefinite "re-writing" of the text as suggested by Derrida's view of *différance*. That is, to the extent that one must rediscover the meaning of the text for *us today* this "re-writing" occurs. And so Macquarrie writes: "Actually, the Christian faith has extended itself both in time and space because of its ability to interpret itself

---

98. Macquarrie, *Twentieth-Century Religious Thought*, 449, 450.
99. Ibid., 467, 468.

in ever new categories."¹⁰⁰ These categories must offer interpretive tools to unlock the meaning of the text of scripture, and therefore Macquarrie's view of scripture is that it cannot stand on its own.

Again, there is no doctrine of *sola scriptura* in Macquarrie. However, allowing for the community of believers to agree upon an interpretation does mean that an "end" comes to this "re-writing," but this is certainly an indefinite end: at most it is provisional and always ready to be reformed. It is a communal and confessed attempt to apply a meaning to "today." Macquarrie does accept that there is *in the text* a meaning, and therefore, this quest for meaning is what drives the interpretation. Therefore, to the question "is there meaning in this text?" Macquarrie answers affirmatively. He insists upon a meaning that continues to be the foundation—the primordial meaning—for the gathering of the Church. This meaning is not a projection, but a reception. "Scripture, as bringing again the disclosure given in the primordial revelation, has a stability and even a certain kind of objectivity as over against the vagaries of individual experiences in the community."¹⁰¹

We have already commented that in Macquarrie's philosophical theology one will find a *destruction* of tradition, a "philosophy with a hammer," however there is not only dismantling, but constructing. Macquarrie's approach attempts to break down barriers to progress in theology, entrenched dogmatisms, while remaining open to and preserving that which is beneficial and needful—*dogma* in the etymological sense of *dokein moi*, "my conviction." In this way, Macquarrie's conversation with the tradition of theology and philosophy fits the description of deconstruction that he gives of Derrida's approach:¹⁰² it simultaneously destructs and constructs.

Having said this much, Macquarrie's criticism of the theological tradition is always accompanied by a *repetition* of tradition in that Kierkegaardian-Heideggerian sense of "thinking with," of contributing and building something new, a repetition that does not merely "look back" in some sort of Platonic retrieval, but looks ahead toward further possibilities, toward a *telos* but always with the *arché* in mind: we are always thinking *with the beginning*.

---

100. Macquarrie, *Principles*, 11.

101. Ibid., 10.

102. Macquarrie, *Twentieth-Century Religious Thought*, 467.

Generally, "repetition" implies "going into some experience that has been handed down in such a way that it is, so to speak, brought into the present and its insights and possibilities made alive again."[103] Here we must comment on a departure from Derrida's idea of repetition. Macquarrie's and Derrida's intentions differ. Macquarie is a philosophical theologian who uses language to move closer to God and in doing so to avail himself to the manifestation and presence of the Holy ontologically and phenomenologically. His curiosity regarding the divine notwithstanding, Derrida's notion of the trace and *différance* is meant to show that this very theological project especially as it is grounded in repetition is self-defeating. However, I have tried to show that Macquarrie's underlying ontological assumptions which permit his new style philosophical theology have as much credibility phenomenologically as Derrida's claims for his method, which has been characterized in this book as a surrogate ontology, a hauntology of the trace.

And here in lies the difference. The determining factor is where one finds faith, trust, conviction. For Macquarrie this is faith in that which is Holy in and through God (Being), who gives himself in an outpouring of grace and love. This is a stabilizing factor Macquarrie finds lacking in ontologies that reduce Being to an ongoing omnipotent process of repetitive play, always and endlessly deconstructing only to arrive at further difference. Such a view, as we have identified above, Macquarrie would identify as unfaith. Macquarrie finds meaning and unity to be equiprimordial with disunity, sheer contingency. Why? He "sees" it in the phenomena, and has faith it is the case.

And what of Derrida's faith? Can we simply relegate it to the category of unfaith as Macquarie might have us do, along with others who have nihilistic tendencies, those whose language reflects a dismantling of creation, like Nietzsche or Sartre or Lyotard? Is this where Derrida belongs? Certainly Derrida speaks of faith. And what does he say: *je ne sais pas, il faut croire*. Certainly deconstruction has as its goal to show the fallibility, limits, and contradictions in truth and knowledge. So he must make room for faith. Faith in a *khora*, a desert place, faith in the anonymous, in God without God, faith in these places and disseminations is where deconstruction takes us as it equally reduces atheism and theism to undecidablity. This is faith in and through the trace and *différance*. Is deconstruction, therefore, faith? Is faith deconstructable and

---

103. Macquarrie, *Principles*, 92.

therefore the unfaith of undecidability? However we interpret Derrida, his faith, it would appear, is preserved through repetition, the multiplicity and the play of being. Now here, I suspect, Macquarrie would accuse Derrida of a calculative form of reasoning. Undecidability is possible if one is always coldly deconstructing, detached and abstracted from the all too human realities that move us to resolution, a leap of faith is needed to end the repetition of either/or. If a decision awaits you, and this seems to be implied in the conundrum of undecidability, and you do not rationally resolve for one option over another, a leap of faith is the possibility that awaits. And if you do not leap, are you dithering? Not leaping, therefore rejecting faith? If a repetitive deconstruction leads to a detached undecidability is this not the result of a detached calculus of reason? In either case, to dither or to relentlessly deconstruct one is removed from the commitment that is faith.

Macquarrie is not deaf or blind to paradox any less than Derrida is. But for Macquarrie faith is a paradox in that a faith commitment is both a free choice—and therefore a leap—and yet is a possibility because it is given to us through the initiative of Being (God). The fact that it is not one or the other, neither one nor the other, does not mean we wait in a waste land of deferral, but we recognize (which is only possible through repetition) we are on both sides encompassed by the gift which is faith through the letting-be of Being (God). This is the dialectic that is integral to the repetition of revelation (phenomenology), of our throwness as beings-in-the-world. This is the *fons et origo* of faith, and this is constitutive of the conversation with those who stand at the impasse of faith and unfaith.

There is a connection between Macquarrie's view of discourse and dialectic and that of repetition, in that the goal is to engage with one another and to move forward in a fruitful and productive way in the quest for meaning and the experience of faith.

Both repetition and conversation involve the social character of thinking and speaking. Said again, both repetition and conversation are movements of an individual in community, whether the community or individual is contemporary or historical. Any thinking is thinking *into* and *with* already expressed ideas.[104] So however creative an individual's thinking may be, it is a response to what has come before and this is very much a conversational movement: a dialectical activity. As previously

---

104. Ibid.

mentioned, the idea of conversation is also a heuristic used to represent a movement in Macquarrie's theology related to the recovery of truth, to the path to salvation: conversation is a working out of salvation and its association with prayer cannot be overlooked in this context. Having connected repetition to conversation, it is time to isolate some characteristics of conversation that permits us using it as a heuristic.

We revert to etymology: a Heideggerian gesture. "Conversation" originates through the Latin word *convertere*, which means to "turn round, transform." A compound verb, *convertere* is formed from *com-* and *vertere*, to "turn," related to the English word *convert*, and as we will explore further, "reform." The past participle, *converses* gives us the noun *converse*, meaning "opposite" and therefore appropriate in our connection with dialectic. *Vertere*, through its specialized form *vertare*, refers to "repeated action," and therefore to "repetition," a key element in Macquarrie's theology. From this specialized form, we get *versari*, to "live," to "occupy oneself." With the prefix *com-* we arrive at *conversari*, to "live" and "dwell" and "associate with others." From here we pass through the Old French, *converser*, into English, where originally it and its derivative, *conversation*, meant "dwelling" and "social life." The modern sense of "conversation" as talking with another comes into play only in the late sixteenth century,[105] but in any Heideggerian inspired thinking, "conversation" cannot be very far from "being," and "thinking," both of which are significant in Macquarrie's theology.

We speak of "conversation" as a "(re)turning," connected to the biblical view of *metanoia*. By(re)turning we mean a "new beginning" in the Christian life which is oriented toward the future, but which is lived through the participation in those teachings originally revealed to us through Christ and testified through scripture and tradition: and here we have the connection as well to *conversion* and *reforming* our life according to the call of the Gospel. This occurs through thinking and discussing the play of possibilities that we confront dialectically and accordingly in terms of Macquarrie's sense of "repetition."[106] However, this dialectic activity and repetition takes place primarily in the discourse-situation and is a communal activity. Therefore, we are in our spiritual quest answering the call and desire to dwell in the community of faithful thinkers and speakers of God. Macquarrie's dialectical theology in a new style has

---

105. Ayto, *Dictionary of Word Origins*, 135.
106. Macquarrie, *Principles*, 90.

called us to do exactly this and to engage others so they may join in the active life of theology, of "God-Talk."

# Bibliography

Ayto, John. *Dictionary of Word Origins*. New York: Arcade, 1990.
Barth, Karl. *Evangelical Theology: An Introduction*. Translated by Grover Foley. London: Weidenfeld & Nicolson, 1963.
Betz, John R. "Beyond the Sublime: The Aesthetics of the Analogy of Being (Part Two)." *Modern Theology* 22 (2006) 1–50.
Blond, Phillip, ed. *Post-Secular Philosophy: Between Philosophy and Theology*. London: Routledge, 1998.
Bradshaw, Tim. "Macquarrie's Doctrine of God." *Tyndale Bulletin* 44/1 (1993) 1–32.
Bultmann, Rudolf. *Theology of the New Testament*. 2 vols. Translated by Kendrick Grobel. New York: Scribner, 1955.
———. *What Is Theology?* Edited by Eberhard Jüngel and Klaus W. Müller. Translated by Roy A. Harrisville. Fortress Texts in Modern Theology. Minneapolis: Fortress, 1997.
Calvin, John. *Institutes of the Christian Religion*. Translated by Henry Beveridge. Peabody, MA: Hendrickson, 2007.
Caputo, John D. *Demythologizing Heidegger*. Indiana Series in the Philosophy of Religion. Bloomington: Indiana University Press, 1993.
———. *On Religion*. Thinking in Action. London: Routledge, 2001.
———. *Philosophy and Theology*. Horizons in Theology. Nashville: Abingdon, 2006.
———. *Prayers and Tears of Jacques Derrida: Religion without Religion*. Indiana Series in the Philosophy of Religion. Bloomington: Indiana University Press, 1997.
Caputo, John, et al., eds. *Questioning God*. Indiana Series in the Philosophy of Religion. Bloomington: Indiana University Press, 2001.
Caputo, John, and Michael J. Scanlon, eds. *God, the Gift, and Postmodernism*. Indiana Series in the Philosophy of Religion. Bloomington: Indiana University Press, 1993.
Charlesworth, Max. *Philosophy and Religion: From Plato to Postmodernism*. Oxford: Oneworld, 2002.
Cox, Harvey. *The Secular City*. Princeton: Princeton University Press, 2013.
Derrida, Jacques. *Adieu to Emmanuel Levinas*. Translated by Pascale-Anne Brault and Michael Naas. Stanford: Stanford University Press, 1999.
———. *The Gift of Death*. Translated by David Wills. Chicago: University of Chicago Press, 1995.
———. "How to Avoid Speaking: Denials." In *Derrida and Negative Theology*, edited by Harold Coward and Toby Foshay, 73–142. Albany: SUNY Press, 1992.

———. *Of Grammmatology*. Translated by Gayatri Chakravorty Spivak. Baltimore: Johns Hopkins University Press, 1979.
———. *Limited Inc*. Translated by Jeffrey Mehlman and Samuel Weber. Evanston, IL: Northwestern University Press, 1988.
———. *Speech and Phenomena*. Translated by David B. Allison. Evanston, IL: Northwestern University Press, 1973.
———. *Writing and Difference*. Translated by Alan Bass. London: Routledge, 1978.
De Vries, Hent. *Philosophy and the Turn to Religion*. Baltimore: Johns Hopkins University Press, 1999.
———. *Religion and Violence: Philosophical Perspectives from Kant to Derrida*. Baltimore: Johns Hopkins University Press, 2002.
Eagleton, Terry. *The Illusions of Postmodernism*. Oxford: Blackwell, 1998.
Fish, Stanley. *Is There a Text in this Class? The Authority of Interpretive Communities*. Cambridge: Harvard University Press, 1980.
Frei, Hans W. *Types of Christian Theology*. Edited by George Hunsinger and William Placher. New Haven: Yale University Press, 1992.
Gadamer, Hans-Georg. *The Beginning of Philosophy*. Translated by Rod Coltman. New York: Continuum, 1998.
———. *Gadamer in Conversation*. Translated by Richard E. Palmer. New Haven: Yale University Press, 2001.
———. *Heidegger's Ways*. Translated by John W. Stanley. Albany: SUNY Press, 1994.
———. *Philosophical Hermeneutics*. Translated by David E. Linge. Berkeley: University of California Press, 1976.
———. *Truth and Method*. Translated by Joel Weinsheimer and Donald G. Marshall. New York: Continuum, 1989.
Gilson, Etienne. *The Spirit of Thomism*. New York: Harper & Row, 1966.
Hamilton, William. "The Death of God Theologies Today." In *Radical Theology and the Death of God*, by William Hamilton and Thomas Altizer. https://www.religion-online.org/book-chapter/the-death-of-god-theologies-today-by-william-hamilton/.
Hankey, Wayne J. "Theoria versus Poesis: Neoplatonism and Trinitarian Difference in Aquinas, John Milbank, Jean-Luc Marion and John Zizoulas." *Modern Theology* 15 (1999) 387–415.
Heidegger, Martin. *Being and Time*. Translated by John Macquarrie and Edward Robinson. New York: Harper & Row, 1962.
———. *Discourse on Thinking*. Translated by John M Anderson and E. Hans Freund. Harper Torchbooks. New York: Harper & Row, 1966.
———. *Identity and Difference*. Translated by Joan Stambaugh. Chicago: University of Chicago Press, 1969.
———. *Introduction to Metaphysics*. Translated by Gregory Fried and Richard Polt. New Haven: Yale University Press, 2000.
———. *Kant and the Problem of Metaphysics*. Translated by James S. Churchill. Bloomington: Indiana University Press, 1962.
———. *On the Way to Language*. Translated by Peter D. Hertz. New York: Harper & Row, 1962.
———. *Pathmarks*. Edited by William McNeill. Cambridge: Cambridge University Press, 1998.

———. *The Phenomenology of the Religious Life*. Translated by Matthias Fritsch and Jennifer Anna Gosetti-Ferencei. Bloomington: Indiana University Press, 2004.

———. *The Question Concerning Technology and Other Essays*. Translated by William Lovitt. New York: Harper & Row, 1977.

———. *What Is Called Thinking?* Translated by J. Glenn Gray. New York: Harper & Row, 1968.

Horner, Robyn. *Jean-Luc Marion: A Theo-logical Introduction*. Burlington, VT: Ashgate, 2005.

Husserl, Edmund. *Cartesian Meditations: An Introduction to Phenomenology*. Translated by Dorion Cairns. The Hague: Springer, 1977.

Jenkins, David. *The Scope and Limits of John Macquarrie's Existential Theology*. Acta Universitatis Upsaliensis: Studia doctrinae Christianae Upsaliensia 27. Uppsala: Uppsala University Press, 1987.

Kant, Immanuel. *Critique of Pure Reason*. Translated by Max Muller and Marcus Weigelt. Rev. ed. New York: Penguin, 2008.

Kearney, Richard. *Anatheism: Returning to God after God*. New York: Columbia University Press, 2011.

———. *The God Who May Be: A Hermeneutics of Religion*. Indiana Series in the Philosophy of Religion. Bloomington: Indiana University Press, 2001.

———. *Poetics of the Imagining: Modern to Postmodern*. 2nd ed. Perspectives in Continental Philosophy 6. New York: Fordham University Press, 1998.

———. *The Wake of the Imagination*. Problems of Modern European Thought. New York: Routledge, 1998.

Kee, Alistair. *The Way of Transcendence*. Harmondsworth, UK: Penguin, 1971.

Kee, Alistair, and Eugene Thomas Long, eds. *Being and Truth: Essays in Honour of John Macquarrie*. London: SCM, 1986.

Kierkegaard, Søren. *The Concept of Anxiety: A Simple Psychologically Orienting Deliberation on the Dogmatic Issue of Hereditary Sin*. Edited by Reidar Thomte. Kierkegaard's Writings 8. Princeton: Princeton University Press, 1980.

———. *Concluding Unscientific Postscript*. Translated by Howard V. Hong and Edna H. Hong. Kierkegaard's Writings 12. Princeton: Princeton University Press, 1992.

Kisiel, Theodore. *The Genesis of Heidegger's* Being and Time. Berkeley: University of California Press, 1993.

Levinas, Emmanuel. *Basic Philosophical Writings*. Edited by Adriaan T. Peperzak. Studies in Continental Thought. Bloomington: Indiana University Press, 1996.

———. *Collected Philosophical Papers*. Translated by Alphonso Lingis. Pittsburgh: Duquesne University Press, 1987.

———. *Ethics and Infinity: Conversations with Philippe Nemo*. Translated by Richard A. Cohen. Pittsburgh: Duquesne University Press, 1985.

———. *God, Death, and Time*. Translated by Bettina Bergo. Stanford: Stanford University Press, 2000.

———. *Of God Who Comes to Mind*. Translated by Bettina Bergo. Stanford: Stanford University Press, 1998.

———. *Otherwise Than Being*. Translated by Alphonso Lingis. Pittsburgh: Duquesne University Press, 1998.

———. *Totality and Infinity: An Essay on Exteriority*. Translated by Alphonso Lingis. Pittsburgh: Duquesne University Press, 1969.

Long, Eugene Thomas. *Existence, Being and God*. New York: Paragon, 1985.

Löwith, Karl. *Martin Heidegger and European Nihilism*. Edited by Richard Wolin. Translated by Gary Steiner. New York: Columbia University Press, 1995.
———. *Nietzsche's Philosophy of the Eternal Recurrence of the Same*. Translated by Harvey Lomax. Berkeley: University of California Press, 1997.
Lyotard, Jean-François. *The Postmodern Condition*. Translated by Geoff Bennington and Brian Massumi. Minneapolis: University of Minnesota Press, 1984.
Macquarrie, John. *Christian Hope*. London: SCM, 1978.
———. *Christian Unity and Diversity*. London: SCM, 1975.
———. *Christology Revisited*. London SCM, 1998.
———. *The Concept of Peace*. London: SCM, 1973.
———. *Existentialism*. London: Penguin, 1972.
———. *An Existentialist Theology*. London: SCM, 1955.
———. *The Faith of the People of God*. London: SCM, 1972.
———. *God and Secularity*. London: SCM, 1968.
———. *God Talk: An Examination of the Language and Logic of Theology*. London: SCM, 1967.
———. *A Guide to the Sacraments*. London: SCM, 1997.
———. *Heidegger and Christianity*. London: SCM, 1994.
———. *The Humility of God*. London: SCM, 1978.
———. *In Search of Deity*. London: SCM, 1984.
———. *In Search of Humanity*. London: SCM, 1982.
———. *Invitation to Faith*. London: SCM, 1995.
———. *Jesus Christ in Modern Thought*. London: SCM, 1990.
———. *Martin Heidegger*. London: Lutterworth, 1968.
———. *Mary for All Christians*. London: Collins 1991.
———. *The Mediators*. London: SCM, 1995.
———. *Mystery and Truth*. Milwaukee: Marquette University Press, 1973.
———. *On Being a Theologian*. London: SCM, 1999.
———. *Paths in Spirituality*. London: SCM, 1972.
———. *Paths in Spirituality*. 2nd ed. Harrisburg, PA: Morehouse, 1992.
———. "Postmodernism in Philosophy of Religion and Theology." *International Journal for Philosophy of Religion* 50 (December 2001) 9–28.
———. *Principles of Christian Theology*. 2nd ed. London: SCM, 1977.
———. *The Scope of Demythologizing*. London: SCM, 1960.
———. *Stubborn Theological Questions*. London: SCM, 2003.
———. *Studies in Christian Existentialism*. London: SCM, 1966.
———. *Theology, Church, and Ministry*. London: SCM, 1986.
———. *Thinking about God*. London: SCM, 1975.
———. *Three Issues in Ethics*. London: SCM, 1970.
———. *Twentieth-Century Religious Thought*. London: SCM, 2001.
———. *Two Worlds Are Ours*. Minneapolis: Fortress, 2005.
Marion, Jean-Luc. *Being Given: Toward a Phenomenology of Givenness*. Translated by Jeffery L. Kosky. Stanford: Stanford University Press, 2002.
———. *God Without Being*. Translated by Thomas A. Carlson. Chicago: University of Chicago Press, 1991.
———. *The Idol and Distance*. Translated by Thomas A Carlson. New York: Fordham University Press, 2001.

———. *In Excess: Studies of Saturated Phenomena*. Translated by Robyn Horner and Vincent Berraud. Perspectives in Continental Philosophy. New York: Fordham University Press, 2002.

———. *Reduction and Givenness: Investigations of Husserl, Heidegger, and Phenomenology*. Translated by Thomas A. Carlson. Evanston, IL: Northwestern University Press, 1998.

———. "The Saturated Phenomenon." Translated by Thomas A Carlson. *Philosophy Today* 40 (1996) 103–24.

McKnight, Edgar V. *Postmodern Use of the Bible: The Emergence of Reader Oriented Criticism*. Reprint, Eugene, OR: Wipf & Stock, 2005.

Merleau-Ponty, Maurice. *Phenomenology of Perception*. Translated by Colin Smith. New York: Humanities, 1962.

Milbank, John. *The Word Made Strange: Theology, Language, Culture*. Oxford: Blackwell, 1997.

Morgan, John H., ed. *On Being a Theologian*. London: SCM, 1999.

Morgan, Michael. *Cambridge Introduction to Levinas*. Cambridge: Cambridge University Press, 2001.

Morgan, Robert, ed. *In Search of Humanity and Deity: A Celebration of John Macquarrie's Theology*. SCM, 2006.

Morley, Georgina. *John Macquarrie's Natural Theology: The Grace of Being*. Burlington, VT: Ashgate, 2003.

Murchland, Bernard, ed. *The Meaning of the Death of God*. New York: Vintage, 1967.

Newey, P. S. "Revelation and Dialectical Theism: Beyond John Macquarrie." *Colloquim: The Australian and New Zealand Theological Society* 22 (1989) 37–44.

Nietzsche, Friedrich. *Beyond Good and Evil*. Translated by Helen Zimmern. Mineola, NY: Dover, 1997.

———. *On the Genealogy of Morlas/Ecce Homo*. Translated by Walter Kaufmann. New York: Vintage, 1989.

———. *Thus Spoke Zarathustra*. Translated by R. J. Hollingdale. New York: Penguin, 1969.

———. *Twilight of the Idols/The Anti-Christ*. Translated by R. J. Hollingdale. New York: Penguin, 1968.

Naugle, David. *Worldview: The History of a Concept*. Grand Rapids: Eerdmans, 2002.

Pratt, Douglas G. "Existential-Ontological Theism and the Question of the Relatedness of God: Macquarrie Revisited." *Colloquim: The Australian and New Zealand Theological Society* 17 (1984) 26–33.

———. "The Imago Dei in the Thought of John Macquarrie: A Reflection on John 10:10." *Asian Journal of Theology* 3 (1989) 79–83.

Rahner, Karl. *Foundations of Christian Faith*. New York: Seabury, 1978.

———. *Hearers of the Word*. London: Sheed & Ward, 1969.

———. *Theological Investigations*. Vol. 1. New York: Crossroad, 1982.

———. *Theological Investigations*. Vol. 4. New York: Crossroad, 1973.

———. *Theological Investigations*. Vol. 5. New York: Crossroad, 1970.

Raschke, Carl. *The Alchemy of the Word: Language and the End of Theology*. Missoula, MT: Scholars, 1979.

Ricoeur, Paul. "Approaching the Human Person." Translated by Dale Kidd. *Ethical Perspectives* (1999) 145–54.

Robinson, John A.T. *Honest to God*. Louisville: Westminster John Knox, 2018.

———. *The New Reformation?* London: SCM, 1965.
Schleiermacher, Friedrich. *The Christian Faith.* Edinburgh: T. & T. Clark, 2016.
Schrag, Calvin O. *The Self in Postmodernity.* New Haven: Yale University Press, 1997.
Shakespeare, Steven. *Derrida and Theology.* Introduction by Paul T. Nimmo. Edinburgh: T. & T. Clark, 2009.
Silverman, Hugh, ed. *Derrida and Deconstruction.* New York: Routledge, 1989.
Smith, A. D. *Husserl and the Cartesian Meditations.* New York: Routledge, 2003.
Smith, James K. A. "Determined Violence: Derrida's Structural Religion." *Journal of Religion* 78 (1998) 197–212.
———. *The Fall of Interpretation: Philosophical Foundations for a Creational Hermeneutic.* Downers Grove, IL: InterVarsity, 2000.
———. *Introducing Radical Orthodoxy: Mapping a Post-secular Theology.* Grand Rapids: Baker Academic, 2004.
———. "A Little Story about Metanarratives: Lyotard, Religion, and Postmodernism Revisited." *Faith and Philosophy* 18 (2001) 261–76.
———. "Re-Kanting Postmodernism? Derrida's Religion within the Limits of Reason Alone." *Faith and Philosophy* 17 (2000) 558–71.
———. *Speech and Theology: Language and the Logic of Incarnation.* New York: Routledge, 2002.
———. *Who's Afraid of Postmodernism? Taking Derrida, Lyotard, and Foucault to Church.* Grand Rapids: Baker Academic, 2006.
Steiner, George. *Martin Heidegger: With a New Introduction.* Chicago: University of Chicago Press, 1987.
Taylor, Mark C. *After God.* Chicago: University of Chicago Press, 2007.
———. *Altarity.* Chicago: University of Chicago Press, 1987.
———. *Erring: A Postmodern A/theology.* Chicago: University of Chicago Press, 1981.
Van Buren, John. *The Young Heidegger: Rumor of the Hidden King.* Studies in Continental Thought. Bloomington: Indiana University Press, 1994.
Vanhoozer, Kevin J., ed. *The Cambridge Companion to Postmodern Theology.* Cambridge Companions to Religion. Cambridge: Cambridge University Press, 2003.
Vattimo, Gianni. *After Christianity.* New York: Columbia University Press, 2002.
———. *Belief.* Stanford: Stanford University Press, 1999.
Ward, Graham. *Barth, Derrida and the Language of Theology.* Cambridge: Cambridge University Press, 1995.
———. *True Religion.* London: Blackwell, 2003.
Webster, John. "Barth, Modernity and Postmodernity." In *Karl Barth: A Future for Postmodern Theology?*, edited by Christiaan Mostert and Geoff Thompson, 1–28. Adelaide: Australian Theological Forum, 2000.
Westphal, Merold. *Overcoming Onto-Theology: Toward a Postmodern Christian Faith.* New York: Fordham University Press, 2001.
———, ed. *Postmodern Philosophy and Christian Thought.* Indiana Series in the Philosophy of Religion. Bloomington: Indiana University Press, 1999.
Wyschogrod, Edith, and John D. Caputo. "Postmodernism and the Desire for God: An E-mail Exchange." *Cross Currents* 48/3 (Fall 1998) n.p. Http://www.crosscurrents.org/caputo.htm.
Zuidema, S. U. "The Idea of Revelation with Karl Barth and with Martin Heidegger: The Comparability of Their Patterns of Thought." *Free University Quarterly* 4 (1955) 71–84.

www.ingramcontent.com/pod-product-compliance
Lightning Source LLC
Chambersburg PA
CBHW051739230426
43670CB00012B/2091